ENDORSEMENTS

"Great read, unusual in that Navy Flight Surgeons seldom comment on life on the carriers. Superbly written ... another perspective of Navy Life at sea and a doctor's wonderful memoirs."

— Warm Regards, Captain Dan A. Pedersen (USN, Retired), Founder of the "TOPGUN" Navy Fighter Weapons School in 1969 and Skipper of USS Ranger (CV-61) in 1982.

"These recollections are familiar to me at different times and places... and are a treasured memory. Readers will find this book most interesting while greatly admiring the dedication, expertise and service of a Flight Surgeon."

— Mike Bristow, Naval Aviator, Experienced A-7 Pilot with over 200 Carrier Landings.

".... thoroughly enjoyed reading...I could relate to a number of the stories... other aviators will be struck with memories."

— Tom Petillo, U.S. Naval Academy '66, Naval Aviator, Fellow Mediterranean Sailor.

"There I Wuz" paints a candid picture of a flight surgeon's naval career and experiences on an aircraft carrier. This insider provides fascinating stories of life in a carrier "city" and insights as to what makes Top Gun pilots tick. Throughout, the author's humor is guaranteed to bring a smile to your face."

— David R. Sobel, Medical Defense Attorney and Award-Winning Playwright.

THERE I WUZ

A Navy Flight Surgeon's
View of Naval Aviation

A Personal Potpourri of Navy Facts and
Lore; Medical Perspectives and Tales;
Personalities, Psychology and Philosophy;
Tragedy, Humor and more … an Insider's View
of the Inner Workings of Naval Aviation.

James A. White, III, M.D. (LCDR, USNR)

ARCHWAY
PUBLISHING

Archway Publishing books may be ordered through booksellers or by contacting:

Archway Publishing
1663 Liberty Drive
Bloomington, IN 47403
www.archwaypublishing.com
844-669-3957

Interior Image Credit: Reade Spivey

ISBN: 978-1-6657-1021-3 (hc)

Library of Congress Control Number: 2021915078

Printed in the United States of America.

Archway Publishing rev. date: 09/09/2021

Dedication

To Linda …. who spurred me to start …. and to finish.
……. and to the men and women of Naval Aviation.

CONTENTS

XII FLIGHT SURGEON ASHORE

XIII NAVY RESERVES

XIV APPENDIX

PRELUDE

NAVY POEM

BY THE AUTHOR

Entrenched in those medical studies,
With few other goals; Ahoy, young boy,
The Navy calls ... your fantasy soul,

Siren song as a summer extern,
Then active after a year intern.
Ancestors all had served with such pride,
And to my knowledge not one had died.

Navy ships seemed better than Nam,
Took the oath and signed, "Here I am."
Adventure began with west coast delight,
Carrier day-cruise clinched Navy in flight.

Some of the folks along the way
Left fond remembrance to this day,
But for happy memory's sake,
Others are best gone in the wake.

Young men with machines, danger, and risk,
Challenge themselves with thrills that persist.
Look back with great pride …. that you had the ride,
Exciting sensations …. while serving your nation.

Thinking back … I surely can say,
Would do it again …. any day.
To shipmates and youngsters who may,
Go Navy …. and …. Anchors Aweigh.

THERE I WUZ

That was how most of the stories began. Almost every day one or another of my pilots would relate something unusual about his recent flight. It could have been a warning light, a strange vibration or noise, maybe just an unusual cloud formation, another aircraft, a ship below .... whatever.

The comment "There I was" referred to being in flight somewhere in the sky. Usually, the pronunciation of the last word sounded more like "wuz" as in "There I wuz." It was an appropriate opening for a story description because there is no other spatial reference while flying in a jet plane in the vast sky over a vast ocean.

We were on a modern super-carrier with daily flight operations, including sometimes all night. The incredible action, noise and visual panoply of launching and recovering jet aircraft on a moving windswept steel deck was always amazing and exhilarating, but sometimes could become routine and repetitive. It was always fascinating and strangely mesmerizing, perhaps because of the constant danger and risk of disaster. High speeds and powerful machines breed potential for mishap. Although during launch operations the regular thump of the steam catapults was heard and felt throughout the ship, they often became routine and just blended into the background regardless of what you were doing.

There is an old saying among aviators that "flying an airplane is ninety percent boredom and ten percent sheer terror." There is truth in that statement. Most of the "there I wuz" stories fell into the ten percent group. The pilots were relating something untoward that had happened such as a fire or other warning light on the cockpit instrument panel. It was not infrequent during hops for a warning light to pop on causing momentary concern. After checking all around and finding no real problems, most pilots would pull the circuit breaker and mumble, "prob'ly be all right." Usually, it was ... and the other air crew would dutifully respond with "Roger that."

But it undoubtedly was the momentary fear and worry of the inflight incident ... and the unspoken relief that all was well now ... that prompted the "there I wuz" stories. The stories were not only just part of casual conversation, but also an important way of communicating experiences. It was a way of sharing knowledge and learning among the amazingly close-knit brotherhood of the aviators in a squadron. The macho-bravado, all-competent mindset of the pilots would not allow expression of fear or failure. Sharing an incident story allowed relief and release from some of the tensions in what might have been a close call. The story also served as an educational and warning function for the squadron group.

Unfortunately, when a real disaster occurred, there was no one to tell the "There I wuz" story.

PREFACE

WHY AM I WRITING THIS BOOK?
BECAUSE "THERE I WUZ."

Young doctors are a remarkable sort. First, they must be intelligent and motivated to gain entrance to medical school. Then they must apply both characteristics diligently for four years without letup. Finally at around twenty-four or so they have earned the M.D. affixed behind their names and are as proud and happy as people can be after accomplishing some challenging goal. Many career choices beckon with exciting anticipation and expectation for the future. Specialty choice is a major consideration. Even family practitioners take a residency now for two or three years because the body of medicine has become so large it cannot be grasped in just the four years of medical school.

Few physicians choose to serve in the military. Those who do quite often choose that route because they have enrolled in a military subsidy program that pays full tuition and expenses during medical school plus monthly personal military pay. This accrues a year-for-year active-duty obligation. With additional year-for-year accruals for residency it makes sense for some to continue along with a twenty-year or longer military career. Yet there is always a shortage of physicians for the military.

It was different during the Viet Nam conflict years. Most every physician went in the military one way or another. If you wanted to complete residency first, the Berry Plan offered deferment and then your military time would be in the specialty in which you trained. General medical officers in all branches had an obligation of two years active duty. The option that appealed to me was to enroll in the Navy Flight Surgeon program. The reasoning and decision proved to be valid and looking back it was a particularly good decision. This book should be proof enough because I hope to relate how exciting and rewarding my Navy experience was in every respect.

This book has several aspects. Throughout the book is the ongoing narrative of my personal navy experiences and circumstances as they happened. So, it is an autobiography of my life during the time I served as a Navy doctor.... almost three years of active duty over a nine-year span.... memoirs of a wonderful time of life, to wit,

(1) summer medical student extern at the Oakland Naval Hospital (Oak Knoll) in Oakland, California [July and August 1963],

(2) physician student flight surgeon in SFS Class 112 at the Naval Aerospace Medical Institute in Pensacola, Florida [January-June 1966],

(3) staff flight surgeon with Carrier Airwing Seven (CVW-7) based ashore at Naval Air Station (NAS) Oceana in Virginia Beach, Virginia and deployed to the Mediterranean Sea et al aboard the supercarrier *U.S.S. Independence (CVA-62)* [July 1966 – June 1968] .... and then later

(4) as a reservist at NAS Alvin Callender Field in Belle Chase, Louisiana [1968-1972] including

(5) two weeks active-duty training in Norfolk and Virginia Beach, Virginia in each of the summers of 1969, 1970 and 1971 [including the Naval Aviation Safety Center.]

This book is also filled with stories of the many and varied happenstances. Some are unique to my own personal experience, some are general that could have and often do happen to others, some are speculative. I have enjoyed relating many of these stories in social conversation ever since leaving the navy nearly five decades ago. Some situations are funny, some sad; some are unique, some routine .... and some are tragic.

DISCLAIMERS

Accuracy and correct information have been attempted throughout the book. There may be errors or omissions that a naval historian or Naval Aviator might find regarding naval hardware, procedures, dates, and various other details. Please forgive the author as much of this is written from memory without serious research. The intent of this book is not to be a definitive discussion of facts, but rather to provide an overview of what it was like to be a navy flight surgeon during the late 1960s. I hope as you read it, everything will "Prob'ly be all right" so you can "Roger that."

There were many people during my time in the Navy that I remember with great fondness and mostly their names herein are those persons' real names. Some names have been fictionalized and some omitted, usually for obvious reasons.

Additionally, the book is written as a collection of observations by an insider who has "been there, done that." I have not been shy about opinions and bits of philosophy, taking full responsibility for them.

As to acknowledgments, recognitions, appreciation and thanks to those who made my navy experience memorable and successful .... thank you. The people who served with me in the navy and who made the experience enjoyable, rewarding and enlightening have a permanent warm and special place in my memories... thank you. To those who encouraged me, assisted in the writing and ultimately enabled the publishing of this book …. thank you. No one writes a book alone even though there are long hours spent alone in the writing. You know who you are, so THANK YOU! to all. Special thanks go to my artistic granddaughter Reade who prepared the maps, sketches and diagrams.

I welcome any suggestions, additions, corrections, or comments but will not appreciate abject criticism or random bitching. Thus declared on this 79th anniversary of Pearl Harbor Day.

Anchors aweigh, me hearties.
Go Navy.

JAW, 7 December 2020

INTRODUCTION

This book first is a personal narrative of about three years active duty in the U.S. Navy. So that makes it a partial autobiography. It covers a span of ten years including time in Navy Reserves and gaps in service. The title, THERE I WUZ, derives from observing, learning and participating as a Navy Flight Surgeon. Refer to the "THERE I WUZ" page for how and why it was selected.

No matter how rigid a military operation might be organized and operated, it is no better than the people involved. Each sailor has his own perspective and his own personal life.... so, every THERE I WUZ story is highly personal.

More importantly this book relates an insider account of the operations of Naval Aviation. If you have ever seen a movie of carrier flight operations, you already know how exciting and how complex it is. Neither a movie nor a book, nor many books, could fully describe the living, breathing life on a carrier. With all the excitement and glamor of the movies life on a carrier is also hard work, drudgery, fatigue, boredom, claustrophobia, and a whole lot more difficulties not described on the wide and full color movie screen.

A modern supercarrier is the culmination of a century of innovation, engineering, physics, mechanical development, trial and error, electrical and electronic advancement, systems improvement and much more. Lives were lost in the process. The result is an amazing complexity of interwoven systems which must coordinate one with the others for an effective whole. Add five thousand individuals into the operation with all their skills, knowledge, and experience ... or lack of it ... it is simply a magnitude which is hard to grasp.

A large part of this book deals with life on an aircraft carrier. The perspective is that of a Navy Flight Surgeon, a physician and medical officer. A great many other perspectives would come from the other five thousand men of many ranks, training, and experience. A good portion of the narrative attempts to describe flight operations, how they work and the psychology of those who are at personal risk to accomplish it.

The medical discussions, tales and perspectives are those of one physician. The other flight surgeons and ships company physicians on the Indy would have their own stories of various happenings of medical interest ... plus there are many other aircraft carriers. Some of the medical incidents are serious, some funny, some tragic .... but I hope all are interesting.

I have attempted to maintain continuity and logical progression but some skipping and jumping around is inevitable. The reader is asked to cut some slack where needed. The goal has been to give the reader insight into Naval Aviation and an understanding of how it all works. I hope it is also entertaining .... because it certainly was for me when ....
THERE I WUZ.

James A. White, III, M.D.
Alexandria, LA, 7 December 2020

I

WELCOME TO THE NAVY

A THOUSAND EYES

ALL SYSTEMS GO. Strapped in and ready. You see the rev-up signal from the Catapult Officer, then hear the roar as jet engines wind up and you feel the vibrations of 35,000 pounds of thrust quivering against the holdback …. pilot salute, yellow-shirt hand to the deck…. then whoosh as you lean into the acceleration…. zero to 130 plus knots in a few hundred feet. The catapult shuttle bridle drops away with a faint click and you are airborne into the vast sky above a vast sea with a sudden feeling of relative weightlessness and quiet. Adrenalin pumps with the omnipresent exhilaration and your senses absorb everything even though you cannot comprehend it all. The sky and sea are sometimes bright blue, sometimes grey, sometimes black as ink, but with every launch from the carrier there is a feeling that cannot be fully described in just words. A thousand eyes were watching your catapult shot. At first only a few people saw you climb into the jet fighter on deck and strap into your ejection seat harness. As you taxied into position for hookup to the catapult more and more eyes were watching including many on television screens all over the ship. Once airborne perhaps a few eyes watch you fade into the distance before they all shift to the next jet to be launched. Before launch you are the focus of attention but in the air, you are just a blip on various radar screens. The thousand eyes will return later when you lower your tail hook, pick up the meatball and follow the glide path to an OK-3 trap.

So here begins a reminiscence, memoirs if you will, of my personal experiences as a Navy Flight Surgeon. It was an exciting time of life, an exciting time of history and an exciting place to be. Anchors Aweigh. THERE I WUZ!

TAIL-HOOKED

A TYPICAL SATURDAY afternoon at the Nu Sigma Nu medical fraternity house on St. Charles Avenue was relaxed. As medical students at the Tulane School of Medicine in New Orleans we were hard-working and dedicated or we did not graduate. However, except for the marathon runups for a big exam it was important to have some down time. The usual pattern was to work full bore from noon Sunday to noon Saturday and then have twenty-four hours each weekend for R & R, the military term for rest and relaxation. Activities varied with the individual and included an amazing variety of sports, partying, and other activities. Partying included serious attention to alcoholic beverages, girls, and shenanigans. Some just took the opportunity for a nap to recover from a long week with little sleep. A good nap also enabled more intense partying on Saturday night.

We had Saturday morning classes in the first two years of medical school and in the last two clinical years there were some classes, teaching rounds on patients and the surgery Bullpen. This "Bullpen" was a clinical teaching hour from 11:00 AM to noon conducted usually by the chairman of the Department of Surgery. The entire junior and senior classes would be present, several hundred of us. Three senior students would be assigned a selected patient at about ten AM and would have an hour to take a history, do a physical examination and then present the case to the chairman and the amphitheater audience. It was a great learning opportunity but could be incredibly stressful if you were one of the presenting students.

However, it was the end of the academic week and we wasted no time leaving when the Bullpen was over. The Nu Sigma Nu house was a huge old mansion at 5018 St. Charles Avenue that housed forty of us, mostly two to a room. We ate all our meals there except weekday lunches and Saturday evening dinner. Saturday lunch was always ready as we rushed in from downtown Bullpen and it was usually sandwiches of some kind…. hot dogs one week, hamburgers another, cold cuts sometimes and always plenty of potato chips, pickles, and other nibbles.

Now you may be wondering what all this has to do with a book about my Navy experience. It has everything to do with it because one Saturday at the NSN house about halfway through my junior year in the spring of 1963 just as we were finishing lunch Johnny Yarborough walked in wearing his dress white Navy uniform. WOW! There is something about a tall, trim man in a Navy dress white uniform that is impressive almost beyond description. The image is one of confidence and power with elegance and grace. Johnny was five years older, from Pickens, Mississippi and had a soft-spoken warm personality. He was well-known by the many SAE and NSN brothers who followed him at Tulane because of his accomplished record and open friendliness. Johnny was a Navy Flight Surgeon on active duty and stopped by to say hello. To this day I do not know if he just came by for a social visit or if he was there to recruit for the Navy …. maybe a little of both … but he recruited me. I was "tail-hooked" and soon to be launched into a stint with Naval Aviation.

Johnny was bubbling with enthusiasm and excitement about his experiences in the Navy. He regaled us about naval aviation, flying, carrier life and lots more. This was the era of military buildup in Viet Nam, and we all knew that some form of military experience was in our futures. I had never really thought much about it because premed and medical school on the seven-year fast track pretty much occupied one's perspective. All my family had served in the military in every generation for several hundred years, so it was something that had always been just a given, but not once had any specifics occurred to me.

Johnny Yarborough's stories and discussions certainly made a lot of sense. It would be far better to serve as a Navy flight surgeon on an aircraft carrier than in a bunker in Viet Nam under enemy fire. (More on that later.) So, THERE I WUZ, minding my own business as a medical student, but with that chance encounter I was hooked, should we say "tail-hooked."

Soon thereafter I applied for the Navy. There were two choices for being a naval officer during medical school. One could enroll to be paid as an Ensign all through medical school which entailed additional active-duty time later …. a year on active duty for each year of being paid during school. Without being paid, one just served a standard two years on active duty. So off to the Customs House on Canal street I went for an induction physical exam and being sworn in as an Ensign. The Navy offered several summer externships on active duty at various Naval hospitals. I had missed some summer travel with classmates due to my father's terminal illness with cancer, so visions and vistas for a summer externship beckoned. There were several options on both east coast and west coast. I chose the Oakland Naval Hospital in California. It proved to be superb in every respect.

I have written a separate narrative of "The Summer of 1963" with extensive details. My medical school roommate and lifelong close friend Art Lochridge and I arranged to meet in Denver three days after medical school classes were over in late May. We drove all over the west for a month then Art flew back to his summer externship in Denver, and I reported to the Naval Hospital in Oakland the end of June. The bay area including San Francisco was so special that the following year I chose to do my internship at the Southern Pacific Memorial Hospital in San Francisco and so did Art.

OAK KNOLL

THERE I WUZ …. footloose and fancy free as the cliché goes starting a wonderful summer in the Bay Area. I had arrived in Oakland a few days early and found an apartment for the summer. I had my set of Navy orders in hand as I reported for active duty for the first time on the appointed date. It was a totally new experience that was filled with anticipation and excitement. Now I had my own "ice cream suit" …. a.k.a. Navy dress white uniform…. although we wore Service Dress Khaki uniforms for daily work, taking off the tunic at the hospital to wear a physician's white lab coat. That summer was exciting and rewarding at many levels and the Navy aspects are related here.

It was easy to adapt to navy life. The hospital environment was not unlike other hospitals. Although it was a military organization, the professional hierarchy was like others with senior officers being the senior doctors. We deferred to them as much for their knowledge and experience as physicians than for their military rank. The doctors were all in the Medical Corps as opposed to being Navy line officers. Line officers wore a star on their uniform (on shoulder boards for dress whites, on their sleeves for dress blue uniforms) while Medical Corps physicians wore the oak leaf with an acorn in the center. Line officers were in the navy chain of command while Medical Corps officers were advisory. The hospital also had a cadre of Medical Service Corps officers. Their insignia was an oakleaf with a branch at the bottom. These were the administrators who ran the hospitals much like any other hospital. The Dental Corps insignia had two smaller acorns at the bottom of the oak leaf. There was the Nurse Corps, mostly women in those days, and their uniforms sported an oak leaf without nuts…. and this engendered numerous male-chauvinist-pig jokes.

There was a large contingent of enlisted corpsmen who were trained as laboratory technicians, radiology technicians, respiratory therapists, patient care assistants and many other specialized fields which are so necessary for hospitals anywhere. Enlisted uniforms showed not only the person's rate, but also the field of specialty. After learning all the insignia, it was easy to understand just what function each person served at the hospital. The Oakland Naval Hospital also employed some civilian personnel to fill in gaps in care where military personnel were not sufficient.

The Oakland Naval Hospital was also known as Oak Knoll Naval Hospital and usually just called "Oak Knoll." Built in 1942 during World War Two to care for military personnel wounded in the Pacific theater the hospital was an interesting arrangement of a few administrative and central core buildings and a series of long wooden barracks buildings which housed most of the patients. The buildings were all connected with covered all-weather but open-air walkways. Patients were taken from the barracks wards to central surgical suites, radiology facilities and other departments on rolling gurneys. So, the arrangement was different from most hospitals which have rooms and wards connected with hallways in one large building. Oak Knoll was spread out with covered walkways connecting everything. The whole site was 167 acres and included lots of open space in the rolling hills. [A modern high-rise hospital building was constructed in 1968 to accommodate Viet Nam war needs. The entire Oak Knoll hospital facility was closed in 1996 and the main high-rise building was imploded in 2011. All the barracks structures were removed. The Officers Club was preserved for later restoration.]

We were quickly oriented to the military protocols, but it wasn't that much of a military environment. There was little to no saluting. Patient care overrode everything.

As externs and not yet licensed physicians we were not "on call" in the evenings and weekends, so just worked regular hours on weekdays. That provided lots of time off to explore the bay area, particularly driving across the Bay Bridge to San Francisco for its many delights.

It did not take long after arrival at Oak Knoll to be introduced to the Officers Club. Lunches were delicious and inexpensive. The traditional Happy Hour was remarkable. Drinks were twenty-five cents each with no tax so for a dollar one could get well schnockered ... and during Happy Hour when drinks were half price, fifty cents would do the same trick. (On days we were going across to San Francisco we skipped happy hour and left directly after the workday ended.) We learned the long Navy tradition of removing your cover (hat for you landlubbers) when entering the O-club else the barkeep would ring the ship's bell and you had to buy a round of drinks for everyone in the bar.

There were many interesting Navy experiences that summer at Oak Knoll. Our most famous patient was Fleet Admiral Chester Nimitz who was in his late seventies. Word went around that he was there as a patient and where his room was located. Curiosity drew me there and he was very cordial in signaling me into his room as I peeked around the corner. Turned out he just wanted some more ice in his water pitcher.

Another interesting experience was meeting an attractive young lady who was a Medical Service Corps officer, just out of college and a little younger. We were both ensigns and new in the navy. She "took a shine" to me and we had a few dates. It was fun to not be solo when visiting various attractions in the bay area such as Zack's turtle races in Sausalito. Zack's was a lively bar/restaurant and one of the "in" places for young people to meet. The parking lot at Zack's was make-out city.

Another unique place was the First and Last Chance Saloon in Oakland's Jack London Square. It was a fun place to visit for several reasons. First it had a history back into the 1800s and had survived the earthquake of 1906…. but the earthquake caused one part of the building to sink a little and the bar had a tilt sufficient that beer or drinks could easily slide down to the customer at the other end. That was fun and unique. The saloon is still in operation currently.

The other fun thing was that a loudspeaker was installed in the women's restroom. When an unsuspecting lady excused herself to "powder her nose," the barkeep would turn on the microphone and start a chat at about the time she was "using the facility" . embarrassing to the lady who was the butt (pun intended) of the customers' hilarity. In retrospect this was a terribly incorrect thing to do to naïve customers, but some young women who knew about the set-up had a wonderful time teasing back with funny repartee. I wonder if this is still happening over fifty years later.

The summer continued with good medical experience and a thorough orientation into Navy life with all its traditions, protocols, etiquette, and lingo. (Little did I know how valuable this exposure and navy experience would be in Pensacola over two years later.)

There were quite a few differences in hospital work that summer. First the hours were so much more relaxed with essentially just daytime work on weekdays. There was no need for late night studying for examinations. The workday was over early with lots of summer daylight remaining for various activities. The officers club bar after work with its two-for-one Happy Hour was certainly different from the rush home to study in medical school. Another first for me was receiving a very satisfactory paycheck. I was on the low end of the officer pay scale as an ensign with no years of service, but it was the first pay of my medical career. Also, in the early sixties, inflation was not the nasty it became in the seventies, so the pay was quite comfortable for me as a single young man.

CARRIER AVIATION

THE MOST EXCITING Navy experience of the summer of 1963 was a day-long dependents' cruise on the *U.S.S. Ranger (CVA-61.) Ranger* was the third of four Forrestal class super carriers and the first with an angled deck planned from the beginning. After that day at sea on the *Ranger,* I was tail hooked again. My destiny as a flight surgeon and carrier sailor was cinched. Later in this history will be details and memories of the days and months that I lived, worked, and served on the *U.S.S. Independence* (CVA-62) which was the fourth and last Forrestal-class supercarrier. *Forrestal* was CVA-59 and *Saratoga* was CVA-60.

A dependents' cruise was an interesting evolution. It was an opportunity for the entire 4,000 plus men of the crew to show their wives, children, family and/or friends what they did while away at sea for such extended periods of time…. sort of a "bring your child to work day." *Ranger* had just returned to its home port in Alameda after being deployed in Asia. It was scheduled for dry dock overhaul in August so sometime in July the dependents' cruise was scheduled.

The word went around Oak Knoll, and everyone interested signed up for the day-cruise. We boarded early in the morning and sailed in high spirits from Alameda, through San Francisco Bay, under the Bay

Bridge, then the Golden Gate Bridge and into the Pacific Ocean toward the Farallon Islands.

THERE I WUZ …. aboard a navy ship, a mighty aircraft carrier … with excitement and anticipation so thick you could have peeled it off my face. In a way it was almost like a huge picnic on a big steel boat. There were certainly more dependents than crew and everyone was in a festive mood. The weather was perfect. The ship's crew were professional, efficient, and simultaneously friendly and welcoming. Their role as hosts did not detract from their respective job performance. The families and various guests were in civilian clothes so were easily distinguishable from navy personnel. My excitement was as great as anyone's, but it seemed important to show it less. The excitement of being on the ship was almost beyond description.

All the medical personnel from Oak Knoll were hosted by the ship's Flight Surgeons and we enjoyed a tour of "sick bay" which consisted of all the medical facilities onboard. Coffee was everywhere and donuts. For lunch, the mess decks served hot dogs, hamburgers, potato salad, chips, and all the usual picnic foods. I do not recall if the two officers' wardrooms were open for visitors, but probably. After the early lunch, a demonstration of flight operations was planned.

Two F-4 Phantom fighters were launched with catapult shots and it was exhilarating. Unfortunately, that was the last festive moment of the day because one of the F-4s crashed and killed both the pilot and the RIO (radar intercept officer) …. within sight of the carrier and with both their families watching. Our flight surgeon rushed to the families of his squadron aircrew who had been killed. At first there was shock and disbelief among the thousands who saw the accident but then grief followed rapidly. Gloom descended on the ship and everyone aboard. We went back to Alameda in low spirits now and little did I know that a few years later we would lose eight aircrew in flight ops off the *Independence*. Carrier flight operations are a dangerous proposition. THERE I WUZ …. exposed for the first time to the hazards of naval aviation and the reality of death from flight operations. It is an unwelcome awareness and feeling.

SAN FRANCISCO BAY AREA

I HAD A small apartment off base but did not spend much time there except to sleep and maybe fix a simple supper some very few evenings. San Francisco and the bay area were beckoning. To describe how much I went to "The City" this little record-keeping statistic is interesting. The toll on the San Francisco-Oakland Bay Bridge was twenty-five cents for a round trip. You paid the quarter on the way west into the city, but the return trip had no toll. I kept records and spent just under $30.00 on tolls that summer. That calculates to about 120 round trips across the bridge and back that summer. It was a short and exhilarating drive and gasoline was cheap. The night life, sightseeing, food, culture and so much more were eye-opening. The restaurants and their cuisine variety were amazing … and prices were very reasonable.

I thought nothing about driving across for example to sight-see the 49-mile drive after work, returning to Oakland to pick up a date …. then back to the City for dinner and some nightlife until the wee hours. On weekend days there might be three or more trips into San Francisco or other attractions in the surrounding areas. An enthusiastic active young single man of twenty-three was on the move. Here are some highlights of the summer.

Golden Gate Bridge ... was and is the famous orange suspension bridge that is as iconic for San Francisco as the Eiffel Tower is for Paris, Big Ben for London, and the Roman Colosseum for Rome. That summer I drove across the bridge many times to enjoy attractions north of the peninsula. (See below for Sausalito, Muir Woods, Mount Tamalpais, Tiburon, wine country and more.)

Twin Peaks ... were two small mountain tops south of downtown San Francisco and the highest points of the peninsula. A road wound up the mountains to a small parking lot and then you could climb and scramble up the loose rock to the top of one or both peaks. The views of the bay area were spectacular on a clear day, but there was no point in going on foggy days.

Sausalito ... was a small residential community just across the Golden Gate Bridge and circling around to the right and winding down to the waterfront. Sausalito was an artist's community with many shops and galleries all along the waterfront. There were many houses perched everywhere on the hills above the marina. Driving up and around the narrow serpentine roads was fascinating. Nearly every home had a fabulous view of The City as San Francisco was called by those in the know. (It is considered totally uncouth to call it "Frisco.") Multiple restaurants beckoned including The Glad Hand, Ondine, Alta Mira Hotel Restaurant and others. The history of Sally Stanford's Valhalla restaurant was remarkable. Sally was the madam of a brothel on Nob Hill for some years, then bought, refurbished and reopened the restaurant and bar in Sausalito. She eventually became the beloved mayor of Sausalito and there is a fountain dedicated to her on the waterfront. We went there for drinks but to my knowledge there was no brothel activity in 1963.

Muir Woods ... Named for the famous conservationist John Muir this is a grove of immense native redwood trees just north of the Golden Gate Bridge in Mill Valley. It is a U.S. National Monument operated by the U.S. National Park Service. This remains a must-see for anyone visiting the bay area. The trees are astounding, immense, inspiring and almost overwhelming.

Mount Tamalpais ... is a peak just north of Muir Woods and it offered fabulous views back to San Francisco. The most incredible sight happened there on one visit. It was a sunny clear day but the ocean to the west had a heavy layer of dense fog. San Francisco is famous for being foggy and what happened that afternoon explained why. The fog (a.k.a. surface cloud) was pouring over the coast range of hills like a waterfall. The fog was also flowing through the Golden Gate, over and under the bridge just like water. I must have taken twenty or thirty photos ... wide-angle, telephoto, varying f-stops, etc. to make sure I would have a good one. The best one was enlarged and framed.

Tiburon ... is another village at the tip of a small peninsula on the north part of the bay. To get there you must drive up and around from Sausalito, but the trip is worth a visit to Sam's Anchor Café. The "dining room" is an open dock with fabulous views of Angel Island, Alcatraz and the skyline of The City. It is worth a trip for their pinnacle version of Crab Louie salad although plenty of other fresh fish dishes there are excellent. Crab Louie has been famous in San Francisco for over a century. The essence of the salad is a generous portion of Dungeness crabmeat heaped on shredded or chopped lettuce and layered with Louie Dressing which is a creamy piquant hybrid of thousand island and Russian styles. Usually steamed asparagus, tomato wedges, cucumber slices and/or hard-boiled eggs are served on the side of the plate.

Napa and Sonoma Valley Wine Country and Winery Visits ... It would take an entire book to relate everything here. [One day maybe I'll write such a book.] Suffice it that in the summer of 1963 this was an important part of bay area explorations. I was on an enthusiastic pilgrim's discovery tour of anything and everything related to fine wine. The many tasting rooms at the wineries everywhere were eye-opening for a novice. This phase of the summer at Oak Knoll cemented my life-long fascination, appreciation and involvement with wine.

Telegraph Hill ... and its Coit Tower are one of the icons of San Francisco. Originally semaphore signals from the hill down to the harbor alerted people of a ship arriving through the Golden Gate. Telegraph

Hill has long been a tourist must see. Nearly the whole of San Francisco is visible: the Golden Gate Bridge of course, the Bay Bridge on the other side, Fisherman's Wharf down below, Nob Hill, Russian Hill and Lombard Street snaking down, Oakland and Berkley across the bay to the east, Treasure Island, Yerba Buena Island, Alcatraz, Angel Island, the north shore of San Francisco Bay …. Telegraph Hill offers grand vistas in every direction. With the constant cool brisk breeze, it is exhilarating to stand there for a while and soak in The City and the bay area. Ever since that summer of 1963 it has been a favorite and first place to go when returning to San Francisco. Frequently I have taken a bottle of Champagne to enjoy while soaking in the vistas. In 1990 I even arranged to marry my second wife on Telegraph Hill.

Lombard Street … is a fun one-block drive down from Russian Hill to the North Beach area. There are eight hairpin turns and the short drive is almost like a carnival ride. There is no way to know how many times I drove down Lombard Street that summer and since. Continuing east Lombard is the access street to Telegraph Hill. Going west from the serpentine part Lombard joins Highway 101 at Van Ness Avenue.

Cable Cars … are another iconic feature of San Francisco. The California line goes both ways up and over Nob Hill along California Street in an east-west direction. It is larger and good transportation but the most fun is riding the Powell & Hyde cable car from Market Street to Fisherman's Wharf and return. It is something of a dream ride. Standing on the running board, hanging onto a vertical pole, leaning in and out as cars pass, riding up and down the hills while enjoying the ever-changing views (including looking down Lombard Street to Telegraph Hill as the cable car goes up or down its tracks on Russian Hill), watching the carman (a.k.a. "grip") use the levers to grip the moving cable beneath the street, listening to the unique cable-car bell and its mesmerizing tune …. it's easy to get addicted to riding the cable cars. In the 1960s the fare for a single ride was fifteen cents. Now it is $8.00 and mostly only tourists ride. There is now an annual contest for best bellringer among the car operators.

Golden Gate Park ... was special with open vistas, athletic fields, grazing bison and a plethora of wildlife, museums, architecture and more.

Stern Grove ... was a sunken little 33-acre valley below street level on the back side of Twin Peaks. Eucalyptus trees scented the air and there was amazing quietness and lack of wind in the sunken grove. A special treat was an open-air classical music concert on a sunny Sunday afternoon while enjoying a picnic lunch with good wine. We sat on the grassy slopes.

Other Attractions ... were amazing in variety and inexpensive availability.

1. The Fairmont Hotel with its posh lobby and revolving bar at the top of the outside glass-enclosed elevator was memorable. I discovered the delicious Gimlet there. The Mark Hopkins Hotel across the street on Nob Hill had a bar at the top which also commanded grand views and where the Dubonnet cocktail was another discovery.

2. There were the posh homes on Russian Hill and Pacific Heights. The architecture of most and grandeur of some were remarkably interesting.

3. The Presidio army base was beautiful. There were large open spaces and many small trees everywhere with the various buildings scattered here and there among the 1,500 acres that enveloped the approach to the Golden Gate Bridge. The Letterman Army Hospital was there but we didn't have much interaction from Oak Knoll. The Presidio Officers Club served excellent food at very reasonable prices. It was a great place for dinner and I recall some great steaks. The army base and hospital are now closed and the Presidio is a park.

4. San Francisco Giants baseball games at Candlestick Park.

5. Several of us from Oak Knoll played a round of golf at an up-and-down hilly golf course just south of Stern Grove.

6. Ice Skating at the old historic Sutro Bath House was a new experience for a southerner.

7. Watching seals on Seal Rock with binoculars from Cliff House at Point Lobos was fascinating.

it just went on and on and I was certainly like the proverbial "kid in a candy store." I saw it all and tried to sample as much as possible. One day I went fishing at Lake Berryessa with Jim Edwards who was a classmate at Tulane medical school and a navy extern at Oak Knoll that summer.

FOOD AND WINE

THE MENTION OF fishing demands a short discussion about the variety and quality of seafood in the bay area. How can I remember and describe it all? Impossible. New experiences included abalone, Dungeness crab, the tiny Olympia oysters and the huge Pacific oysters … and flat fish of every kind. Sand dabs were a new variety. The cioppino fish stew is a San Francisco Italian-American creation which is much like the bouillabaisse originating in Marseille. Multiple restaurants on Fisherman's Wharf were a little touristy but mostly offered high quality seafood. Those walkaway cocktails of crabmeat or tiny shrimp were quick and fun but less quality inclined.

Memorable restaurants and foods would include:

1. Tadich Grill … was and is the oldest restaurant in California, specializing in seafood and lots more. It was a favorite. Really fresh fish grilled to perfection over a charcoal grill with a little olive oil and lemon undoubtedly is one of the great culinary dishes ever.
2. Sam's Grill was like Tadich Grill but less fancy and less historic. However, state of the art seafood was served there also.
3. Schroeder's (downtown) and The Embers (on Telegraph Hill) were noted for German cuisine. It was fun to park on Telegraph Hill under Coit Tower and walk down to the Embers.

4. <u>Jack's on Montgomery Street</u> was one of my favorite restaurants. It was the second oldest restaurant in San Francisco behind only Tadich Grill. Jack's was one of the few restaurants which served the miniscule and uniquely flavorsome Olympia oysters. That's where I discovered sand dabs and Bar-le-Duc jelly (made with currants) that is great with most any cheese after a meal. The Dungeness crab was superb there also. There were small private rooms on the second floor and the rumor was that they were available for assignations.

5. For <u>Chinese</u> cuisine there were multiple choices in Chinatown and all were good. A discovery was dim sum which is a streaming variety of little dishes offering small servings of many foods. It is analogous to a *degustation* menu in France.

6. <u>Japanese sushi</u> was another new culinary vista and there were multiple restaurants for it.

7. <u>Ernie's and the Blue Fox</u> were the "high end" venues. Ernie's was famous for plush red wall coverings and French cuisine. They also served steaks, roast beef and hearty dishes. The Blue Fox was likewise expensive and its menu was upscale. Their famous dish was a small game bird roasted in clay. The clay was cracked away at table to yield the succulently moist bird.

8. The <u>Glad Hand</u> was a tiny restaurant in Sausalito. It was a small houseboat moored to the dock and was famous for its Green Goddess salad dressing.

9. <u>Ondine</u> in Sausalito was upscale like Ernie's and the Blue Fox, but newer without the long history. Its location was a prominent outcropping on the road down to the town.

10. The <u>Alta Mira Hotel</u> in Sausalito offered a fabulous open-air deck with views of The City. Their Sunday brunch with mimosa cocktails was special.

11. <u>Fior d' Italia</u> (Flower of Italy) in North Beach offered the pinnacle of Italian cuisine much of which was new to me.

12. <u>Garden Court of the Palace Hotel</u> (Sheraton now) … Originally an interior open court to receive horse-drawn carriages, it had

been covered over with a fancy domed roof. Their buffet was magnificent and it is where I discovered steak tartare.

13. <u>Sourdough Bread</u> was everywhere and quite a new taste. Served with sweet cream unsalted butter it just complimented and complemented all the other foods.

14. <u>Irish Coffee at the Buena Vista Café</u> (located between Fisherman's Wharf and Ghiradelli Square) was always welcome in the cold, foggy, windy clime that is S.F. The coffee was strong and hot and the spike of Irish whiskey certainly was warming, especially if having several.

15. Late night and wee hours <u>steak burgers</u> were a staple. They were grilled in the open air on a real charcoal grill set out on the sidewalk in front of a restaurant in North Beach where all the nightlife was centered. You could smell the aroma from blocks away and it enticed you to walk over and indulge. That was undoubtedly why they set up the grill outside. After a little partying and a few beverages young men seem to always be hungry. [Years later, on the carrier, we routinely enjoyed "MidRats" (our jargon name for "midnight rations" …. about which more later.]

Those trips to the wine country and various wineries ignited a fire in my psyche. I was "tail-hooked" again as the pursuit of fine wine and wine knowledge became a lifelong passion. I was no different from many Americans who are raised on milk and soft drinks, then in the early stages of wine exploration, prefer sweeter wines. There is truth in the old saying that "the more wine you drink, the drier and redder it gets." My favorites that summer were Chateau Lasalle by Christian Brothers, sweet Semillon blanc by several wineries and Moscato Amabile by Louis M. Martini. All three are sweet dessert wines. I bought some "splits" (1/4 bottle size) of the former to take back to Louisiana as souvenir gifts for family and friends.

The summer ended much too soon but at least the drive back

to Louisiana was enlivened by a stopover in Las Vegas and a visit to my sister, May Louise, in San Antonio, Texas where her husband was in Air Force Flight Surgeon training. (only about 6-8 weeks in the Air Force with no actual pilot flight instruction.... compared to six months in the navy culminating with solo flight in a T-34.) So back to New Orleans and the senior year of medical school at Tulane. When internship matching rolled around, it was a slam-dunk to choose the Southern-Pacific Memorial Hospital in San Francisco for internship. Art Lochridge selected the same internship so we continued our friendship there.

June of 1964 was momentous. First was graduation and adding MD after my name. Later that month was marriage, a honeymoon in the Virgin Islands and driving to San Francisco for the year of internship.

By now it should be obvious that the two months as a medical student navy ensign extern at the Oakland Naval Hospital in the summer of 1963 was a magnificent and spectacular time of discovery for me. I don't think that is unique. The Navy and other military service introduces many to new vistas in adult life. Compliments of the U.S. Navy I was launched into a new phase of life exploration.

TIMING MY NAVY
ACTIVE-DUTY SERVICE

MY NAVY CAREER began with commissioning as an ensign in the inactive reserve in the early sixties while in medical school. I went for the induction physical exam in the old Customs House on Canal Street in New Orleans and I was sworn in there. (Later during residency as a physician and after navy active duty I would perform the physical exams there as a moonlighting job.) My status was inactive reserve until January 1966 except for the two months at Oak Knoll in July/ August 1963.

I was late to apply for Flight Surgeon School during the internship year. Consequently, the class starting in July 1965 was already filled so I was given the choice of starting in the October class or the January 1966 class....... Somehow a flash of inspiration struck me!! Two years active duty was my obligated agreement plus the six months in Pensacola for Flight Surgeon School. That would put me starting residency in July 1968 whether I enrolled in the October or the January class.

THERE I WUZ ... I had been working straight through the three-year pre-med fast track then four years of medical school and the internship .... eight years of intensive academic effort. That summer at Oak Knoll had really been the only break. Although it had been a wonderful change of pace and respite from almost continuous hard work, certainly I must have had some innate understanding of the long eight years of effort. In addition, toward the end of the internship Virginia had thrown her birth control pills into San Francisco Bay just under the Golden Gate Bridge. We had decided to start a family.

SIX MONTHS OF R & R

SO, THERE I WUZ …. suddenly realizing that this would likely be the only time in an entire lifetime that I would be able to take off for six months and have no responsibilities for children and no medical responsibilities. It was another slam dunk. I signed up for Student Flight Surgeon (SFS) Class 112 to begin in January 1966. That flash of inspiration …. was it serendipity? Genius? Dumb Luck? Who knows?

I borrowed some money and we planned our six months. First would be six weeks of leisurely driving to see both families and assorted friends with visits in Louisiana, then New Jersey. Next would come a few weeks in New England. We would sail to Europe the last week of August and we booked passage on the Holland America ship *Rotterdam*. We planned a few weeks in England driving all over and with significant time in London. Then we would take a ferry to the Continent and drive around for about three months. Ultimately, we drove 10,000 miles and went as far as Istanbul …. which I would visit later in the Navy when *Independence* anchored in the Bosphorus.

We shopped for a car in San Francisco and arranged to take delivery in London. We selected a Triumph TR-4A in British racing green. It cost just under $3,000. Our passage on the *Rotterdam* had been budgeted at $400. each for tourist class, but the travel agent made a mistake or had a misunderstanding and booked us First Class and it could not be changed. The cost was $700. each. That extra six hundred dollars was a lot of money for our budget at the time...... BUT it did include all taxes and gratuities AND the highest end food you can imagine. It's a long side story but we had caviar at every meal including breakfast and all manner of exciting gourmet cuisine. One of the most expensive wines on the wine list was Chateau Margaux 1955 at $6.00 per bottle. It was wonderful. Kick it up a notch in the wine tasting experience and knowledge department. The wine list on the *Rotterdam* was extensive and inexpensive. We indulged in lots and lots of them. That mistake booking in First Class was both a miracle blessing and a curse. It opened a new vista of fine food and wine .... and at the same time spoiled me forever after.

Fast forward to December. Virginia was pregnant with Elizabeth (Paris in September.) We had about two weeks to visit in New Jersey and Louisiana between the return flight from London to New York and beginning active duty in Pensacola. I'm not sure where but somewhere at a party I ran into Gene Berry. He was a longtime close friend from undergraduate SAE days and medical school at Tulane. We both interned at Southern-Pacific in San Francisco. Our new wives had become friends as well. Gene had applied early enough to be in the July Flight Surgeon Class 110. After graduating with his flight surgeon wings and leaving Pensacola he had a few weeks leave before deploying on the carrier *Roosevelt.* Our paths crossed by sheer accident. More serendipity as it turned out because Gene Berry saved my bacon!

HOW GENE BERRY
SAVED MY BACON

THERE I WUZ about to launch my active-duty career in the Navy and Gene scared the socks off me. It seems that the Marines had redesignated an air wing in November 1965 and after expansion and training it would deploy to Viet Nam. The Pensacola Flight Surgeon Faculty had announced to Gene's class that nearly all the January 1966 class of new flight surgeons would be assigned to the Marine Air Wing upon graduation in June. (It turned out that 29 of the 35 U.S. physicians in my class did indeed go with the Marines to Viet Nam…. including my medical school roommate Art Lochridge. Only six did not. One of the 29 was killed in Viet Nam.)

Gene explained that billets were assigned by order of position in the graduating class. The top person would have first choice of all available billets. The second-ranked physician would have the next choice … and on down the line. Yep! Gene saved my bacon by scaring the socks off me. He put a Motivation on me with a capital "M" in bold, large format. Study, study, study was the message/suggestion/warning. Pensacola would be no country club duty like that summer at Oak Knoll. In fact, I studied more diligently at flight surgeon school in Pensacola than I did in medical school and was fortunate to get an aircraft carrier assignment.

In due course we went to Pensacola right after Christmas to find an apartment suitable for a studying maniac and his pregnant wife. We found a delightful place at the Bayshore Apartments. It was a little more expensive than other choices but it was new, clean, had an elevator and a good view of Pensacola Bay from the sixth-floor unit we rented. We were now a two-car family and the Bayshore was close to the main gate of the Pensacola Naval Air Station (NAS) so not much time would be wasted commuting.

II

FLIGHT SURGEON
TRAINING

NAVAL AEROSPACE
MEDICAL INSTITUTE

I REPORTED FOR duty at the Naval Aerospace Medical Institute (NAMI) the last week of December and thus began my active-duty service as a Navy Flight Surgeon. Classes began 3 January 1966 at 0700. [Note that I have herewith shifted to military date and time designations. :)] We had orientation presentations and introductions of the faculty members. The various elements of our training were detailed including an overview of the six months program with a calendar of events and planned graduation day. The daily routines and schedules were discussed. We received study materials with a few textbooks. Maps of the NAS and NAMI building were distributed and discussed including the Officers Club location. Everyone was in high spirits with this new adventure which was so different from standard medical school and hospital work. Most everyone (except me) was looking forward to a relaxed program with time for golf, tennis and a variety of recreational activities available in the area both through the navy and in other venues.

We had time to meet and greet all the others in our class. There were two doctors from Argentina who upon graduation would be the only two flight surgeons in the Argentine navy. They would rotate every six months on the single Argentine carrier. We had one doctor from France who would be stationed on Corsica after graduation. The thirty-five U.S. Navy doctors were from an assortment of medical schools and with many different individual circumstances. Some were single, some married, some had children …. most were mid-twenties and just out of internship. Art Lochridge, Bob Blews and myself were medical school classmates at Tulane and Art was my roommate for two years.

Of course, everyone was in uniform. We had previously all received our uniform allowance with instructions on what to purchase and where to get it. We were required to have service dress blue, dress white and service dress khaki uniforms with khaki and white covers. Military formal attire (equivalent to a tuxedo) was not required. I think everyone was a lieutenant and sported two standard stripes on their shoulder boards and sleeves as appropriate along with the oakleaf and acorn medical corps embroidery as mentioned above. We had rank and medical corps pins for our shirt collars. We also had "fore and aft" covers for use with flight suits which were also required. We were not required to have swords like line officers because we were considered non-combatants. That was good because swords were expensive and not included in the uniform allowance. Someone joked that we could always sling scalpels to our belts with shoelaces if necessary. After the lowkey and relaxed orientation we headed for lunch at the O-club. Compared to medical school this was going to be a "piece of cake" and I might well have been the only one savvy about the marines in Viet Nam. Because of that this was going to be a serious competition when the word got out. In Navy jargon "the word" meant information, official and otherwise. It could also be called "the skinny," "the scoop" or especially "scuttlebutt" which could be truth or rumor. [Scuttlebutt has an interesting origin.]

The six months break I had enjoyed is known in the Navy as "R & R", rest and relaxation. It turned out to be a good thing. Most all the other doctors in SFS Class 112 had been working as physicians during the six months, many working some weekends and nights, covering emergency rooms and the like. Upon finding the very relaxed atmosphere and low-key academic pursuits, no one was the least worried about studying at this point. There would be no classes or requirements for Saturdays, Sundays, holidays or nights. It was a Monday through Friday classroom format with a leisurely lunch break (I seem to recall several hours.) and early finish each afternoon. Happy Hour at the O-club beckoned for some after class and alcoholic drinks were handily available during O-club lunches.

The first three weeks of classes covered naval history, protocol, etiquette et al. We were expected to learn saluting, rank order for getting in and out of boats, uniform regulations, formal visitation procedures at new duty stations, relationships with senior officers and their spouses. There was a lot of material but it was non-challenging. My two months at Oak Knoll was invaluable and provided a good base of experience and understanding. I studied carefully and diligently. The tests were mostly multiple choice. I routinely scored a full hundred-point grade on these tests. Those who didn't study at all scored 92 - 94 or so with ease. No one was the least concerned at that point. Compared to the difficulties and stress of medical school and internship this NAMI instruction was going to be a crip course.

After three weeks the aerospace medical classes began. We had instruction in ophthalmology and vision in aviation; hearing, audiology, vertigo, disorientation, pressure changes; altitude physiology including pressure chamber runs; psychology, neurology and psychiatry; cardiology and electrocardiography; even fields like dermatology, pediatrics, radiology, sexually transmitted diseases, family counseling and a plethora of areas related to being a physician for navy personnel and their families. Many of the latter areas were just short passing orientations. The real emphasis was on the areas important to pilots and flight. Classes also included carrier operations overview including catapults, arresting cables, tailhooks, flight paths and Fresnel lenses and just a whole lot of exposure to Naval Aviation.

THE WORD IS OUT AND
THE PRESSURE IS ON

AFTER ABOUT THREE weeks everyone became aware of the Marine Air Wing and the large number of us to be assigned to it and a tour to Viet Nam. I can't say that panic set in but everyone became a lot more serious. Meanwhile I had developed intense study habits. Most days I would take a sandwich or other lunch in a brown bag and study through the lunch break, sitting in the TR-4 munching and reading until time for class to start again. When class was over, I would go straight back to the Bayshore and start studying. Virginia would bring me mini-sandwiches, snacks, coffee, etc. and I just worked straight through to bedtime. There was no television time, we didn't go out to eat, even on weekends I studied. In essence about all I did for the bulk of four or five months was go to class, eat, sleep and study. They never caught me!

Do the math like this. One person scores 100 points on 20 exams while person two scores 92 points on the same tests. Then for the next 200 tests both people score 100 on all tests. Who do you think will have the higher average score? They never caught me!

When duty station/billet selection time came along in June I was fortunate to be able to select Carrier Airwing Seven (CVW-7) based at NAS Oceana in Virginia Beach, Virginia and deploying aboard *U.S.S. Independence (CVA-62)* to the Mediterranean. [The "C" in these designations means "carrier", V means fixed wing aircraft, W is for wing-size unit, A is for attack.]

THE CURRICULUM

NAVAL AEROSPACE MEDICAL INSTITUTE

STUDENT FLIGHT SURGEON Training Program ... The Naval Aerospace Medical Institute (NAMI) has many mission goals besides training physicians to be flight surgeons in the fleet. NAMI does research in flight physiology and other aspects of aviation. There is a residency in aerospace medicine and there are other programs. Here is a quote of the <u>Purpose of NAMI</u>:

To Support Navy and Marine Corps aviation units through expert aeromedical consultation, services development and application of aeromedical standards and training of aeromedical personnel for operational assignments.

The discussion in this book is only regarding the training of flight surgeons and how it was in 1966 when THERE I WUZ enrolled in Student Flight Surgeon Class 112. Undoubtedly there have been changes in the curriculum since then. I don't recall the exact week by week classes and training exercises as they evolved. It was a complex and comprehensive curriculum. The goal was to prepare physicians to be Navy Flight Surgeons who would be competent in supporting naval aviation. This involved multiple phases. We began the day for the first month or so with an hour-long outdoor drill session. A Marine Drill Sergeant gave us an abbreviated version of boot camp training. It was essentially an overview so we would understand the navy indoctrination of enlisted personnel. Those of us who had some boy scout experience already knew about left face, right face, about face, etc. Those without previous exposure were funny and awkward with the marching drills. We laughed a lot at some of the goofs. The Marine sergeant had a good sense of humor. He knew it was just a familiarization course for a bunch of docs.

After the hour of drill, we stood in formation outside the building while Commander Gregg conducted the orders of the day.... schedule for that day, announcements, question and answer opportunity, etc. One day one of the docs raised his hand to ask a question and upon being recognized, said, "Sir, we're not having fun, sir." Of course, there was uproarious laughter from the group. A lot of this drill instruction was tongue-in-cheek anyway because it was only for orientation and overview. Nobody expected a bunch of doctors to be proficient at close order drill.

Commander Gregg was the administrator of the flight surgeon training program but was not senior in rank. Some of the "professors" who taught the academics were full "bird" Captains. CDR Gregg was really a "good guy" and his intent was to see everyone succeed. He was friendly, low key and encouraged informality around the protocols we were learning. He was more of a guide and friend to us all than an authority figure. We of course respected his rank, seniority, experience and responsibility for our training but he was a good leader and motivator rather than an authoritarian. We liked him and responded to his friendly guidance.

A typical day involved classroom academics for three or four hours after the drill session, then a generous lunch break followed by practical hands-on training of various sorts for the rest of the day. (See details below.) The drill sessions only lasted a month or six weeks then we began directly with Dr. Gregg's muster and announcements. The day ended when the practical training was over, sometimes by three or four o'clock, never past five.

Academic classes included flight physiology, especially regarding vestibular phenomena from motion and from pressure changes. There was a lot of material and emphasis on vision in aviation. We studied cardiovascular effects of flight including G-forces. We had long lectures and discussions about the psychology of flight, of aviators and the stresses of an extremely dangerous occupation. Overall, the academics reviewed what we already knew from medical school and then how it applied to aviation. Course sections included Ophthalmology, Otolaryngology, Cardiology, Psychiatry, Neurology, Dermatology and all the other specialty areas. Some particulars of the various sections are as follows:

1. Ophthalmology … importance of precise vision in aviation, refraction, retinoscopy, night vision, monocular depth perception and the "bomber's moon," diseases and injuries of the eye, etc. This was really a major section with considerable emphasis.

2. Otolaryngology … vestibular apparatus, effects of motion, motion sickness, Coriolis effect in flight and techniques to avoid it, dizziness and vertigo from other causes, Eustachian tube function and dysfunction, lots more. Hearing and auditory communication were studied including disorders and compensations.

3. Cardiology … gravity forces (widely called G-forces), high and low blood pressure, arrhythmias, electrocardiograms, physiologic stresses of flying, etc.

4. Pulmonology …Lung function, altitude and pressure changes, altitude sickness, oxygen use, safeguards in naval aviation, et al.

5. Psychiatry and Psychology … emotional and mental stresses of flying, fear of death, management when friends are killed, handling pilots with "close calls" and again a lot more including the personalities of pilots and aircrew, their motivations,

relationships with families and friends, stress relievers, et al. More major emphasis here.

In total the academic parts of navy flight surgeon training were superb. In a systematic way but remaining relatively low-key the curriculum reviewed each topic from the medical aspects then applied it to aviation. The material was filled with lots of practical information and how to handle various situations we would encounter in the fleet with our pilots, aircrew and even their families.... including some aviation aspects of enlisted support personnel. There were discussions of general medical conditions not related to flight but commonly seen in military and especially carrier situations. It was an enlightening and rewarding six months.

The academics were not difficult but they rapidly became challenging when the "word got out" about Marine/Viet Nam assignments. The examinations were easy. One could score over ninety points out of the perfect one hundred just from listening in class and with no study. But study we did and sometimes nearly everyone would score 100 on an exam.

A NOTE ON THE PSYCHOLOGY
OF MILITARY UNITS

DESMOND MORRIS IN his writings, in particular "The Naked Ape" and "The Human Zoo," described the psychology of human herds and small group identity. The military has understood these principles for thousands of years and Naval Aviation is organized around those principles. The operational unit in naval aviation is organized as the squadron. Each squadron is composed of about thirty officers or a few more and about two hundred enlisted, divided into smaller groups each responsible for an area such as maintenance of the aircraft (mainframe, engines, ejection seats, etc.), weapons, avionics, equipment (oxygen systems, parachutes, etc.), et al. Each squadron has twelve to twenty aircraft. A carrier air wing consists of eight to ten squadrons or detachments. [A detachment of a parent squadron ashore such as helicopters and air early-warning aircraft (with radar domes) have fewer aircraft, officers and men.] Total complement of aircraft on a deployed carrier is between 75 to 100 aircraft with airwing personnel of a bit over 2,000. More about all this later.

Small groups of people function more efficiently than larger groups for several reasons. Mainly the members of smaller groups know one another better, likes and dislikes, habits, skills, history, family, etc. ….

just like small groups in civilian life. This enhances teamwork with specific goals in sight. It also makes delegation of responsibility more direct and the same for accountability. Being mostly all young men (now women also) in their early twenties there is lots of competition. If you saw the movie "Top Gun" you will understand completely. There is significant competition but at the same time cooperation, togetherness and team orientation in the shared common goals. While the individuals compete within the small group, they identify with, defend and promote the overall squadron unit. The squadrons compete against one another in similar fashion while maintaining their common mission teamwork on the carrier.

Okay-Three is Ten Points ... The best example of this inter-squadron competition is the scoring system for landing on the carrier. A carrier landing is known as a trap. The basic idea is to lower the tailhook on your aircraft, land on a pitching deck at the right place, at the right angle, at the right speed and lined up with the center line of the carrier's angled deck.... to engage your tailhook with one of the large steel arresting cables stretched across the deck (three now, four when I deployed.) The cable plays out as it absorbs the weight and speed (35-50,000 pounds and 130 knots) and slows the aircraft to a stop.... and even pulls it backward a bit. After doing this successfully you have made a trap and scored ten points if every aspect was correct and your tailhook caught the number three cable. Each pilot's scores are logged and the whole squadron's averages are in competition with the other squadrons.

The difficulty comes when the ship is pitching, rolling or yawing * .... in any combination and sometimes all three ... sometimes at night .... sometimes in the rain and strong wind .... sometimes all of that. At least the ship always turns into the wind for launches and recoveries. This provides more airspeed lift with less power from the engines and a decreased closing rate plane to ship. It also eliminates crosswinds ... usually.

Over the course of a cruise a pilot may have a hundred or more traps and over a career many more. Of all the skills a naval aviator must acquire and perfect …. and become proficient at performing as a routine without adrenaline-spurting shakes …. carrier landings are the most physically and mentally taxing … and the most hazardous. [See old stories #1 and #2 below.]

In the spirit of friendly small-group competition among squadrons and among individuals within a single squadron, every trap is given a numerical score between Zero and Ten. If you perform a perfect approach and arrest on the number three wire at which you are aiming, your score would be "okay three" which earns 10 points. If you are slightly long and catch the four wire, that's an "okay four" which is also 10 points. If your approach was wobbly, too low and hazardous, or if you catch the number one or number two wire, then fewer points are earned. If you "bolter", meaning you miss all the wires and have to "go around" i.e., fly the race-track pattern and do another approach…. you get a Zero on your score tally. Over the course of a cruise each pilot has an average score and added together yields the squadron average. It's an ongoing friendly competition. [I had a senior F-4 Phantom pilot (A.L.) who had all ten-point "okay three" traps for the entire cruise. During down time he went to his room and painted oil-on-canvass scenes while listening to classical music. He was not the usual jet jockey.]

* **Pitching** is when the ship rocks up and down lengthwise causing the flight deck bow and stern to rise and fall. This may cause you to hit the fantail (rear of ship) or overfly the arresting cables no matter how perfect your approach. **Rolling** is like a pencil rolling on a flat surface so that the flight deck changes from horizontally level to a slant one way, then another. **Yawing** is when the bow and stern are going back and forth horizontally so that the fantail and flight deck are moving side to side in the ocean.

> Old story #1 … If a lawyer makes a mistake, he sends his client to jail; if a doctor makes a mistake, he sends his patient to the undertaker; if a minister makes a

mistake, he sends his congregation to hell …. but if a carrier pilot makes a mistake, he kills himself.

Old story #2 … (Fondly told by Naval Aviators to Air Force Pilots) "Anybody can land on a stationary two-mile runway."

NAVAVBREVFAM

PART OF THE training in Pensacola was learning how to read, understand, discuss and use navy abbreviations.... which are myriad and widely used. Along the way we also became familiar with jargon, common terms and other traditions. Those will be found in other sections and the Glossary.

I just made up the title of this chapter. NAVAVBREVFAM means "Naval Aviation Abbreviation Familiarization." It is no less confusing than many common navy abbreviations. Some are quite simple and easy to pick up. Examples would be CO for Commanding Officer, XO for Executive Officer, CPO for Chief Petty Officer, CDR for Commander, LCDR for Lieutenant Commander, etc. Some are straight forward but a little mysterious until you are "in the know." Examples would be CINCLANT and CINCPAC which mean Commander-in-Chief Atlantic and Commander-in-Chief Pacific.

Then there is SOPA which remains confusing because it has a double meaning that depends on where you are. It means officially the Senior Officer Present Afloat, but it can also mean Senior Officer Present Ashore, although sometimes that is written SOP(A). It is also used to mean Standard Operating Procedures Afloat AND Standard Operating Procedures Ashore. Maybe a professional career navy person can elucidate this one a little. There is also SOFA which means Status of Forces Agreement and there is SO which means Special Warfare Operator, a.k.a. US Navy SEAL, which also implies you know that means "**Se**a, **A**ir, **L**and." Yep, it takes a heap-o-learnin' to become fluent as a savvy sailor…. and once you do get comfortable with the lingo you are BRAVO ZULU (a.k.a. BZ), meaning "well done."

We weren't concerned much with SECNAV but BUPERS and BUMED were important to us. The COD was important. COD meant Carrier Onboard Delivery and it was the term we used for the propeller support plane that shuttled back and forth to the carrier from various shore stations. The COD brought personnel onto the ship and took them ashore when needed, for example emergency leave when someone had a death or serious illness of a spouse.

[I arrived on the carrier in the COD on a flight from Rota, Spain to the *Independence* which was at sea just off Barcelona. It was my first trap.]

Enough about abbreviations for now. They will be used liberally throughout this book without explanation and the reader is invited to refer to the glossary as often as needed.

Let's proceed on to the FAM parts of the training program for flight surgeons in Pensacola. FAM means "familiarization" and is a training element which does not expect to have the student learn to be an expert in something …. or even proficient … or even comfortable …. but at least familiar with it. We had a great many FAM training exercises during the six months including PRIFLY at the end where we did multiple FamHops in the exact same training program at Saufley Field where naval aviators are taught to fly.

FAMEX =
FAMILIARIZATION EXERCISES

[I just love making up these abbreviations because the Navy has so many and to this day, I still don't understand a lot of them… so making up new ones is sort of a diabolical revenge.]

MOST OF THE afternoons in Pensacola at the flight surgeon school were utilized as training exercises for our bunch of docs who were new to the navy and mostly slimy pollywogs at that. We had so much to learn if we were to be effective in our roles as physicians and officers in the Navy and particularly in Naval Aviation. The following section details stand-alone topics and discussions of FAMEX in which we participated. They are not in any order. Some were one afternoon training, some multiple days. All were exciting and valuable.

As previously noted, we had academic classroom work every morning, then a lunch break and after lunch we met at a designated time and at various designated places around NAS Pensacola such as the pressure chamber, the gym, the swimming pool, the ejection seat trainer, et al. We were met usually by a chief. (Chief = Chief Petty Officer = CPO.) There is an old saying that the CPOs run the Navy and there is great truth to that. The CPOs are both expert and experienced in their fields.

They know how everything works and how to fix it when it doesn't. (More on this later.)

When meeting a CPO instructor for the day he would introduce himself and give us an overview of the afternoon's topic, equipment, exercise, whatever. This might involve a lengthy lecture or it might just be a brief welcome as we began the exercise. In lots of cases, we had already received classroom instructions about the session.

DILBERT DUNKER

Starting with one of the most dramatic and most difficult exercises is appropriate. The Dilbert Dunker was developed during World War Two to train pilots how to egress the cockpit of an airplane which has been ditched in the water. This was before the days of jet aircraft and ejection seats. Propeller aircraft would usually turn upside down upon contact with the water. It is not an easy feat to exit the cockpit underwater, upside down, wearing full flight gear including helmet, strapped into the seat with strong harness and with connected radio wires et al. Also, the instrument panel was tightly over your knees with your feet on the pedals and with the stick between your legs. If you don't do it right, you don't get out and you drown. The Dilbert Dunker was designed to teach pilots how to do it right.

The huge bulky Dilbert Dunker "machine" is perched above the deep end of the swimming pool. It is a steel open cockpit simulator ... exactly like an airplane cockpit but without the glass overhead. The dunker cockpit is mounted on two strong steel rails which descend into the water far enough for the entire cockpit to be submerged. At the end of the track the rails are configured so that the cockpit flips forward and turns upside down. The forty-five-degree angle of the rails ensures that you hit the water at 25 miles per hour, go underwater and rapidly invert. Talk about a THERE I WUZ situation ... this is it.

We reported to the indoor swimming pool in full flight gear.... orange jump suit, boots, helmet. The CPO in charge welcomed us and explained the procedures and rules. There were half a dozen enlisted sailors assisting the chief including two or three in wet suits with face masks and SCUBA diving equipment. The required protocol was to climb the ladder and into the cockpit in full gear, then the staff strapped you into the harness and connected your communication wires. (We were given already-wet helmets to use so that we would not get our own wet.) Upon your signal that you were ready they released the dunker and down you accelerated into the drink. Almost immediately you found yourself hanging in the harness upside down. Not only did you have to egress safely, but you also had to do it exactly right according to instructed technique. The divers were watching you both for safety and to observe if you did it right. If you got out safely, but didn't do it properly, you had to repeat the dunker dive as many times as necessary to get a thumbs up from the divers.

The accepted technique was as follows:

1. Take a good deep breath just before hitting the water and hold it.
2. When the cockpit stopped upside down, do nothing until the bubbles subsided.
3. Then remove the communication wires first, then unbuckle the harness.
4. Then grab the "overhead" steel rim of the cockpit (below you underwater) with both hands and pull yourself further down deeper in the water until you are clear of the cockpit.
5. Next swim laterally up and away from the cockpit at a forty-five-degree angle to the surface. This was to insure you cleared the burning fuel likely to be on the surface in a ditching situation.

Some of our class made four or five trips down to dunker hell before getting it right. I was successful on the first try.... for two reasons. First, I didn't want to do it more than the one time and, I wanted a high score on my record to keep out of Viet Nam. It was a double strong motivation to listen carefully to the instructions and go over them in my mind in preparation, then follow them to the letter. Also, since I wasn't first, I could watch the others.

Several of the class became disoriented, couldn't get out of the harness and the divers had to release their harness for them and pull them out while giving them oxygen via mask. The thumbs down meant the student had to "go around" again…. sort of like a bolter on the carrier…. and again, and again until they did it properly. It took the entire afternoon for all thirty-eight of us to successfully complete the exercise. I can tell you that my thumbs up on the first try was a beautiful sight indeed.

IN THE OCEAN INSIDE

THE WORD "NAVY" derives from Greek and Latin, then through French. It means ship or boat and more specifically a group of them. Where there are ships, there is water. The surface of our earth is 71% water, mostly oceans but also lakes, rivers, etc. Entire volumes would be required (and many have been written) to describe the varied aspects and considerations regarding oceans. Although our small group of physicians was in training to be FLIGHT surgeons, we were also going to be sailors, navy men. Except for periods of shore duty, we were going to spend a lot of time on the seas.

Leave it to the Navy to put a piece of the ocean indoors. In the case at Pensacola, it was the Olympic-size swimming pool enclosed in a huge building much like an aircraft hangar. It was the site of several training exercises. The Dilbert Dunker at one side of the deep end of the pool was the most dramatic training exercise but the others were more grueling and more important.

First, we studied oceans in the classroom…. overview, water survival, safety and lots more. After all we would not only be onboard a ship in a vast ocean, but also flying over it far away from the ship and its rescue capabilities. We learned that even in eighty-degree water your survival time was limited, so getting into a life raft and out of the water as soon as possible was important. We learned that if a pilot was down in the colder ocean with water at forty degrees or so like in the Arctic Ocean, survival time was twenty minutes. If wearing an anti-exposure suit (a.k.a. "poopy suit" … more about this elsewhere), survival time was extended to sixty minutes. If a rescue boat or helicopter had not retrieved a downed pilot quickly, he could be a goner even after successful ejection and parachuting. Our classroom orientation included a survey of potential situations, procedures and techniques for safety and survival, and lots more.

Also, once we deployed to the fleet one of our major functions would be to educate and train our pilots and other flight crew about the medical aspects of all these safety and survival topics. The classroom work was comprehensive and it prepared us for the "lab" …. which was that big chunk of ocean in the hangar. On multiple afternoons we reported to the indoor pool where the instructor team was waiting to put us through the paces. Required training included ocean survival. We had to tread water and float for ten (or was it twenty?) minutes in full flight gear. That might not sound like a long time but in full flight gear it was not as easy as it sounds. Another exercise was the survival swim. We had to do laps in the pool, wearing flight gear, and swim several miles, was it five?

Another day we practiced the technique of jumping from a ship high above the water. The flight deck of a carrier is twenty stories above the water! The training pool had a large platform about twenty feet high (or was it thirty?) extended out from the edge. We had to jump off the platform into the water, again wearing our flight gear. To pass we had to demonstrate the proper techniques else we had to keep repeating the jump until we got it right. Essentially the idea was to avoid injury as much as possible. The proper technique was to jump feet first, legs and ankles tightly crossed and locked, both hands firmly holding the groin and head straight or slightly back. The risks of the water impact were flailing and broken arms and legs and/or a hard blow to the groin or to the face. Jumping feet first minimized the risk of a broken neck, head injury or flail chest. I was a happy swimmer when one successful jump earned me the beautiful thumbs up.

I found the high jump more stressful than the Dilbert Dunker, the long-distance survival swim or any other of the water exercises. I must say that the instructor team was professional, helpful and friendly. They respected the physician group and wanted us to succeed. We rapidly developed respect for their expertise and skill in getting us all qualified. Usually, it took all an afternoon for the entire class to complete the day's exercise. We were able to socialize and get to know one another while watching the others and waiting for our turn. That was probably part of the intended training as well although not formally in the curriculum.

NOTE: Fortunately, when deployed later in the fleet I did not need any of the water survival skills …. although I almost did in the Mississippi River in 1969, about which more later.

GETTING HIGH AT NA-MIGH (NAMI)

WE ALL DID it. We were required to do it. We got high to observe its effects and we watched the others do it. We also did it for the fun of it. We got high in groups of five or more and we gave each other high-fives while we were high. This makes perfect sense when you realize we are talking about the high-altitude pressure chamber training.

Again, we started with the classroom academic study of high altitude. The higher you go above the sea level surface, the lower is atmospheric pressure and the lower is the oxygen concentration. That has remarkable effects on people. Up to about 5,000 feet there is not much to notice. Between 8,000 to 10,000 feet subtle effects begin. The higher you go the more profound are the effects of low oxygen pressure.

Common symptoms are headache and light headedness, shortness of breath, disorientation, loss of coordination, nausea, lethargy, and eventually cerebral edema, coma and death at the highest altitudes.

This refers to the acute altitude changes of aviation. People who live and work at high altitudes compensate over time by building higher levels of red blood cells to carry more oxygen around the body. "Mountain sickness" is a well-known term for not being acclimated to altitude.

In naval aviation and particularly in jet aircraft there are often rapid changes in altitude so an oxygen mask with 100% oxygen is standard required procedure for aircrew. (Combined with G-forces a low blood-oxygen level can have dramatic and serious effects including death.) So, we studied pulmonary physiology at length in the classroom with emphasis on its application and importance in aviation.

Then off we went one afternoon to the pressure chamber. That's a misnomer because it's really a low-pressure chamber and its proper name is Hypobaric Chamber. (Not to be confused with a hyperbaric chamber used for medical conditions.) The unit is a large steel rounded chamber with numerous windows for observers. Using vacuum pumps, the pressure within the chamber can be lowered progressively to simulate the oxygen pressure at the various altitudes. Gauges record everything much like submarines monitor pressure at depth.

The training exercise was called a "chamber run." Five or six of us would go into the chamber with the ever-present instructors/safety staff. The entrance would be sealed and we would be seated, donning oxygen masks. We all breathed 100% oxygen for a bit to purge nitrogen from our bloodstreams, thus preventing decompression sickness (the "bends") from occurring during the ascent. Then the pumps started decreasing pressure to simulate increasing altitude in the chamber. We continued with 100% oxygen until the simulated altitude was up to around 25,000 feet conditions.

One or two of us at a time would remove our mask and begin trivial tasks such as playing solitaire with a deck of cards, writing our name on a tablet or two student subjects might face off and start playing "patty-cake" with their hands. We were looking to determine the "Time of Useful Consciousness" which varies with the individual. Those still wearing oxygen masks and those observing from outside through the viewing ports were watching the test subjects' behavior to note decreasing coordination and any other signs and symptoms. The safety staff were vigilantly standing by to replace someone's oxygen mask in the event of unconsciousness. On signal we replaced our O2 masks and the next two

docs would remove theirs and so on until everyone had a turn. One of
the teaching goals was for everyone to try to understand his own subtle
indications of early hypoxia before the time of useful consciousness was
exceeded. Observers found amusement in the discombobulations of the
subjects. We all learned a great deal about altitude, pressure, oxygen, et
al which would be a significant part of our flight surgeon responsibilities.
Everybody passed the chamber run exercises which were a valuable
experience.

Another part of the "chamber run" was to test everyone's Eustachian
tube function. This had two considerations. First was a simulated rapid
decompression as if a cabin door blew off an aircraft or if the canopy
blew off a fighter jet at high altitude. The second was clearing of the ear
on descent from altitude which is frequent in military aircraft.

We of course had studied pressure changes and middle ear
clearance in the classroom section on otolaryngology. * With sudden
decompression the ambient pressure rapidly decreases dramatically
and if the Eustachian tube cannot accommodate the change, severe
vertigo can result. In the other direction decreasing altitude causes
increasing atmospheric pressure and if the Eustachian tube can't
accommodate that by letting air pressure up into the middle ear space,
again, severe vertigo, intense pain in the ear and even a ruptured
eardrum can occur.

If you have done some air travel you probably know that going up in
a plane is usually not a problem as air can get down the Eustachian tube
and out of the middle ear space without a problem. However, descending
can be a big problem because it is much more difficult for air to get up
the Eustachian tube into the middle ear. Stretching of the eardrum
is painful so the Eustachian tube must open frequently to relieve the
pressure buildup. If it's not spontaneous from yawning, chewing gum
and the like, a Val Salva maneuver is required to force air into the middle
ear space. (You might have noticed that babies on a plane often start
crying from the ear pain on descent. The crying provides relief from
release of the pressure.

*The otolaryngology section was taught by Dr. B-------- who was a senior navy captain. He was interesting, informative and professional but his accent was so thick that one could hardly tell the difference when he said "ear" and "air" ... so he spelled the word each time: "The air, A-I-R, in the middle ear, E-A-R, has to freely move in and out through the Eustachian tube." Dr. B----- also took glee in telling how he once "busted" the son of the CNO (Chief of Naval Operations) for a Eustachian deficiency. The young man was in training and couldn't clear his ears well so Dr. B---- put him in the pressure chamber and "crashed" it.... 25,000 ft. to sea level in a few seconds. The young man flunked the test and was "busted" out of the flight training program. This is known as the NAMI Whammy.

THE EJECTION SEAT
TRAINER WAS A BLAST

THIS WAS A most interesting training exercise. As usual we had didactic information beforehand. The ejection seat evolution has been a necessity. With slower earlier propeller-driven aircraft when something went wrong a pilot "bailed out" by just jumping from the cockpit and deploying his parachute. With the advent of higher-speed aircraft this became impossible because of the extreme forces involved.

The earliest ejection seats were manufactured by the Martin-Baker company (British, since 1929.) The ejection seat is essentially a steel seat frame with cushions, harnesses, etc. which has been fitted with an explosive charge to blast the seat with its strapped-in pilot up, out and away from the aircraft. The force of the explosive charge must be sufficient to clear the pilot safely and for many years pilots suffered compression fractures of the spine when ejecting.

Another problem was when an aircraft had a sink rate, i.e., was falling faster than the ability of the seat to eject the pilot safely. Early seats required certain minimums of altitude and/or airspeed to safely function. Modern seats have "zero-zero" capability meaning you can be sitting in the cockpit on the runway or deck with "zero-zero" altitude and speed and the ejection will project you high enough for the parachute to deploy and float you safely to the ground. That extra power also helps when an aircraft has a sink rate.

To prevent more and more extreme force shock to the pilot, modern ejection seats have rockets connected with the explosive charge so that on ejection enough additional height/distance can be achieved without so much shock to the pilot. Compression fracture rates were lowered with this development.

Then there is the problem with the canopy over the aircrew person. In the movie "Top Gun" what killed "Goose" who was "Maverick's" RIO (Tom Cruise's 'back-seater' Radar Intercept Officer) was impact with the canopy on ejection. Several mechanisms have been used to solve this problem. The canopy can be blown off in its entirety, it can be exploded to break it into pieces or the seat can have spikes to puncture it. Usually, the first way is best.

How is the ejection seat activated? There are two large steel loop "handles" attached to the seat, both having yellow and black spiral stripes to make them stand out for quick identification. The preferred handle is above the pilot's head going from side to side and when pulled forcefully down it carries with it a nylon cloth face curtain designed to protect from wind forces on ejection. If the situation is such that a pilot can't reach overhead, the second handle is between his legs on the front of the seat bottom. All the oxygen hoses, communication wires, anti-gravity lines, etc. are designed for quick disconnect on ejection.

After ejection when at the peak of the trajectory the seat automatically separates from the pilot and the parachute deploys. The parachute pack is attached to the seat harness into which the aircrewman sits and "straps in." The harness and parachute stay with the pilot when the seat separates.

In fore-and-aft pilot/RIO configurations the rear seat is automatically ejected prior to the front seat to prevent what happened to Goose, i.e., impact with the canopy or pilot overhead. Both seats are equipped with ejection handles. So, if the pilot ejects, the rear-seater is automatically ejected first, then his own seat ... but if the rear-seater ejects, the pilot is not ejected …. unless the rear-seater specifically activates a control to be used when the pilot is incapacitated and cannot eject himself.

With all that complicated and intricately coordinated equipment you may be wondering just how much an ejection seat costs? They are expensive …. several hundred thousand dollars.

Another part of our training during this segment was devoted to parachutes. We went to the parachute "loft" which is a large area with long tables where parachutes can be spread out, sewn, repaired, etc. Then using specific techniques, the parachutes are carefully folded and put into their casings with fittings for strong attachment to the parachute harness. The parachutes obviously must be quite strong, but lightweight nylon parachute cord is famous for its strength. The harness is strong wide nylon webbing with quick-release metal buckles. Every pilot is totally dependent on the professional competence of the parachute packers.

Speaking of professionals … the instructor staff in each phase of training in Pensacola was highly competent, skilled and motivated, dedicated to teaching us what we needed to know and friendly in responding to questions.

Back to the ejection seat trainer. We reported in full flight gear including helmet and steel-toed boots. It was outdoor so a good-weather day was selected. The seat was mounted on a rail at a slight angle backwards and extending up twenty or thirty feet. The seat was equipped with only a one-third explosive charge for obvious reasons. Our training exercise consisted of each of us in turn strapping into the seat harness and demonstrating that we understood all the parts of the system. Instructors watched and guided us carefully to be sure everything was correct. What a tragedy if a physician fell out of the seat at thirty feet in the sky.

The same protocol is followed in jet fighters on the decks of aircraft carriers. When you climb up and into the cockpit, strap yourself into the harness, connect all your hoses and wires… then one of the plane attendants leans into the cockpit and pulls on all your fittings, etc. to be sure everything is okay… then gives you that wonderful thumbs up. It's too loud for verbal communication in that environment.

So, THERE I WUZ strapped in the ejection seat trainer with "all systems go." With my own thumbs up signal the ejection seat was fired and BAM …. I was thirty feet in the air. It was better and more amazing than any carnival ride. After a brief interval, the seat with me in it was slowly lowered back down the rail to the starting ground position. Unstrapping and exiting was simple enough and the next student strapped in for his blast into the big blue above. It was a fun day besides being educational, interesting and exciting. What a blast!

THE BEAT GOES ON ... MORE
AVIATION "FAM" TRAINING

IT IS DIFFICULT to remember all the phases and specific areas of instruction and "FAM" (familiarization) training promulgated (good navy/military word) during the Flight Surgeon school at NAS Pensacola because it was comprehensive, thorough and very well executed. The physician officer faculty were quite knowledgeable, mostly skilled teachers and had the practical experience of having been flight surgeons in the fleet themselves. The program was organized in similar fashion to a college science course: classroom lectures, followed by laboratory experience. The physician officers presented the lectures and classroom teaching while the practical hands-on "lab" training was done by a large group of enlisted sailors, each of whom was expert and competent in a particular area. Usually, they were chiefs and first class rated sailors who had thoroughly learned their fields and were delighted to pass their knowledge along to the docs.

LOX ... After studying the physiology of altitude and oxygen, then the learning-lab of the Hypobaric Chamber, next was the fam-lab of oxygen supply for air crews. We were introduced to oxygen masks and the accompanying hose, how to wear it, how to connect it and all the practical considerations. We learned all about LOX which is the abbreviation for liquid oxygen. The current system in use in the fleet was described and demonstrated. The big spherical cylinder containing LOX is colored bright green. O2 supply is as important to high-altitude, high-performance aviation as the fuel, communications, et al.

G-SUITS … In the classroom we studied gravity forces (G-forces) and how they affect fliers. One "G" is the effect of the normal gravitational force of the earth. With centrifugal events at high speed the number of G's or gravitational force on the body goes up dramatically in jet aircraft, particularly when engaged in air combat maneuvers (ACM, a.k.a. dog fighting.) With G-forces blood is forced into the lower extremities and abdomen, depriving the brain of adequate blood-oxygen which causes loss of consciousness, a.k.a. blackout. A partial blackout is known as a grey-out and usually losing one's peripheral vision is the first thing noticed. Making an acute turn in a jet is often referred to as "pulling G's" (likely derived from pulling back on the stick for the turn.) Pilots learn to recognize their own symptoms from pulling G's and how to counteract the effects.

Modern pilots are equipped with anti-gravity harnesses known as G-suits. A G-suit looks a little like a garter belt with legs. It is worn low on the hips and is fastened around both legs. There are air bladders over the abdomen, thighs and calves. The G-suit is plugged into an air pump fitting in the cockpit. When G-forces are "pulled" the bladders are inflated automatically in proportion to the G's. This causes pressure on the large muscles of the calves, thighs and the lower abdomen to prevent pooling of blood from the G-forces. Pilots also learn how to tense their muscles and abdomen to enhance the G-suit effect and thus increase the number of G's they can tolerate. We had thorough show-and-tell demonstrations and instruction one afternoon.

Anti-Exposure Suit … Essentially this is a big rubber balloon shaped like a person and worn by air crewmen to protect against the effects of cold-water immersion. The suit is made of neoprene much like a wetsuit. They are usually bright orange. The purpose is to extend survival time in icy water while awaiting rescue. Their common name in the navy is "Poopysuit" because it is impossible to take a restroom break from the cockpit of a jet fighter. So, if, as and when such relief is necessary, pilots just let 'er rip. Even if no relief functions are required on a flight, one usually loses about five pounds of sweat because when not in icy water the suits are hot. After a flight most aircrew remove their poopy suits in the shower, turn them inside-out, wash thoroughly and hang them to dry for the next flight. One is not to ask about the aromas commonly found in poopy suits.

FITNESS, FOOD AND SYNCOPE

IT WAS IMPORTANT to achieve good physical fitness while in Pensacola…. for three reasons. First, I was a little out of shape. During medical school I participated in competitive badminton regularly whenever there was time. Also, we "ran the stairs" at Big Charity hospital and at our young age we really kept in good shape. During the internship not so much and that six months of R&R in Europe between internship and Pensacola resulted in less activity and putting on a few pounds. The second reason was that part of our grades (thus rank in class, thus being able to avoid Viet Nam in the Marines) would be determined by scores on physical training exercises…. running, swimming, etc. The third reason was to be trim and fit whether I billeted on a ship, a Naval Air Station or Viet Nam.

After Gene Berry "saved my bacon" I started on a bacon and butter diet, a.k.a. Low Carbohydrate Diet. The medical physiology of keeping your carb intake below 100 grams daily, preferably below 60gms, was to deprive Krebs Cycle of the energy of metabolism thus forcing your body to draw on previously metabolized energy. The excess calories you have previously metabolized and not used have been stored as fat. It's sort of like a bear hibernating and living off the summer's fat storage. A low-carb diet is not healthy long term but quite effective short term and that was exactly what I needed. One of the side effects and hazards of the low-carb diet is the keto acidosis you induce. When you mobilize the fatty triglycerides and use them for your day's energy, a byproduct is ketones and acidosis of the bloodstream. It is like diabetics who don't metabolize sugar for lack of insulin. Many develop ketoacidosis. You can smell it on their breath and it affects them adversely in many ways.

On the other hand, it is a fun diet while you are doing it because you can eat lots and lots of meat, but you must skip the potatoes and the bread. Non-starchy vegetables are okay, desserts are out. You can "butter your bacon" but no toast. You can drink alcoholic beverages all you want except no beer and no sweet mixers. In my case I was not imbibing much because of all the studying. An occasional glass of good dry red wine was a real treat.

Since I was eating lots of meat but no carbs, sandwiches were out. Some days I took a lunch to eat in the car and study but sometimes I did have lunch with others in the O-club. There I discovered London Broil which for some reason was new to me. Essentially it is beef (originally flank steak), marinated a little, broiled or grilled, then cut in thin slices against the grain. Yum. I had that whenever at the O-club and it fit perfectly with the low carb diet.

Well, all was well, weight was coming off, fitness was going up and there were no problems until that day in the gym. Our assignment was to run up and down the basketball court four times while being timed for a fitness grade. I was determined to score well and gave it all the speed and effort I had. On the last leg before finishing, I collapsed and sprawled out on the gym floor. THERE II WUZ. I had exhausted my glycogen stores and just passed out. It must have been something like an insulin coma event. I recovered rapidly and scrambled across the finish line to get a reasonable time score. That's the story of FITNESS, FOOD AND SYNCOPE.

LOOKING THE PART

FEW OF THE physicians enrolled in my student flight surgeon class had any prior experience in the Navy. My two months on active duty as a summer extern at Oak Knoll Naval Hospital gave me something of a leg up. I already had uniforms and knew how to wear them. I understood lots of navy protocol, navy history, terminology and what was expected in general of a naval officer and of a physician in the navy. It was an immediate advantage.

Upon medical school graduation I had been immediately promoted from Ensign to Lieutenant. As physicians we all held the rank of full Lieutenant with two wide stripes on our shoulder boards and sleeves of our dress blues. A naval officer must have dress whites, service dress khaki and service dress blues. Officers in naval aviation are known as "brown shoes" because the original flight personnel uniforms were green with brown shoes. The green uniforms were phased out including the brown shoes, but the name stuck. Non-aviation navy officers are known as "black shoes." Sometimes aviation personnel use the term in a semi-derogatory way. Aviation personnel, both officer and enlisted, are also sometimes called "Airedales" and black shoes sometimes use it with a sarcastic tweak.

On arrival in Pensacola, we were outfitted additionally with orange flight suits, helmets, steel-toed boots and other flight gear. We would use these all during our training in Pensacola and later at our duty stations. The initial few weeks of classroom instruction was designed for us to learn the intricacies of being an "officer and a gentleman."

Knowledge of saluting protocol was important. First was how to salute properly then when to offer a salute, when to return one and when a salute wasn't required and even improper. Standing for senior officers was sometimes appropriate, sometimes not.

Table manners were expected. Knowledge of navy traditions around the table were reviewed such as how to use the side-handled coffee pot on a ship. There are a lot of formalities and gentlemanly behavior expected of naval officers because of the long history thereof.

Discussions included when to wear your cover, when not, when to remove it, etc. (Landlubber readers have already been told that a navy cover is a hat.) Besides the white and khaki round covers with medallion, we also as flight personnel used the fore-and-aft soft cover which could be folded flat and hooked over a belt or stuffed in a flight suit pocket to use when wearing a flight suit. (Sometimes this cover was crudely called a "piss-cutter" but I'm not sure why.) Your rank pin was affixed to the front of this cover.

Some of looking the part of a naval officer was natural, some just learning how to wear the uniform, some learned by instruction, some by trial and error and some by occasional embarrassment if you did it wrong. Anchors aweigh, Go Navy …. THERE I WUZ.

EGO STRENGTH, RISK-TAKING, FLIGHT SURGEONS AND SHRINKS

ONE OF THE most interesting and valuable segments of flight surgeon training was the one on psychology and psychiatry in aviation. Our instructor was Dr. R---- who was a physician psychiatrist and a senior "bird" Captain Navy Flight Surgeon. He was highly experienced both in his specialty and in its applications in Naval Aviation. Besides teaching student flight surgeons, he served as psychiatrist for Naval Aviators and the students in all the training programs in Pensacola. Dr. R--- was a superb teacher possessing knowledge, wisdom beyond that and experience …. plus, patience, understanding and a friendly desire to prepare us for our roles as confidants, physicians and therapists for our naval aviators when we had earned our wings.

That last sentence is a mouthful trying to describe the psychology/ psychiatry section in Pensacola. First, we examined naval aviation from a broad scope. It is exciting and it is dangerous. It is challenging and it can be fatal. It is mentally and emotionally stressful and can push pilots beyond their tolerance. The psychological aspects of carrier aviation are crucial to its success.

If you saw the *Top Gun* movie, you will recall the first scene in which a naval aviator turned in his wings because he had lost his nerve worrying about his wife and young child at home. The stress and danger of carrier aviation had overwhelmed him and his ability to cope. That's the reason Maverick (Tom Cruise) went to 'top gun school' in California. The movie was filled with the psychology and psychiatry of naval aviation: the competitiveness among pilots even as they share small group identity and camaraderie; both humor and bravado as ways to manage stress and worry; the call signs and nicknames to establish individuality within a group occupation; the emotional decompensation Maverick experienced when his RIO Goose was killed; family emotions; relieving stress with sex …. the movie was a study in psychology and psychiatry although most viewers have no inkling of that. Most viewers are enthralled by the excitement, the bigger-than-life spectacle of naval aviation … even the fantasy of it.

Although fictional, in fact the movie was almost a documentary because real life naval aviation is exactly like the movie depicted …. except for that first scene. Naval aviators don't get to be at the top of their profession and flying in combat situations, then suddenly worry about their family at home. If they couldn't "hack" it, they would have "washed out" long before that level. Naval aviators would rather fly that phallic symbol in the sky than just about anything else in life. Later in this book I will relate some events to illustrate exactly that because THERE I WUZ.

Meanwhile back in Pensacola, THERE I WUZ in Dr. R ---'s course on psychology and psychiatry in naval aviation. We were provided several books as refreshers of the basic knowledge of psychiatry and psychology we had learned in medical school. One was Eric Erikson, MD's *Childhood and Society* (1950) which detailed the eight stages of psychosocial development and lots more pertinent background material. Another book was Erik Berne, MD's book, *Games People Play* (1964) which had a great section on Transactional Analysis. Additionally, there were reprints of articles and other materials that Dr. R--- felt were valuable in our learning curve for naval aviation.

Somewhere along during the course one of our class asked Dr. R----, "Since carrier aviation is so dangerous, why do people do it?" In his wisdom Dr. R--- smiled knowingly and responded, "As long as there are challenges young men will test themselves against them regardless of the dangers and risks."

That is also the underlying basis for a well-known old navy saying. After flying in the fleet for ten or more years and as they mature and become more senior, most pilots have seen friends get killed.... like Goose in *Top Gun*. Most have compensated well and continued as competent aviators, but a little more aware of the hazards. [The same is true in many military combat situations.] At a certain point in an aviator's career, they leave regular active daily flying ("the fleet") and move along to staff positions and command roles (a.k.a. "a desk job.") The old saying is, "**Naval aviators leave the fleet with great nostalgia, but no regrets.**" How true !!! because THERE I WUZ and witnessed it on many occasions.

Let's talk about ego strength. Erikson believed that "a sense of competence motivates behaviors and actions." If an individual achieves a sense of competence in each stage of psychosocial development, that adds to feelings of self-worth and mastery which is called ego strength. It is mandatory in naval aviation. It is not the foolish optimism of a devil-may-care Pollyanna attitude. It is the mature inner knowledge that with hard work and diligent application one's "Self" can achieve mastery of exceedingly difficult skills and tasks. This could also be called self-confidence, relaxed competence, proficiency and many other names. Naval aviation reeks with all that .... and not just in the pilots, but also in thousands of enlisted support personnel, both ship's company blue jackets and Airedale technicians. Almost to a man (and now woman) people in naval aviation have a sense of pride about what they do and their role in the success of the mission. Call it ego strength if you will.

Day after day, week after week, nearly all the time ... emphasis is placed on training with discussions on skills, demonstrations and practice, drills and exercises, contingency planning … all with the goal of developing competence and confidence up and down the line and across the board. More on this later in the book.

Carrier aviation is a dangerous proposition. Not only flight crews have risks. The carrier is a big steel container filled with powerful machinery. The catapult, the arresting cables, the ship's engines, the anchor and chains, stationary aircraft with and without propeller blades or jet wash, flight deck activity, rolling, pitching and yawing in high seas, overhead crane loads, electrical and hydraulic systems, etc., etc., etc. …. the list is almost endless…. and all can be dangerous. * If you don't have at least a modicum of self-confidence, a.k.a. ego strength, you should be somewhere else.

*When the 1MC blasts "General Quarters, General Quarters" and everyone is running to "Man Your Battle Stations," even with the orderly traffic flow of "up and forward to the Starboard; down and aft to the Port," there is the hazard of bulkhead high hurdles, a.k.a. "knee knockers," and nearly always some injuries show up later in sick bay.

Air Sickness … There are two basic causes of air sickness: 1) physiologic vertigo originating in the vestibular apparatus of the inner ear (and others) and 2) psychological aerophobia (fear of flying.) The second type is an anxiety disorder that may not be only fear of flying itself but also phobias of height (acrophobia), tight spaces (claustrophobia), etc. Nausea and vomiting are common with both types. Sometimes both types are present simultaneously.

There are a significant number of SNAs (student naval aviators) who begin with some element of aerophobia. Most overcome it with "exposure therapy" …. regular and repeated flying with the instructors. Those who don't overcome it, regardless of the cause, "wash out" early. There is another old navy saying that Dr. R--- told us, "Aerophobia doesn't occur on solo flights."

The Essence of a Flight Surgeon … There is a strong undercurrent and firm belief in naval aviation that pilots are super-competent, that they can perform well under even the most difficult situations, that they can handle stress, almost that they are invincible. This is especially felt by and expected of naval aviators who are also Naval Academy graduates. Naval Academy aviators are expected to be superheroes. The truth of course is that all are humans and subject to the same emotions as everyone. Some handle stress better than others but none are invincible. Now to whom does an aviator turn when he is having subtle or even obvious difficulties handling stress? There is no spouse onboard for sharing. It is certainly not macho-acceptable to voice any anxieties or fears to his peers. Some casual chatting and sharing of "THERE I WUZ" stories might be helpful, but no expression of weakness or worry is acceptable. Even the squadron commanding officer who is charged with the health, safety and well-being of his flight crews is not an acceptable sounding board. He might think less of the pilot who is expressing emotions and/or the pilot might think he would. Also, even if the CO is sympathetic, he might be of no help.

Enter the flight surgeon. Physicians are the traditional people in whom emotionally troubled people confide. Problem: aviators are a close-knit fraternity. Not the least part of their small-group identity is their mutual sharing of risk and danger. They just will not trust nor confide in anyone, including a physician, who doesn't share that with them. To be effective a flight surgeon must fly with his pilots, learn and know the intricacies of their jobs, understand the stresses and share the risks and dangers. He must become a friend, a comfortable and familiar person, a peer …. and to achieve that he flies with his pilots.

Stand back and think about it. Pilots (and nearly everyone else on a carrier) are healthy young men. They don't take medications. They really don't need physicians and medical care except for the occasional injuries, infections or other physiologic ailments. [A well-trained, competent and experienced hospital corpsman could take care of most problems.] However, there is considerable emotional stress onboard a carrier. That is not just the risks and dangers of flight operations and not just the air crew. It is also both officers and enlisted sailors living in cramped quarters, with no women, with no alcohol, with the intrinsic latent aggressiveness of young men. It's almost a miracle that there isn't much discord.

The flight surgeon's major responsibility is the emotional health of his aircrews.

Let's elaborate on that a little more. We know carrier aviation has intrinsic risk. We know that high levels of skill are required to manage those risks and avoid mishaps. Even with pinnacle skill and experience safety always demands complete attention and concentration during high performance tasks such as taking off and landing on the carrier (and operating the various machinery that enables it.) The slightest distraction or lapse of attention can result in disaster.

[All eight aircrew deaths on my eight-month cruise in 1966-67 on *Independence* were caused by lapses in attention and concentration. More about that later in the book.]

An effective flight surgeon cannot just wait and hope a stressed pilot will come to him to confide problems. The flight surgeon must be an active observer. He must know the normal behavior, attitudes, speech, et al of his squadron members. He must notice changes in behavior whether by omission or commission. He must understand mood swings and the reasons behind them. He must have some understanding of aircrews' families and home situations. Often the stresses of stateside problems are more influencing than those of carrier ops. An effective flight surgeon must not only observe and diagnose when emotional/mental stresses are affecting a pilot, but also the flight surgeon must know how to broach it with the pilot and arrange a mechanism of time and place in which the pilot will confide his troubles. (More on this with some specific examples later in the book.)

Call it preventive medicine if you like. Call it accident prevention. Call it performing the duties of health and safety. Call it whatever you want, it is the **essence of an effective flight surgeon.**

What else did we learn in Dr. R---'s shrink sessions? Lots. We studied the progression of maturity among aviators. The attitudes and emotions of Ensigns who are recent college and flight training graduates are far different from second and third tour LCDRs and Commanders. Knowledge of the typical maturity progression is important for management of both standard medical issues and of "shrink" considerations. Flight surgeons serve as physicians to the Captain of the Ship and the Admiral of the Task Force (and their wives when onboard or ashore at ports of call). Both are also naval aviators who just don't fly much anymore but have more stresses of responsibility than the active aircrews.

We had an overview of abnormal psychiatry: how to recognize and diagnose and how to treat. With such a large group of people on a carrier there were undoubtedly going to be some paranoia, some schizophrenia, some obsessive-compulsive behavior, some passive-aggressive personalities, some anti-social behavior, some self-destructive behavior and the whole gamut of mental disorders. We were going to be the duty psychiatrist wherever we were assigned.

Looking back at Dr. R---'s course in Pensacola, it was more valuable in later medical practice after the navy than was the psychiatric training and exposure in medical school …. and we had a fine psych department and education at Tulane. Maybe that was because it was "add-on" learning; maybe because I was older, more mature and experienced; maybe because it was not only about abnormal psychiatry, but also normal people with situational problems. Whether one or all of these, it was just a magnificent educational experience. Thank you, Dr. R---.

SAUFLEY SNA PRIFLY – TRARON ONE – T-34B MENTOR

 AREN'T NAVY ABBREVIATIONS fun? … only if you are savvy to their meaning! Saufley Field was an 866-acre auxiliary air station about ten miles northwest of NAS Pensacola and was where SNA's (Student Naval Aviators) did their PRIFLY (Primary Flight Training) in TRARON ONE (Training Squadron One (VT-1)) in the T-34B Mentor single-engine propeller aircraft.

The first Four plus months in Pensacola covered the medical aspects of naval aviation … academic classes in the mornings and "FAM" sessions in the afternoons. Then the Navy taught us to fly. The significance of this is that Air Force flight surgeons do not have actual flight training. We went through essentially the same first flight training syllabus as all the naval aviators. It was six weeks and our last big training block. The flight training at Saufley Field was great and it was culminated with a CARQUAL day cruise on *U.S.S. Lexington (CV-16.)* Following that was our gala graduation in late June and off to our duty stations.

The SNA syllabus at Saufley began with ground school in the classroom where we learned the basics of aerodynamics and flying … air foils, lift, physics, history, components of aircraft and their functions, types of engines and how they worked, propulsion mechanics, current aircraft, etc..... a huge amount of valuable information. We studied full days in the classroom at first then split days with some classroom and the rest of the day on the flight line learning and flying in the T34B. We learned ground safety around the aircraft and we learned safety procedures in the air.

Each of us was assigned a naval aviator flight instructor. They had to be brave souls to take a bunch of docs under their wings and teach us to earn our wings. The squadron patch of TRARON ONE shows a large adult eagle perched on a ledge watching a small, young newbie eagle learning to fly. Some of our physician student flight surgeons were no more accomplished in their flying skills than they were in the close order drill exercises. In years past a young student flight surgeon had killed himself at Saufley in a flight accident. Bravo for the instructors.

After the initial ground school basics, the syllabus essentially went day by day .... first discussing what the plans were for that day, what we were to accomplish and then going out to the flight line to do them in the aircraft. The T-34B Mentor was a wonderful aircraft. It was basic in its controls, simple to understand and extremely stable in the air. You could put the airplane in just about any position, including a stall, then take your hands off the controls and the Mentor would right itself, stabilize and keep flying straight and level.

Obviously the first thing to learn was takeoff and landing. There were several outlying airstrips used for practice. I seem to recall Silverhill, Summerdale and Loxley. We flew mostly in southern Alabama between Pensacola's Saufley Field and Mobile Bay, always keeping south of the new interstate highway (I-10) under construction. That red dirt roadbed was a great landmark from the air. We learned "touch-and-goes" to practice the approach and landing techniques. One would roll the wheels on the tarmac, then add power and climb out again, going around the racetrack pattern for another touch and go. My favorite was Silverhill.... which was also the site of solo flights at the end of the syllabus. Since there were so many of us, we needed lots of airspace and lots of auxiliary airstrips. None of these had any personnel or ground facilities. I think that was planned so in case we crashed we wouldn't hurt anyone but ourselves. Likely also the instructor group met for briefings each day before we came out to the flight line. They undoubtedly took us all to different airspace segments for safety …. ours and theirs. The instructors surely swapped "There I Wuz" stories about the idiosyncrasies and goof-ups of their doctor trainees.

We learned and practiced many aspects of flying from the basics to the advanced aerobatics. We learned preflight inspection of the airplane … what to inspect and look for, what might be dangerous and should ground the plane. In the cockpit we learned the importance of checklists, routine procedures, testing the controls before takeoff, checking gauges and fuel, communications both within the aircraft and with base at Saufley … all of it and more. My instructor (LT D.L.) was an excellent teacher and quite helpful with my learning curve. On one takeoff I couldn't seem to get enough airspeed and climb rate and was puzzled about it. He said, "Did you forget something?" Immediately I noticed that I had forgotten to retract the landing gear, so of course the drag prevented speed and climb. He had known from the beginning but had said nothing to let me figure it out.

Once we mastered the basics, we advanced to the most fun part of the syllabus … aerobatics. We learned about and performed hammerhead stalls, spins, loops, rolls, the Immelmann maneuver, the Split-S and lots more. [Later in the fleet my favorite in an F-4 Phantom jet fighter was the Split-S …. whooo-eee.]

I qualified for solo flight but my instructor was not allowed to permit it because the regulations required perfect 20/20 vision. My vision wasn't much off, but it was not 20/20, so no solo. Dang. I was disappointed.

Overall, the learning curve and training experience at Saufley PriFly was highly beneficial. It gave us an understanding of naval aviators and how they trained. It gave us an appreciation of flight, aircraft and all the ancillary aspects such as maintenance, communications, et al.

Note: Over the years Saufley evolved into other iterations. The aviation training shifted to Saufley just being an outlying field from Whiting Field PRIFLY. Other non-aviation naval training utilized some of the facilities. In 1988 a federal prison was established there. A temporary landfill operation caused some major problems. In 2016 the Gulf Power Company leased 366 acres and installed a 50-megawatt solar-power farm. Saufley is no longer used for aviation.

MORE FAM AFTER
SAUFLEY PRIFLY

NAS WHITING FIELD, T-28S ET AL, HELICOPTERS,
LEXINGTON CARQUAL CRUISE

WE HAD NOW learned about aerodynamics and aerobatics, engines and ailerons, rudders and radios, …. and so much more ……. and we had learned to fly the T-34B Mentor. The next step was familiarization with other aircraft in the fleet and then a day on a carrier watching real at- sea flight operations.

We went to NAS Whiting Field which is in Milton, FL a little northeast of Pensacola. After a brief classroom overview of the T-28 Trojan we had a FAM Hop in it. The T-28 was much more powerful than the T-34 and was very impressive to us as newbies. Just looking at the 9-cylinder, 1500 horsepower radial combustion engine was impressive and there were three propeller blades. The flight performance was a huge jump up from the Mentor.

We learned that Student Naval Aviators (SNAs) who were to transition into jets would go to NAS Meridian in Mississippi to fly the T-2 Buckeye single engine jet. We did not go there, but just confined our learning to lecture and textbook. We learned that SNAs generally had several options or pipelines in training. They could transition to jets. They could continue with propeller planes including ultimately multi-engine planes in the fleet like the P-2 Neptune and P-3 Orion patrol and Anti-Submarine Warfare airplanes. These were land based and not carrier aircraft. NAS Whiting Field also was the training facility for another branch and pipeline for naval aviators .... and for Marine Aviators.

Helicopters ... SNAs and SMAs learned to fly those dragon-flies-in-the-sky .... rotary wing aircraft .... helicopters. We studied those rather intensively and I expect it was because so many of our class of docs would be with the Marines and likely have much more exposure and use of helicopters.

Helicopters are fascinating. The lift comes from the same airfoil configuration of the blades as on fixed-wing aircraft. Lift on fixed wingers comes from forward speed. Helicopters get their lift from rapid rotation of the blades overhead (speed AND PITCH) without any forward speed required of the body of the helicopter. Small problem however ... without the tail rotor with its horizontal control the body of the helicopter would be unstable and just spin around. The tail rotor in a way is like the tail elevators/stabilizers on fixed wing aircraft. The direction that the main overhead rotor blades point is controlled by the cyclic stick for pointing fore or aft and port or starboard. We learned about the "collective" which is the lever to the left and below the seat of the pilot. The collective changes the pitch of all the rotating blades the same amount and at the same time to increase or decrease lift ... sort of like flaps do for fixed wings. There are four control mechanisms in helicopters. The other two are the throttle for power control and the pedals to control the tail rotor.... the rudder petals on fixed wing craft similarly point the nose left or right. The throttle is on the collective lever much like the power grip on the handlebar of a motorcycle. It always takes two hands on the controls to fly a helicopter.

One of the especially important things we learned was the danger of rotor blades. Just like propeller blades on fixed wing aircraft the rotor blades of a helicopter are extremely dangerous. You don't really see them but must be always aware. Many fatalities and serious injuries have occurred when people inadvertently walked into spinning blades. A reasonable analogy might be when physicians learn about maintaining a sterile field. Bacteria are unseen but they are always there. The physician must develop an innate, automatic awareness and the unconscious habits of keeping germs out of the field. Aviators must do the same with rotating blades …. and for that matter also with rotor wash and jet wash.

We had several hops in helicopters, maybe four or five. They were my first helicopter rides and were simply great. It's a different sensation and the aerodynamics are different. Later in the fleet were many more opportunities to fly in helicopters. One of the most interesting aspects of all was the ability to land a helicopter safely after total loss of power. My instructor insisted helicopters were safer than fixed wing aircraft for that very reason.

Auto-rotation …. is the name of that characteristic. Essentially if power is completely lost, the overhead blades continue to rotate rapidly because of the rushing air on their airfoil surfaces as you lose altitude. The blades are free-spinning and at just the right moment before impact with the ground, the pilot pulls up on the collective and the rapidly increased pitch of the blades causes a huge uplift from the momentum of the spinning blades as they "bite" the air, thus landing the helicopter gently on the ground. I am positive you must be experienced in this because if you pull up the collective too soon OR too late … or too little or too much …. you're a goner …. because that momentum of the free-spinning blades is only good for one time.

Learning about helicopters was fascinating and flying in one was wonderful. When a helicopter hovers motionless, i.e., without any forward/backward/left/right/up/down movement it almost feels like you are floating in the air…. except there is constant small movement (and vibration) because the pilot is making constant minor control changes and adjustments to maintain that relatively fixed position. That is why it is called a hover. Maintaining a steady hover is the most difficult part of flying a helicopter. The hover and the autorotation are significant differences from fixed wing aircraft. Please recall that the "V" in squadron and ship letter designations means "fixed wing while "H" means helicopters.

U.S.S. Lexington (CV-16) … Our day-cruise on the "Lex" was both fun and educational. The Lex was an older carrier constructed during WWII and commissioned in 1943. It was used in Pensacola for training only and mainly for student pilots to qualify for carrier operations, i.e., to learn how to land and launch on a carrier and to repeat it enough to be competent. Landing on a carrier is the most difficult and dangerous skill needed by a naval aviator. Of course, the navy as usual had an abbreviation for that. Everyone "in the know" simply called it "CarQuals" which meant Carrier Qualifications. Whenever a group of SNAs needed CarQuals the Lex would sail for the day and provide that training. To graduate and earn his Wings of Gold and to become a Naval Aviator, each SNA was required to "qualify" on the carrier. It was the culmination of their intensive training program. The schedule of our class of SFSs (abbreviation for student flight surgeons in case you forgot) was coordinated so that we could go out with the Lex to observe and be introduced to carrier operations in real time. For those of our class of physicians who were assigned to Marine squadrons it may have been the only carrier experience in their entire time in the navy.

For me, the *Lexington* CarQual cruise was especially meaningful for several reasons:

1. Carrier aviation was the reason I had signed up for the Navy Flight Surgeon program.
2. After that dependents cruise on the *Ranger* in summer 1963 another day cruise on a carrier was filled with exciting anticipation. So, the Lex cruise was not completely new for me

like it was for most of the class. That made me an "old salt" as
it were.

3. It was essentially the culmination of our training in Pensacola
    before graduation.

4. I invited my first cousin, H. Aubrey White, Jr., M.D. to come
    out to sea with us as my guest. ["Aubrey Jr." was a practicing
    cardiologist in Mobile, AL and maybe enjoyed the Lex day
    cruise more than any of the rest of us.]

5. By this time we had selected billets and I knew that my fleet
    assignment was to Carrier Air Wing Seven (CVW-7) in Oceana,
    Virginia and deployed aboard the supercarrier. *Independence* …
    a carrier flight surgeon!

We all met at the pier, walked up the gang (plank), saluted the
flag, then addressed the OOD (Officer of the Deck) with "Request
permission to come aboard, Sir." With "Permission granted" to one and
all we cast off and steamed into the Gulf of Mexico to prepare for our
aircraft. There is an amazing communication and coordination that goes
on between the carrier and its aircraft. The best example of this sort of
communication and coordination that everyone has seen is the flyover
at a football stadium that is timed to the second to occur exactly as the
singing/playing of the Star-Spangled Banner has finished. Naval carrier
aviation is like that …. and must be for the safety of all. With dozens
of aircraft "in the pattern" (flying in the racetrack-shaped circle above
the ship), each waiting for his turn to roll into the approach, pick up
the meatball and safely trap …. precise and efficient communication is
mandatory.

We were shown all of that. The huge radar capacity to track every
aircraft, plot their constantly moving positions … then both coordinate
and communicate with them … was impressive if not mind-boggling.
A great many Air Traffic Controllers have been trained by the navy.
In addition to the radar center, we had guided tours of sick bay, the
engine room, crew's quarters both enlisted and officer, the island with

the various important control spaces, the catapult and arresting gear machinery below decks, the hangar deck, mess decks, wardrooms, etc., etc., etc. Besides the CarQuals for the SNAs it was a Fam-cruise for the SFSs.

Then flight ops began. Because of my *Ranger* experience was it "old hat for old salt" me? Not on your bippy. For the entire time I was in the navy, carrier flight ops remained exciting, even mesmerizing and I never tired of watching both launches and recovery... and the deck actions which are multiplex and ceaseless. Whether strapped in the aircraft to fly, watching from the island (multiple vantage points including Vulture's Row), in the radar center observing, or even in sick bay working or in one of the wardrooms having a meal (where the sounds were unmistakable) ... flight operations were always fascinating. It is the stuff of a young man's dreams and why *Top Gun* is still my all-time favorite movie.

THERE I WUZ .... onboard the Lex for CarQuals. When you are as excited as a five-year-old at Christmas, it is difficult to appear cool and collected as expected. Even at twenty-six I was one of the older group of people on the ship. Besides that, I was a physician with intelligence, skill and experience. It was important to appear calm and controlled but inside in my soul and psyche I was dancing, singing and giddy with glee. Such is the life of a navy flight surgeon onboard a carrier.

We watched multiple landings and launches as pilot after pilot SNA made the required number of traps to qualify and earn his wings. [See letter I wrote home about CarQuals in the Mediterranean seven months later.] CarQuals are an interesting form of "touch and goes." In the regular version you approach, land, roll the wheels and immediately add full throttle and take off. On the carrier you also approach, land, roll the wheels and throttle full power.... BUT the tailhook and arresting gear pull you to a full stop and even roll you backwards a little. You add full throttle at touchdown just in case your tailhook misses the cable and you need to be at flying speed when you shoot off the front of the angled deck. Also different is that to effect the "go" part of a touch-and-go on the carrier, you must reattach to the catapult shuttle and take a cat shot to relaunch.

After the last plane was launched for its return to base we turned out of the wind and back toward Pensacola. The flight deck was strangely silent with no activity. All gear and apparatus had been stowed and flight deck personnel were below decks for relaxation or other tasks.

Aubrey Jr. and I walked out to the leading edge of the flight deck. We were not alone, but almost. We stood there with the wind in our faces watching the sun get lower on the western horizon and talking about the day's activities. Aubrey, Jr. was about thirty-seven and was speculating if it would be possible to join the Navy or if he were too old. It puzzled me at the time but became clearer later when he divorced from his first wife. Probably Aubrey, Jr. was having enough mid-life stress to cause the speculation about a dramatic change in life and career directions.

After watching the Lex hawser to the pier, we "Requested permission to go ashore, Sir," saluted the flag and descended the gang. (When saluting the flag, we never actually could see it because of the immensity of the ship, but we knew it was flying on the stern when we were at anchor or tied up to a pier in a port. We saluted sternward.)

What a day it was. Exciting, educational, fatiguing and fun. That could be EEFF in navy lingo.

THE MOST MOMENTOUS
EVENT IN PENSACOLA

A NAVY COUPLE BECOMES A NAVY FAMILY

ALL THAT NAVY training was valuable, fun, necessary and much more but it paled in comparison to Elizabeth's birth. We arrived in Pensacola as a young navy couple and left as a navy family. In early January 1966 Virginia was not quite halfway through the nine months of pregnancy. Before Pensacola we had been quite active with travel but then during Flight Surgeon School about all we did was eat and sleep at the Bayshore apartments. I was something of a studying maniac and Virginia was supporting that as previously discussed. While I was at NAMI during the day Virginia did a lot of walking and swimming. Then by and by she was dealing with the last trimester which is notorious for various symptoms. We had selected an obstetrician and hospital so Virginia was getting regular recommended prenatal care.

Late one Sunday in May Virginia began having some low back pain and we speculated that labor was in its early stages. During medical school and internship, I had delivered about a hundred babies so had a reasonable knowledge and experience about it all and was confident we had everything under control. After midnight Virginia had increasing symptoms of labor ... never mind the technical medical descriptions. Sometime in the wee hours she began having significantly stronger and regular contractions. It was time to go to the hospital. I called the obstetrician and jumped in the shower before getting dressed for the drive to the hospital.

About that time Elizabeth was born.... no hospital, anesthesia or medicines ... nothing ... just natural birth in the fullest extent of definition. Elizabeth came out crying and pink. We were incredibly lucky there had been no complications. Vera and Henry (an MD classmate) were also living at the Bayshore. Vera was a nurse. I called them; they came up immediately. We boiled a new dress-whites shoestring, tied off and cut the umbilical cord. The ambulance arrived and we three piled in for a ride to the hospital. The obstetrician came in to deliver the placenta and to make sure all was well. The pediatrician took over Elizabeth. The hospital would not admit Elizabeth to the newborn unit because she had been born outside the hospital and might be contaminated. She went to the pediatrics infant unit.

Both grandmothers came rapidly to Pensacola and were incensed that their first grandchild was "contaminated." They gave me considerable heat for it all. In retrospect my previous experience made me too self-confident. Virginia delivered Elizabeth in forty-three minutes of active labor and about 17 contractions... quite fast for a primipara (mother with her first baby.) Again .... we were lucky!

Our health insurance paid $40.00 for the delivery (pre-inflation 1960s.) The obstetrician insisted I keep it because I had delivered the baby and he insisted that I sign the birth certificate. That was great and rather unusual, only allowed because I was a physician. So that's the story of Elizabeth's birth. She has been a delight since that first breath and cry. The same can be said for her sister Lydia born in New Orleans, December 1968. That time we were in hospital!

BILLETING

AND THE TIGERS OF STUDENT FLIGHT SURGEON CLASS 112

WHEN EVERYONE BECAME aware of the large number of us who would be assigned to the new Marine Air Wing, studying and competition became much more intense. The class rank depended solely on the test scores and grades achieved in academics and in non-academic training exercises such as the Dilbert Dunker, distance swim, timed run, flight training performance and others. There was a group of seven or eight who tried to go beyond just performing well. In younger days they would have been called teachers' pets, brown-noses and the like. The rest of us nicknamed them "Tigers." They were always trying to get attention, asking sometimes-silly questions, trying to impress the faculty and trainers with what studly people they were. We had already figured out that with some diligent study it was typically easy to score a "100" on most of the tests and lots of the class did so. The Tigers believed that their extra efforts would give them an advantage. For example, they arranged a parachute jump one weekend and made sure the faculty knew about it, likely hoping to get some brownie-points. They invited anyone in the class who wanted to join them to do so. Nobody did. Maybe we had already heard that famous Naval Aviator saying, "There is no reason to jump out of a perfectly good airplane."

Toward the end of the six months at NAMI, billeting day was announced and the rules were explained. A list of the available billets would be posted and copies given to us all. We would have a few days to confer with family and friends as to the various choices, research the duty stations if we wanted and then to be prepared to make our selection when our turn came up. Of the thirty-eight docs in Class 112 two were from Argentina and one from France. That left thirty-five U.S. Navy and Marine Corps billets. Twenty-nine were with the Marines. Only six were not. Of these a few were shore stations like Leeward Point in GITMO (Guantanamo Bay, Cuba), NAS Whidbey Island in Washington State and Guam. Two billets were with Airwings and Supercarriers, both on the east coast at NAS Oceana.

On billeting day, the list of class ranking was posted and lists given to everyone. The list showed the class rankings top to bottom with the average score/grade for each person for the entire program. The procedure was to call the names of each person in our class from top man down. When your name was called, you were to be prepared to state your selection. After the selections were sent to BUMED, official orders would be cut for each of us with instructions for date and place of reporting for duty.

The top man in our class selected Whidbey Island. I was extremely happy to get a Carrier Airwing. The dedicated studying paid off.... especially those first few weeks because "they never caught me." A good friend (B. W., MD. who was married with three children) selected the other air wing before me. He had bested me by .002 points on the hundred-point scale. It was hard to not show giddy happiness amongst the glum countenances of those going to Viet Nam including my medical school roommate Art Lochridge. One of our classmates (S.L.) was later killed in a rocket attack in Chu Lai in early 1968.

GRADUATION

GOLD FLIGHT SURGEON WINGS WITH THE
BAND PLAYING AND FLAGS FLYING

THERE IS SOMETHING impressive and almost beyond description at a formal Navy ceremony… especially when everyone is in full dress white uniforms, arranged in formation if standing and carefully ordered if seated. There is a military band also in dress white uniforms. The podium is decorated in red, white and blue. The U.S. flag is prominent and there is an assortment of unit banners and other military flags. There is an old navy saying that the time to leave a unit or a command is "when the bands are playing and the flags are flying." THERE I WUZ … doing that.

There was a section for family and friends, a section for faculty officers and enlisted trainers and of course the section for the graduating physicians. The podium held the various command officers and dignitaries. It was a beautiful day …. weather, spirits, appearance, everything. You have probably seen something like this in the movies. It is impressive!

The band played background music including military marches. As the Star-Spangled Banner began all military people stood at attention in full salute. I don't recall the speeches and the comments of the dignitaries. Someone sang the Navy Hymn. * Then our names were called and we were individually awarded our Gold Flight Surgeon Wings and Certificates with a handshake, salute and congratulations. Pride walked across that stage and it was palpable.

The flight surgeon wings are quite like Naval Aviator gold wings except in the middle is the Medical Corps insignia…. an oak leaf with an acorn in the center and for the wings this was mounted on a round medallion connecting the wings. To this day I recall with fond memories how proud I was to receive those wings and the pride with which I wore them thereafter. *

At the end of our graduation ceremony as we filed out the band struck up "Anchors Aweigh." **

These ceremonies are emotionally moving on steroids. I can't recall the day or date of graduation but it was a gala event and indeed had everything to do with my life for the next two years and after. THERE I WUZ, …. in my Ice Cream Suit …. Qual'ed and Launched.

GO NAVY   ANCHORS AWEIGH   FLY WINGS

---

* My Flight Surgeon wings are mounted in a shadow box frame over my desk as I write. Somehow, I had the forethought to collect colorful embroidered patches from every squadron, Naval Air Station and unit where my navy days took me. Those patches are also mounted in the large shadow box. The bright colors of the logo designs are surpassed only by my memories of how and when they were acquired.

** For just a taste of it, go online and search for the Navy Hymn and "Anchors Aweigh." Listen to a Navy band play them and/or chorus sing them. (More on this later.)

NAMI DENOUEMENT

SO, THERE I WUZ in late June 1966, graduated and newly certified as a Navy Flight Surgeon., proudly wearing my shiny gold wings on the" ice cream suit" dress whites and Service Dress Khaki and the blue uniforms.... and with an exciting deployment in prospect. My "detach, proceed, report" official orders from BUPERS (Bureau of Personnel) were issued in a stack of duplicate originals so a copy can be given to many different people during the transition. We must pack up and move to Virginia Beach... and with a one-month-old daughter added to the family the logistics had been kicked up multiple notches. Active-duty military service and training in Pensacola had "FAM'ed" us to navy life. So, what about these six months in Pensacola at the Naval Aerospace Medical Institute (NAMI) and the flight surgeon training?

Aviation safety ... that's it in two words. The logo of NAMI aptly illustrates the mission. There is a navy shield of sky blue in the background with a circular grid showing the earth in sea blue superimposed in the center. At the bottom is a banner spelling out NAMI. At the top in the foreground is a set of navy Flight Surgeon wings with the Medical Corps insignia in the center. Hanging from the tip of each wing is the tray of a balance scales, much like the well-known "scales of justice." In the left tray is a jet fighter. In the other tray is the figure of a man. It is immediately obvious that the mission of NAMI is balancing the men and machines of aviation.

Quote: "NAMI trains more than 240 aeromedical providers [annually] including aerospace technicians and all categories of Aeromedical Officers." The bulk of these are flight surgeons, physicians with M.D. degrees who will deploy on active duty in the fleet. This includes combat squadrons on aircraft carriers, Marine aviation units, some land-based squadrons serving other functions and shore billets at Naval Air Stations. There are over 260 billets for flight surgeons worldwide. Nearly a dozen foreign military services use NAMI for physician training.

NAMI also offers a two-year residency in Aerospace Medicine. The U.S. Army sends their residents to the program. NAMI sponsors many ongoing research projects to examine the medical, health and safety aspects of flight.

All candidates for Navy and Marine Corps flight training undergo extensive flight physical examinations at NAMI. To earn the "Wings of Gold" proudly worn by navy and Marine aviators each candidate must first pass psychological* and physical examinations to insure meeting the standards required for training and for active duty in high performance aircraft. Also, during the six months in Pensacola student flight surgeons are trained to conduct these flight physicals that active-duty flight crews must pass annually.

* The Aviation Selection Test Battery is used to optimize selection of aviation candidates and minimize attrition. Student flight surgeons receive extensive training in this testing... the tests batteries used, how to score them, how to evaluate the individual candidates and active-duty flight personnel when necessary.

LOGISTICS .... PENCLA TO INDY

WE PLANNED FOR Virginia and Elizabeth to stay with her parents/ new grandparents (Edgar and Betty Hendershot) in Tenafly, New Jersey while I was deployed at sea. It was no simple task to move the family with Elizabeth still nursing, moving two automobiles, the new crib, the old cat Gigi plus all the usual clothes, some kitchen ware, books and papers, etc. We didn't have any furniture as we sold everything when we left San Francisco and our apartment at The Bayshore was furnished. We wanted to visit in Alexandria, LA on the way (out of the way) and do it all in about two weeks between duty stations. We were young so took it all in stride.

We packed up the Starfire including crib and cat, then drove to Alexandria which was about six hours west. My TR-4A stayed in the parking lot at the Bayshore. After a couple of days in Alexandria we took off for New Jersey. We were going to drive just past Atlanta to get a motel on the east side so we wouldn't have traffic the next day. Just about dusk we drove through downtown Atlanta on the Interstate highway and passed the Atlanta Braves baseball stadium. There was a game that night. Hmmm.... we found a motel as planned, checked in and Virginia just wanted to nurse Elizabeth and go to sleep... so back I went solo to watch the Braves game.

Oh! the energy of these young naval aviators. Next morning, we drove straight to Tenafly.

I booked a flight back to Pensacola to pick up and drive the TR-4A back east. My flight was the LAST commercial flight before a nationwide airlines strike. Driving north through Virginia next day I stopped for gas and the weather had cooled off from a front coming through. My casual comment to the gas station attendant was, "It is really cooler here up north." I thought he was going to clobber me. From my perspective in the Deep South, Virginia was further north ... but he was mightily offended that I thought Virginia was in the north. Uneventful trip thereafter...

Except!!! by the time I arrived in Tenafly, wife Virginia had decided and announced that there was NO WAY she was going to stay there with her parents for six or eight months. It was pack up the Starfire again and drive back to Virginia Beach to find an apartment and store my car. We each drove a car in caravan and made it easily in one day. Next day we scoured the area for available places and found a new apartment complex on Colonial Arms Circle, the Colonial Arms Apartments. The one-bedroom apartment was perfect and the price was reasonable. It was in the Hilltop community (west of downtown Virginia Beach) and just north of NAS Oceana for an easy commute on my return from sea duty. With infant baby Elizabeth in arms, we went furniture shopping and bought a bed and a Formica-top dining room table* with four chairs. That was all we could afford at the time. It couldn't be delivered until the next day so we spent the first night on the carpeted floor of the new digs. Next day I found a storage garage and deposited the TR. Lots of navy cars were stored there when their navy owners were at sea. Then after one night on the new bed, Virginia went back to Tenafly and I flew to McGuire AFB.

*The table is still in use in the kitchen at my office on Jackson Street in Alexandria, now fifty-four years later.

Time was getting short for when I had to report to McGuire Air Force Base in southern New Jersey. The *Independence* had sailed for its eight months Med Cruise about the time I graduated in Pensacola so I was to join it when my leave and move were completed. My orders were to fly to Spain on a transport plane of the Military Airlift Command (MAC) to then fly out to join the ship via the COD (Carrier Onboard Delivery plane, a Grumman C-2A.)

On her way out of town Virginia took me to NAS Oceana where a small airplane was to fly me to McGuire for my overseas flight. I was beginning to understand why they give you so many copies of your orders. Everyone must have a copy to authorize everything.

THERE I WUZ at NAS Oceana reporting for duty. The Oceana logistics office or personnel office or main desk or flight officer or whatever/whoever it was (I was too newbie to understand it all) had arranged my flight. I was scheduled to fly to McGuire in a C-45. The pilot was one of the last enlisted aviators in the navy before a college degree was required for aviator candidates. The C-45 Beechcraft was a twin-engine light plane with a tail wheel and canvas panels on some of the tail structures. In production since the late 1930s it was a reliable workhorse sometimes fondly called "The Bug Smasher." It was the pilot and me with one other passenger. We loaded up, received clearance from the tower and off we went. The pilot said, "Dang, someone put fuel into the nose tank rather than just the wing tanks and it's flying a little out of balance. I am going to burn down the nose tank fuel to improve the aerodynamics." That meant little to me as such a newbie. Time went by and we were flying along having a random chatty conversation when suddenly both engines stopped. THERE I WUZ on my first non-training navy flight and we were out of gas in midair. Believe me, **the silence was deafening!** Never before or since have I been so acutely aware of silence. The pilot was straightforward saying, "Dang, forgot to switch over to wing tanks before emptying the nose tank." He promptly turned the fuel tank switch to wings and initiated a midair restart. The engines roared to life …. at least it seemed the loudest and most welcome roar possible. We were back in powered flight. The Wright Brothers would be proud. The rest of the flight to McGuire was uneventful. That one event was certainly enough for me. Jet fighters have the glide path of a free-falling safe. No doubt the C-45 is better but thank goodness we didn't have to test it. It was delightful to step out on the tarmac, grab my gear and thank the pilot for the flight.

At McGuire, a large MAC transport plane flew trans-Atlantic every night, departing about 1900 hours. When I checked in at the scheduling desk with my orders, the Air Force Sergeant shrugged, smiled and said, "Doc, there is no telling when you will get on the manifest to fly. This airline strike has us overloaded and every brother's cousin is backed up waiting for a flight." He suggested I get a room at the BOQ (Batchelor Officers Quarters) and report to him at the scheduling desk every morning at 0800 to see if I would be on that evening's flight. I was on active duty again even though doing nothing but waiting to fly. I explained my situation with wife and newborn who were staying just a short drive away. McGuire was about eighty miles south of Tenafly and a drive of about an hour and a half.

It didn't take him ten seconds to say, "Doc, if you will call me every morning at 0800, I'll carry you as present for duty. Then whenever you get on the manifest you must be here with your gear by 1200 hours. Leave me your telephone number where I can reach you if a sudden vacancy opens a seat for you." Thanking him profusely I called Virginia and she drove down to get me and we were off to Tenafly again. I enjoyed an extra week "on active duty" in Tenafly, New Jersey. Six or seven mornings at 0800 when I called there was no seat. Then one morning my flight was confirmed and THERE I WUZ on the way to Spain and the carrier.

The military transport was "no frills" with maximum seating but was an uneventful flight to the Torrejon Airport just south of Madrid. A small plane from the Rota Naval Base was there to pick me up and take me to Rota. As usual those transatlantic flights are fatiguing with lack of sleep and the time change. I had a big steak at the Officers Club and then crashed at the BOQ to get some sleep. *Independence* was at sea just off Barcelona and I was to fly out next day on the COD. I didn't know it at the time nor know anything about Sherry but Rota is smack dab in the middle of sherry country. It's south of Jerez the capital city and just across the bay from Cadiz.

Refreshed and ready, quick breakfast and I was off. The *C-2A Greyhound* aircraft was a cargo modification of the Grumman twin turboprop *E-2 Hawkeye Airborne Early Warning* aircraft. When the carrier was at sea the COD made daily trips carrying personnel, replacement parts, mail and whatever was needed by the carrier. The COD had a lot more power than the bug smasher and we didn't run out of gas midair.

THERE I WUZ …. and there IT WUZ. After about an hour or so of flying from Rota the pilot said to look out the window. The Indy was a spec in the distance at first, then was larger and larger as we approached. Exciting. We received clearance from the ship, turned into the pattern then lined up for approach. Meatball in view the pilot made a perfect landing on the angled deck. Bravo. It was my first trap on the carrier.

They knew I was arriving and a corpsman met me at the COD. He helped carry my gear down to my quarters then showed me the way to sickbay. I reported to the CAG of the airwing, my boss, then to Commander B--- the senior physician and commanding officer of the medical detachment. Some of the other physicians and a few corpsmen were there. I met Al Cohen who was the other flight surgeon attached to CVW-7 and who was to be my roommate during the cruise.

My life as a navy flight surgeon and with carrier aviation had begun. Yep, it was a long road from the spring of 1963 but THERE I WUZ.

THREE QUOTES IN
PRAISE OF THE NAVY

"I can imagine no more rewarding a career. And any man who may be asked in this century what he did to make his life worthwhile, I think can respond with a good deal of pride and satisfaction: 'I served in the United States Navy.'"

President John F. Kennedy, 1 August 1963, in Bancroft Hall at the U.S. Naval Academy.

"A good Navy is not a provocation to war. It is the surest guaranty of peace."

President Theodore Roosevelt, 2 December 1902, second annual message to Congress.

"The Navy has both a tradition and a future – and we look with pride and confidence in both directions."

Admiral George Anderson, CNO, 1 August 1961.

III

CARRIER AVIATION

IMMENSITY, MAGNITUDE
AND COMPLEXITY

WHERE TO BEGIN? An aircraft carrier with its airwing in full operation is awesome. The power is immense ... not just its aircraft, bombs and rockets but also the engines and machinery that support air operations. Don't underestimate the combined energy, dedication, talent and combined team effort of four or five thousand young men mostly under twenty-five years old. Even in downtime daily life it remains awesome because everyone aboard understands the latent potential. Four or five thousand souls living and working in tight spaces designed for maximum efficiency is also awesome ... and complex ... both from analytic perspective and from actual observation. It is in so many ways quite remarkable.

THERE I WUZ in bigger-than-life real life. Movie writers, directors and producers only wish they could get twenty percent of the action and activity on the screen. So, where to begin? Every individual onboard has a personal life story and a set of talents and skills. It is a wide panoply of humanity. Yet here we all were together on a big hunk of steel floating on the vast sea .... intent on being ready if, as and when we were called to action. We practiced continually all our skills. The Navy calls it drills and training.

In movies everyone has heard the call to General Quarters on a navy ship. In real life it's like that on steroids and makes you realize how many people are on board and how active they can be. All hands (another navy term) literally run to their battle stations. It is imperative that everyone knows the rules: "Up and forward on the starboard, Down and aft to the port." Going the wrong way would be like trying to swim up a waterfall. Try it once and you will never try it again … if you can recover from being runover by a horde of charging wildebeests.

Once "all hands have manned their battle stations" (every single person on the ship has been assigned a place and purpose) we were poised and ready for about anything…. attack, fire, explosion, emergency flight ops, whatever. We were like a coiled human spring. It is only a small part of the immensity, magnitude and complexity of a carrier.

NOTE: Except for General Quarters it was perfectly okay to walk in any direction fore and aft, up and down, whatever was convenient. In contrast to smaller ships the passages and ladders were much wider. Passing other-direction people was easy except for the hatches of which there were many. (More on hatches and knee knockers later.)

I think it was Al Cohen who took me under his wing and gave me a tour of the ship and its various spaces. This required multiple days during the times between medical and flight surgeon duties. First of course was showing me our compartment where we would sleep and enjoy some occasional down time. Being the senior flight surgeon, he claimed the lower bunk and me the newbie was privileged to enjoy the delights of the upper berth. More on the layout and spaces of our quarters later. Part of the intro to our quarters was showing me where the "head" was located and a brief discussion about navy showers. (The water supply on a carrier is more generous than on smaller ships because Indy had eight large conversion stills making fresh water from sea water.)

Of equal importance in the FAM tour were the two wardrooms where officers obtained their chow. The main wardroom was "amidships" and on the main deck, which was four decks below the hangar deck, inboard from the port side passageway…. not too far from sickbay (which I had already toured.) The second wardroom was far forward and just below the flight deck. The main wardroom was open year around even when the ship was in port whereas the forward wardroom was opened to accommodate the large number of officers in the air wing during deployments. We could eat in either wardroom as we chose so we enjoyed the accommodations of both.

Al Cohen took me around to all the squadron ready rooms and introduced me to hundreds of pilots, aircrew and others. He knew them all well. The squadron commanding officers, a.k.a. skippers .... were most cordial and welcoming. The others were equally hospitable. It took me a while to FAM everyone... get to know them, develop friendship, etc. ... essentially living and working with them, becoming part of the team, part of the small-group identity ... which was precisely my role as a flight surgeon and why I was there. Everybody was accustomed to welcoming newcomers because there was a constant turnover and flux of personnel. *

Each squadron had its own Ready Room and they were spread out all over the ship. I think that was for safety as much as anything. Remembering the kamikaze planes and attacks of World War Two, the architects and designers undoubtedly wanted to spread out critical personnel.

The Ready Room was exactly that. It was a large room with comfortable chairs in classroom style facing the podium and display boards. It was where pilots and aircrew would gather in full flight gear and be ready to man their planes at the given signal. Preflight briefings were done from the podium, etc. The Ready Room was also the squadron's lounge, news center, coffee shop, game room and team central. More on ready rooms later.

Early in this discussion I twice asked, "Where to begin?" because of the immensity, magnitude and complexity of an aircraft carrier. It turned out to be obvious...... start with the basics: eating, sleeping, working and a triple-S. What better beginning than the fundamentals of life?

* In military units the usual duty tour is about two years. Rotations

in and out of a unit are staggered so people are regularly arriving and departing. The turnover in personnel on the ship and in the airwing is about fifty percent each year. There is less turnover while a ship is on a cruise, more while in port or stateside at the NAS in the case of Airedales.

STEEL BEHEMOTH

A MODERN SUPERCARRIER is **H U G E**. One could say it is bigger than life, but it IS life. The expected service time of fifty years would be its physical and mechanical life. It is the lives of the 5,000 +/- crew (including airwing) …. and since there is a turnover every two years or so, it's the lives of 100,000 to 125,000+ people who serve aboard during the fifty-year span. It is the life of the two nuclear reactors and all the lights, machines and equipment that they power.

A modern supercarrier also has a unique life of its own. Each carrier has its own personality, develops its own history, its own culture …. all of which is passed from crew-complement to crew-complement in rotation. Each carrier deploys to different parts of the world, is involved in different battles or not, visits different ports, has different accidents, damages, repairs, visitors …. the list of differences goes on and on …. yet in many ways all the supercarriers are the same. The mission is the same, the procedures, protocols and operations are the same and within a class the parts are mostly interchangeable.

Maybe when a carrier is constructed, launched, outfitted, crewed, commissioned and operational that famous line from the 1931 Frankenstein movie applies, "It's alive, it's alive."

Just how big is it? The Ford class carriers are……

1,106 feet long,

134 feet abeam at the waterline and 256 feet abeam on the flight deck.

The height is 250 feet with

25 decks and a

draft of 39 feet.

Displacement is 100,000 long tons.

Power is two Bechtel A1B Nuclear Reactors with four shafts and propellers.

Speed is 30 knots (admitted), likely much more (classified information.)

Aircraft complement is 75-100.

The flight deck is over six acres (6.4176308 for precise-niks.)

That's enough. Complete lists and descriptions undoubtedly cover volumes and volumes which is why the planning and construction of a carrier takes so long. All these statistics are meaningful and important, but difficult to grasp if you haven't had the opportunity to stand on the dock next to a carrier or been aboard one. The size is almost overwhelming.

Suffice it that a supercarrier is one dang big and complicated piece of steel machinery.

BRIEF HISTORY OF
AIRCRAFT CARRIERS

1910	First launch of an aircraft from a stationary ship
1911	First aircraft to land on a stationary ship
	Arresting gear
1912	First aircraft to launch from a moving ship
1915	First catapult
1917	First aircraft to land on a moving ship
1918	First full length flight deck
	Aircraft elevators
	First purpose-built carrier
1922	Transverse arresting gear [USS Langley (CV-1)]
1924	Starboard island
	Hurricane bow
1927	Hydraulic arresting gear
	Lexington Class Carriers began
	World War Two .... Carriers Major Players
1945	Jet aircraft on carriers
1950	Steam Catapult

1953   Optical Landing System
1961   Nuclear Propulsion [USS Enterprise (CVN-65)]
1973   Ski-jump deck
2010   EMALS ... Electromagnetic Aircraft Launch System

THE BIRTH, LIFE AND DEATH
OF AN AIRCRAFT CARRIER

ONE COULD DESCRIBE a modern supercarrier as alive because it is in operation "24/7 and 365" as is the modern expression of "continuously without interruption." Since I am not a naval historian nor a professional in-the-know navy person this discussion is just my opinion of the birth, life and death of a modern supercarrier. Consider that a disclaimer if you like because there may be errors and/or omissions in this description. However, please consider this as an educated opinion because I have "been there, done that" and have been an avid student of carrier aviation ever since.

The modern supercarrier is something like both a beehive and an anthill. When flight operations are in progress thousands of people are in constant motion and activity is everywhere. Aircraft are literally buzzing off and on the ship like bees from their hive while worker ants are scurrying everywhere doing an incredible array of activities necessary to support the bee-flight. When the flight deck is calm and almost deserted, there is still continuous activity within the mighty steel ship. Like any navy ship everything is organized "by the bells" in four-hour shifts. [This tradition dates to before chronometers when time was measured with a thirty-minutes sand glass ("hour-glass shaped") with a bell rung every thirty minutes when the glass was finished and inverted for the next cycle. The bell was rung once, twice, etc. in sequence until eight bells signaled the end of a four-hour watch or duty cycle.] So, there are always people on duty and working at every task while others in rotation are eating, sleeping, relaxing et al.

NOTE: Except for sleeping there is not so much relaxation on a supercarrier because it is a long tradition in the navy that "A busy sailor is a happy sailor." This is a highly practical evolution really because the crew of a supercarrier is mostly young men (now also women) between the ages of eighteen and maybe twenty-five with a smaller contingent a little older and up into their thirties perhaps. Even the commanding and senior officers and senior chiefs are usually not much over forty. (It's a young man's game for several reasons which will be detailed later.) Idle young men tend to get into mischief. Their hormones, the confined spaces, restricted living conditions and proximity to so many others can easily result in conflicts which lead to discontent and fighting. This is much less likely when everyone stays busy at some productive activity. Thus, senior leadership directs activity. Operations and systems requirements make this easy and routine. Thus, we are back to the analogy of the anthill.

So, what about the birth of a carrier? The Navy "brass" is always looking at the big picture of world conditions, national particulars and the overall management of the fleet with its needs and operations…. both its hardware and its personnel. Other branches of the military do the same and there is ongoing competition for funds budgeted for each. Thus, it has always been and likely always will be. Military hardware is expensive. A current Ford class* supercarrier now costs about $14-15 Billion or more and takes at least 10-15 years from planning to commissioning. After the Navy decides the overall fleet requirements and plans, the funds must be appropriated in the national military budget, then the process of construction begins.

In the case of the *U.S.S. Gerald R. Ford (CVN-78)* ["N" = nuclear propulsion] construction officially began 11 August 2005 but ramp-up construction began in early 2007. Modern ship building uses modular techniques so the keel was laid down 13 November 2009. Launch came four years later in October 2013. Finish work and outfitting required nearly another four years when the *Ford* was finally commissioned on 22 July 2017. Since multiple carriers are scheduled in the Ford Class, planning time is decreased and overlapping construction is expected to allow a ship to be commissioned every 4-5 years as the currently serving Nimitz class carriers are retired.

At commissioning, a ship is officially turned over to the Navy. At that point, a carrier is operational with crew 24/7-365 for about fifty years. In the case of my own sea service the Forrestal class *U.S.S. Independence (CVA-62)* had its keel laid in the New York Naval Shipyard in Brooklyn on 1 July 1955, it was launched 1 June 1958 and commissioned 10 January 1959. I flew onboard in July 1966 and by then there were four newer carriers in the fleet …. three in the new Kitty Hawk class and the first nuclear carrier. All the Nimitz class carriers are nuclear.

The life of an aircraft carrier is basically divided into two parts …. sea time and port time. While in port the crew is reduced to a minimum of personnel. There are no aircraft and no flight operations. Some crew are transferred to other ships and other duty, some go on leave in rotation. Only enough crew remains onboard to keep everything functioning.

When underway and deployed at sea the "ships company" complement grows to about 2,600 crew. When the airwing is deployed aboard, there are another 2,000 plus people. So, when operational there are about 5,000 people onboard a carrier and it is a small city afloat. The analogy of an anthill is not unreasonable as there are many passages, corners, spaces, nooks and crannies on the 25 decks. The crew is constantly scurrying in them all doing various activities. During peaceful times training and preparedness exercises are ongoing. During war times such as Viet Nam, Iraq, Afghanistan and others activity is at a peak.

After its active service span a carrier is decommissioned and no longer operational with a crew and combat readiness. The death of a carrier involves three possibilities. It can be sunk. Four were lost in battle during

World War Two. Several have been scuttled and sunk to make reefs or used as targets for training. Five carriers have been preserved as museums in various cities. Most have been scrapped for the steel. *Independence* was sold for one dollar and scrapped in 2019 after forty years of service. I had a certain feeling of loss when that happened because time spent on *Independence* was memorable as this book will attest.

There are currently eleven supercarriers in active service. Ten are Nimitz class plus the *Ford*. Ten or eleven more Ford class carriers are planned to replace the Nimitz class ships as their service span limits are reached. Planning extends to 2058.

*For classes and sequences of carriers ... see chapters World Carriers and Carriers 1966-1968.

STATS .... USS INDEPENDENCE (CVA-62)

Ordered:	2 July 1954	
Builder:	New York Navy Shipyard	
Cost:	$182.3 million	

Laid Down:	1 July 1955
Launched:	6 June 1958
Commissioned:	10 January 1959

Forrestal Class Aircraft Carrier (4th and Last)

Motto:	"Freedom's Flagship"

Displacement:	67.2 Tons, standard
	90.32 Tons, full load

Length:	1,070 feet (39.63 meters)
Beam:	130 feet, waterline
	270 feet, extreme
Draft:	37 feet

Speed:	34 knots [admitted] (63 km/hr., 39 mph)
Range:	8,000 Nautical Miles at 20 knots

Decommissioned: 30 September 1998

39 years, 9 months, 20 days

"Don't Tread on Me" First Navy Jack for oldest ship in the Navy was transferred to Kitty Hawk next oldest active ship.

In "Mothballs" 5 ½ years, Bremerton, WA

Port anchor & both chains used on Nimitz class carrier George H.W. Bush (CVN-77)

Sold for $1.00 on 10 March 2017 to the International Shipbreaking Company for 16,000-mile towing to Brownsville, TX

Arrived in Brownsville 30 May 2017,

Honored in local ceremony

Scrapping completed by early 2019.

(64 years from "steel to steel")

4,000 Nautical Miles at 30 knots

Propulsion: 4 Westinghouse geared turbines, 4 shafts

                     280,000 shaft horsepower

                     8 Babcock and Wilcox Boilers

Complement: 3,126 Ship's Crew   Over 100,000 crew served
                                                aboard Independence

TOTAL   2,089 Airwing   during its active span of service.

5,357   70 Flag Staff

                     72 Marines

Armament: 8 x 5"/50 caliber Mark 42 guns

                     2 x 8 NATO Sea Sparrow

                     3 x Phalanx CIWS

Aircraft Carried: 70-90 total ... of various types.

                     50-75 Fighter/Attack plus

                     Assorted Radar Early Warning, Helicopters, et al

COMISSIONED CARRIERS
1966-1968

WHILE THE AUTHOR WAS "IN THE FLEET"

Supercarriers [Forrestal Class 59-62; Kitty Hawk Class 63/64/66; Enterprise Class 65]

CVA-59	Forrestal
CVA-60	Saratoga
CVA-61	Ranger
CVA-62	Independence [Nickname "Indy"] ... [The author's ocean transportation.]
CVA-63	Kitty Hawk
CVA-64	Constellation
CVN-65	Enterprise
CVA-66	America

Other Carriers [Essex Class 31-38, 45; Midway Class 41-43; Saipan Class 48]

CV-16	Lexington (training only, in Pensacola)
CV-31	Bon Homme Richard
CV-33	Kearsarge
CV-34	Oriskany
CV-37	Princeton
CV-38	Shangri-La
CVB-41	Midway
CVB-42	Franklin D. Roosevelt
CVB-43	Coral Sea
CV-45	Valley Forge
CVL-48	Saipan

WORLD CARRIER CENSUS
2020 (22 TOTAL)

1 each Spain, France, United Kingdom, Thailand, Russia, Brazil, China (7 total)

2 each Italy, India (4 total)

Eleven (11) **United States**

Nimitz Class			Commissioned	Home Port
1.	CVN-68	Chester Nimitz	3 May 1975	Bremerton, WA
2.	CVN-69	Dwight Eisenhower	18 October 1977	Norfolk, VA
3.	CVN-70	Carl Vinson	13 March 1982	Bremerton, WA
4.	CVN-71	Theodore Roosevelt	25 October 1986	San Diego, CA
5.	CVN-72	Abraham Lincoln	11 November 1989	San Diego, CA
6.	CVN-73	George Washington	4 July 1992	Newport News, VA*
7.	CVN-74	John C. Stennis	9 December 1995	Norfolk, VA
8.	CVN-75	Harry S. Truman	25 July 1998	Norfolk, VA
9.	CVN-76	Ronald Reagan	12 July 2003	Yokosuka, Japan
10.	CVN-77	George H.W. Bush	10 January 2009	Norfolk, VA

Ford Class

11. CVN-78   Gerald R. Ford   22 July 2017   Norfolk, VA

                    * Overhaul, Repairs, Refitting in progress

Planned for Future:

CVN-79	John F. Kennedy	2022 Anticipated	Under Construction
CVN-80	Enterprise	2027 Anticipated	Under Construction
CVN-81	Doris Miller	2030 Anticipated	Ordered
CVN-82	(not named)	2034 Anticipated	Ordered

Six or seven more Ford Class carriers anticipated to replace Nimitz Class carriers with the last one to be commissioned in 2058, approximately one every four years.

IV

LEARNING THE ROPES

ONE M C

TEN PERCENT NEVER GOT THE WORD

ON A HUGE aircraft carrier with five thousand men scattered fore and aft, port and starboard, topside and below … in a noisy environment, some working, some asleep …. communication was always difficult but was important, vital and essential. Everyone has seen a movie with a ship's "squawk box" blasting "Now hear this, now hear this …." Well, that is truly how it's done on a carrier.

A supercarrier has 1,600 <u>miles</u> of cable and wiring (you read that right) and 1,400 telephones. Everywhere on the ship are the loudspeakers: in workspaces, in sleeping quarters, eating sites, on the flight deck and hangar deck (extra-large and loud ones), in passageways, in the heads …. everywhere. Take that word 'loudspeaker' and emphasize the first syllable, LOUD. They had to be heard above whatever noise was in the space. If you were asleep, they woke you up. If you were showering, they overrode the water in your ears. Even on the flight deck with jet engines and other machinery in full blast you could hear the loudspeaker.

Its name was "The Number One Master Communications System." We called it the "One MC."

Every thirty minutes the OOD (Officer of the Deck) and his Bosun would sound the bells over the 1MC. One bell for thirty minutes, two bells for the first hour, three for an hour-and-a-half, etc. up to eight bells for the end of a four hour "watch" (shift) which was the normal time for personnel to rotate in 24/7/365 duty stations. Then they started another eight-bell cycle. The bells became so routine we almost paid no attention to them. Not so the announcements.

The 1MC would crackle a little as it was turned on and the mike was keyed. Then the bosun's pipe would whistle the attention call (low sound, then high), followed by the announcement. That's when the "now hear this" could be blasted when appropriate. Routine announcements would just be simply said following the bosun's attention pipe call, but the most important announcements used the "now hear this" preface.

Interestingly, we had a saying, based on truth, that "Ten percent never got the word." Despite the impossibility of not hearing the 1MC wherever you were or whatever you were doing, there were always people who didn't know about the announcement nor follow its instructions. We never knew if they "didn't hear" the announcement, or if they heard it and they didn't understand it, or if they understood it but ignored it, etc. No matter what the cause or facts might have been, TEN PERCENT NEVER GOT THE WORD.

The only exception to this was "General Quarters." Everyone on the ship was assigned a battle station which was exactly that.... where you went in case of battle, fire or another emergency. We had frequent drills to practice procedures such as firefighting. The Medical Department was no exception. The battle station of the senior medical officer and the ship's company surgeon was in sick bay itself. The flight surgeons were dispersed around the ship. As the ranking flight surgeon my roommate Al Cohen had his battle station in the island aid station with a cadre of skilled corpsmen. My battle station was on an O-level far forward at another aid station also with a complement of corpsmen and lots of medical equipment and supplies for emergency care if needed. At the island aid station Al had fresh air and was able to watch whatever was happening on the flight deck. I saw nothing but steel in closed spaces. The only thing relieving boredom was watching the firefighters in their retardant suits uncoil the fire hoses to practice extinguishing a fire. Thank goodness we never had one. Several carriers have had serious fires with loss of life.

Now even if you didn't hear the 1MC "General Quarters" call, you couldn't miss the immediate running to battle stations…. "up and forward on the starboard, down and aft on the port side" which was essential to keep from being trampled. [Lots of knee-knocker incidents happened here.]

So here are some 1MC calls and announcements as I remember them:

General Quarters … *"General Quarters, General Quarters. All hands man your battle stations. Set material condition [whatever it was] … This is a drill (or not), This is a drill…. General Quarters, General Quarters."* FOLLOWED BY TWELVE LOUD GONGS.

I think the double-statement repetition was for emphasis and to show urgency and importance. [That double-statement repetition was common in the movie, *Top Gun*.]

Smoking Lamp … *"The smoking lamp is lit, throughout the ship, in all authorized spaces."*

I never saw or knew what the smoking lamp was … probably a historic reference. I wasn't sure where the authorized spaces were either since I was not a smoker, but probably the authorized spaces were far away from the fuel and other fire hazards.

Sweepers …. *"Sweepers, sweepers, Man your brooms. Make a clean sweep fore and aft. Take all trash and shitcans* to Sponson Eight."* [* See "Bosun's Incident."] Sponson eight was the protrusion from the ship on the Hangar Deck from which the garbage was thrown overboard.

Captain Arriving or Departing (or Admiral) … [Bell struck twice in a couplet, pause, then twice again in another couplet.] *"Captain, Arriving."* or *"Captain Departing."* [Admiral when so.]

There were others that I don't remember. They were mostly related to working day evolutions, mess call, general instructions., etc. The 1MC could be used for routine announcements as well as important and emergency communications.

THERE I WUZ .... always wondering why some sailors never got the word.

AIRCRAFT CARRIER
ORGANIZATION ... THE DIVISIONS

PREVIOUSLY DISCUSSED WAS the "small group identity" that functions best in human productivity and happiness. Desmond Morris' seminal works described the details and psychology. Long before that military and other large organizations have known that small groups work the best. A modern supercarrier is a huge and complex operation with five thousand crew.

The magnitude of those complex mechanical, electrical, physics, engineering, electronic and so many more systems all coordinated into one huge functioning operation is difficult to comprehend. The skills and knowledge of the crew necessary to make it all work together ... and to repair what doesn't work... is likewise amazing. To accomplish the smooth end-product the ship's structure is organized into small units called divisions. Each Division is led by an officer or two with special expertise in that area of functioning along with a chief or two, also expert and very experienced. Each Division has a varying number of enlisted crew at various levels of training from basic beginning to advanced expertise. The number in each division depends on the needs of the area for which that division is responsible. Here is a listing of Divisions and functions. (Please remember that this information is from an observer and one who makes no claim to completeness or accuracy. Please forgive any errors.)

Command ... Carrier Division Admiral with Chief of Staff and about 70 officers and enlisted.

Captain with Executive Officer and a cadre of Department Heads:

1. Operations
2. Navigation
3. Supply
4. Air
5. Weapons
6. Engineering
7. Communications
8. Medical
9. Dental
10. Airwing

Each department had one or more Divisions under its command.

Navigation Division ... Navigation, piloting, and anchoring are primary, but also training and management of Officers-of-the-Deck, protocols for honoring visiting dignitaries, et al.

OC Division ... Air Traffic Control: radar monitoring and tracking, flight schedules, clearance of aircraft after departure and before return, an incredibly important control function for safety.

V-3 Division ... the Hangar Deck division: operating the huge aircraft elevators, the even bigger hangar bay doors, moving aircraft around the hangar bay, maintaining sprinkler systems, water curtains, foam monitors, conflagration stations, et al.

First Division ... Thirty-ton anchors and the three "R's" ... rearming, refueling, replenishment.

B Division ... Operation of the ship's eight boilers which provide steam for propulsion, catapults, electrical generators, et al. Without B Division we would be "dead in the water."

CS Division … Mechanical eyes of the ship: semaphore flags, flashing lights, all visual communication ship-to-ship and ship-to-shore. In the movies you have seen those big round blinkers. It takes skill and knowledge to operate them.

S-1 Division … Supply: a staggering collection of parts and supplies must be ordered, inventoried, retrieved when needed…. from simple nuts and bolts to mysterious black boxes.

Mess Deck Master-at-Arms … Security, peace and tranquility on the mess decks and making sure there are high standards of cleanliness and smooth, efficient service of meals.

Primary Flight Control ("PriFly") … The Air Boss and his assistants coordinate with the CAG and the Airwing to control the flight operations of the fighter, attack, reconnaissance and radar aircraft on the ship… the flight schedules, ordinance carried, CAP assignments, maintaining the meatball, coordinating with the airwing's landing signal officers (LSOs)…. anything and everything to do with flight operations. The Air Boss and his team operate from an elevated tower section in the island where they can see everything.

V-2 Division … The flight deck crew … all those different colored shirts and the mickey-mouse ear protectors you have seen in the movies. (See separate list of the shirt colors and what they signify.) These proficient crewmen operate the catapults, arresting gear, emergency barricade, everything to do with launching and recovering aircraft.

W Division … the ship's gunners, rarely needed but must always be trained and ready. They also must be sure the ship's guns are functional and well-maintained. Practice sessions are interesting and fun.

V-6/IMA Division … part of the flight deck team, wear blue shirts, operate shops and facilities for maintenance and repair of embarked aircraft, complex aeronautical equipment and the ship's C-1A (COD). They are under a particularly heavy load when the ship is doing round-the-clock CAP flight operations.

OA Division … the Weather Team: monitoring, predicting,

tracking and keeping a "weather eye out" ... includes oceanography, upper air observations, winds, tides, all of it.

G Division ... "keep'em rolling," ... the vehicles for handling ordnance, the ship's magazines, ordinance elevators, the ship's onshore vehicles, small arms, ship's saluting battery, et al.

G Division is part of the Weapons Department.

OP Division ... Photographers mates, intelligence officers et al .... They manage the reconnaissance photos taken by the aircraft, control the information, maps and intelligence data in the IOIC.... and they take the candid photos of the cruise.

M Division ... Want to go somewhere? You need M Division. They manage the ships propulsion engines, turbines, gears, shafts, propellers and bearings. Sometimes it's a greasy dirty job in maintaining and managing the ship's 280,000 horsepower.

S-6 Division ... Seven types of aircraft require 7,000 times 7 spare parts... That is about 50,000 <u>different</u> parts. S-6 is responsible for procurement and distribution of engines to electron tubes and all replacement parts.

X Division ... Personnel records, correspondence, public relations, master-at-arms force, religious guidance (including chaplains), library, legal office, mail management, career counselors, onboard TV station (WIND), et al.

H-Division ... the medical department (discussed extensively elsewhere.) ... two ship's physicians, three flight surgeons, all the hospital corpsmen including aviation specialists.

Dental ... Dentists and technicians ... must keep those chompers healthy for chow call.

S-2 Division ...feeding 5,000 hungry young men "three squares," MidRats and more.... resupplying, storing and preserving safely, preparing, cooking, serving, cleaning and maintaining sanitary conditions... the list goes on and on. If you think the aircraft are important, try getting sailors to work without good eats.

S-3 Division ... barbering, cobbling, tailoring, laundering et al.

Small stores, gedunk, camera shop, tobacco shop, etc. Sailors need snacks, toothpaste and retail items by the hundreds and S-3 division looks after the personal needs of the crew.

S-4 Division … Disbursing office, payroll, banking services… especially important to every sailor.

S-5 Division … maintenance of 230 staterooms, serving meals for officers and dignitaries, maintaining wardrooms, et al.

A Division … Emergency generators, evaporators for fresh water, heating and ventilating systems, engineering log room, lots more.

R Division … Jacks of all trades, ready to fix anything, damage control parties, whatever, et al. They are ready to help in any other divisions when needed.

Second Division …Interior Quarterdeck, Highline equipment, and help with the "three R's."

Boat Division … all the small boats, maintenance, operation, protocols, et al.

3rd Division … Assist with the "three R's" and add manpower wherever needed.

E Division … "E" stands for Everything Electrical. That's what they do and it's a big job. Lots of the equipment is highly sophisticated and there is an almost unimaginable amount of it onboard. Miles of wiring, breaker panels, et al.

CR Division … Radio, teletype, morse code, UHF/VHF radio, etc. to link with the outside world.

GM Division … Target drones for training and practice, guided missiles systems of the ship.

5th Division … the 5-inch, fifty-four main battery with magazines and handling equipment … for direct defense of the ship.

Fox Division … the sophisticated radar fire controls for the main battery are their bailiwick.

Fourth Division … Boat cranes for on/off loading, aviation crane ("Tilly") and share other work with the deck divisions.

V-1 Division ... aircraft handling on the flight deck, firefighting and rescue squads.

OE Division ... maintenance of electronic equipment, radar antennae, scopes, et al.

OI Division ... maintaining the "secrets" of the ship ... IOIC... gathering information, including pilotage for entering port, verifying accuracy of aircraft information gathered, et al.

V-4 Division ... red shirt fuels crew to "keep'em flying", lubrication, supply, purity of fuels, et al.

That's thirty-nine divisions on the carrier and I may have missed some. These are ship's company divisions and so do not include the airwing, its squadrons and its many divisions. It takes a lot of specialized, trained, experienced and motivated crew members to sail the carrier 50,000 miles, support the airwing flying 17,000 hours, burn millions of gallons of fuel and supply and consume thousands of tons of stores.... all while keeping everyone safe and healthy.

When you stand back and try to comprehend the magnitude of the whole it is almost beyond what you can grasp in your mind. No wonder it is `broken down into the small units for efficient performance. Coordinating it all together is not an easy task either. Go Navy. Bravo!

BLACK SHOES AND
BROWN SHOES

EVERYONE ON THE ship was on the same team with the same mission. However, there were two distinct groups aboard …. Ship's Company and Air Wing. Each group was proud of their identity and there was always a jocular rivalry between the two groups, both officers and enlisted men. However, to my knowledge there was never any serious conflict between them at any level of rank or rate. There were about an equal number of men in each. However, there were more officers in the airwing because of the pilots and other flight officers.

"Black Shoes" referred to the Ship's Company and "Brown Shoes" to the Air Wing. The terms date back to when early aviators wore green uniforms with brown shoes. Now their uniforms are identical with all naval personnel. The terms "black shoes" and "brown shoes" apply more to officers than to enlisted.

The ship's company black shoes are attached to the ship and are on duty there whether the ship is at sea or in port. For example, our Senior Medical Officer was a flight surgeon, but attached to the ship, not the air wing. Our four-year-residency trained surgeon was ship's company. Both deployed with the ship but stayed aboard when the airwing departed and they still worked in sickbay when the Indy was in port in Norfolk.

In contrast the brown shoes, the air wing, were only onboard Indy when deployed at sea. When the carrier was in port in Norfolk, the entire airwing … officers, enlisted, aircraft, equipment …. everyone and everything were domiciled at NAS Oceana.

That's why there were two wardrooms for officer meals. Without the air wing, only the one main facility was needed. The dentists and their assistants were ship's company. So were most of the hospital corpsmen that supported the physicians whether ship's company or flight surgeons who came aboard with the air wing. There was a small group of Aviation Hospital Corpsmen who were attached to the airwing. They had special training so they could help with flight physicals doing such things as vision testing, hearing testing, et al.

There were some gray areas that only have passing interest. For example, we had a barber shop for the officers with three barbers. They stayed busy with the full complement of black shoes and brown shoes during deployment but I doubt all three were needed when docked in Norfolk. My guess is they were reassigned to the Norfolk base barber shop. Maybe one kept the facility open in port. Please consider this paragraph a WAG.

Most of the airwing officers knew one another because we lived and worked together. Same for black shoes. There was some interaction between the two groups but more at the acquaintance level than friendship level. A good analogy would be students at a college or university. You knew those taking the same courses in the same major better than others in your larger class.

An exception to this was the physicians and Medical Department. We cared for all the personnel onboard so had more interaction. However, since most of the crew both officer and enlisted were healthy young men most of them didn't come to sick bay at all.

Certainly, there wasn't much interaction between officers working in the engine spaces, etc. with pilots and flight crew. They would have meals together sometimes but with two wardrooms that was random …. black shoes did not frequent the auxiliary wardroom much. Everyone wore a name tag and rank insignia even in working khaki uniforms. Flight personnel wore their wings so it was easy to identify who was who.

Anyway, everyone always seemed cordial and cooperative no matter what shoe-group defined them. Even so there was occasionally a comment by a black shoe indicating that he felt the Airedales had a superiority complex. It might have been more an expression of jealousy because flight crew received hazardous duty pay ($200.00 a month) and black shoes did not.

From personal observation there was an occasional pilot or flight officer who seemed irritated or jealous because flight surgeons received both flight pay and professional pay. Professional pay was $250.00 per month…. the navy's opinion of the value of four years of medical school to obtain the MD degree.

So, there was a distinction between black shoes and brown shoes, between ship's company and airwing…. but no one really seemed to care.

Black shoe, brown shoe and sneakers. The individual will go unnamed but I observed one Naval Academy graduate Lieutenant Commander aviator who wore white sneakers with his Dress Blue uniform at a squadron "Hail and Farewell" party hosted by the Commanding Officer in his home. The spouses wore cocktail dresses and it was a formal squadron function…. except for the sneakers. No one said anything. It was probably a joke or maybe a dare. I don't think it affected the individual's fitness report because his navy career continued to flourish thereafter. He later held several important high-profile navy jobs and he retired as a full Captain. Could the sneakers have been responsible for him not being promoted to admiral?

U.S. MILITARY RANKS

BRANCHES OF SERVICE: ARMY, NAVY, MARINE
CORPS, AIR FORCE, COAST GUARD

THERE ARE NINE pay grades for enlisted and ten pay grades for officers. The pay grades are identical in all five branches but the name of the rank varies among the branches. The Army and Marine Corps use the same designations. The Navy and Coast Guard designations are the same. The Air Force has its own rank names. Here following is a listing of the pay grades and the equivalent designations of rank in the five branches.

ENLISTED RATES/RANKS

Pay Grade	Navy & Coast Guard	Army & Marine Corps	Air Force
E-1	Seaman Recruit	Private	Airman Basic
E-2	Seaman Apprentice	Private [Army]	Airman
		Private First Class [Marines]	Airman First Class
E-3	Seaman (SN)	Private First Class (PFC) [A]	
		Lance Corporal [Marines]	

E-4	Petty Officer Third Class (PO3)	Corporal	Senior Airman
E-5	Petty Officer Second Class (PO2)	Sergeant	Staff Sergeant
E-6	Petty Officer First Class (PO1)	Staff Sergeant	Technical Sergeant
E-7	Chief Petty Officer (CPO)	Sergeant First Class [Army] Gunnery Sergeant [Marines]	Master Sergeant
E-8	Senior Chief Petty Officer (SCPO)	Master Sergeant	Senior Master Sergeant
E-9	Master CPO (MCPO)	Sergeant Major	Chief Master Sergeant

OFFICER RANKS

O-1	Ensign (ENS)	Second Lieutenant (2LT)	Second Lieutenant
O-2	Lieutenant Junior Grade (LTJG)	First Lieutenant (1LT)	First Lieutenant
O-3	Lieutenant (LT)	Captain	Captain
O-4	Lieutenant Commander (LCDR)	Major	Major
O-5	Commander (CDR)	Lieutenant Colonel	Lieutenant Colonel
O-6	Captain	Colonel	Colonel
O-7	Rear Admiral Lower Half (RDML)	Brigadier General	Brigadier General
O-8	Rear Admiral (RADM)	Major General	Major General
O-9	Vice Admiral (VADM)	Lieutenant General	Lieutenant General
O-10	Admiral (ADM)	General	General

ROUTINE ROUTINE ROUTINE

THE NAVY FUNCTIONS through routine. Over many years standard operating procedures have been developed for just about everything. The term "ship shape" didn't come into common usage for no reason. Every new wave of incoming sailors is trained, trained, trained to know, understand and follow procedures. It is the military application of "the right way, the wrong way and the Navy way."

Not only is standardization and meticulous adherence to procedures and protocols important and widespread in the general navy, but it is especially important on an aircraft carrier. That big steel behemoth is an amazingly complex machine. With thousands of men aboard who possess widely different levels of ability, skills and experience, if mistakes are made, someone may be injured or killed…. and not infrequently are … both. Repetition is the key to learning.

Couple that with the age of many of those young men who if not busy, may get into altercations. This is another reason why training and repetition is so important. Even the older, experienced "salty dog" leaders continue training and repetition both to keep their own skill levels honed and proficient and to train those following them. Add to all that the fact that personnel turnover is ongoing…. about fifty percent every year.

Not the least consideration is **combat readiness**. When attack becomes necessary (or if attacked) all hands must know what to do and how to do it. Making functions routine removes guesswork, minimizes mistakes and develops efficiency. Effectiveness and survival may depend on it. So, routines must become routine.

It would take hundreds or thousands of huge volumes to describe the innumerable protocols and procedures involved for carrier operations. Many of those volumes do exist in workspaces throughout the ship and they are the basis for training and for operation of the working parts of the ship. Even the concept of trying to discuss everything is way beyond the scope of this book…. which is after all a personal account of …….

THERE I WUZ…. a newly arrived flight surgeon physician assigned to the airwing (for reasons discussed elsewhere) but also working in the Medical Department doing doctor things. I needed lots of training, training, training for everything to become routine, routine, routine.

After four years of medical school and another year of internship my doctor skills were there. After the six months at NAMI in Pensacola my understanding of naval aviation and the role of flight surgeons were there also. Now it was time to put that knowledge into practice.

First it was important to "learn the ropes" (notice how those navy terms have seeped into common usage) of the existing routines in both the Medical Department and the Airwing. My duties as a physician were primary. I was not there as a pilot, but as a doctor. My function and importance to carrier operations was as a physician.

Sick Bay … That was the term for the Medical Department. It was located on the main deck which was multiple decks below the hangar deck. It was 'amidships' which is the steadiest part of the ship in rough seas…. and the most protected in case of attack. The physical spaces were not large, but quite ample and efficiently arranged. (See description and illustrations on pages 205 and 214.)

Sick Call (the name for clinic hours) was every morning at 0800. Sailors would check in with a Hospital Corpsman to register and describe his medical problem(s). Health records would be retrieved from the files and vital signs recorded. Then as in any medical office we physicians would see and examine each patient in turn. If prescriptions were written, we had a well-stocked pharmacy and the Pharmacist's Mate (another well-trained corpsman) would fill it.

The examination room had a table and a large stock of surgical and medical supplies. We would suture lacerations, treat abrasions and other such which were common every day. We had x-ray equipment if we needed a chest plate or to see if bones were broken. We had full equipment for setting and casting fractures. We even had a fully equipped operating room with anesthesia equipment for surgery as needed. Al Taquino was our competent and fully trained surgeon and my internship was "mixed surgery" with wide exposure to general surgery, ENT, urology, OB-Gyn (not needed at sea in those days), orthopedics and other areas. Al Cohen had received some special training in anesthesia before deployment. Some of our corpsmen were trained operating room technicians (scrub nurses.) The senior Hospital Corpsmen, especially the 1st class petty officers and the chiefs, were highly experienced and invaluable. We were ready and equipped for most any contingency. (More details later about surgery on the cruise.)

Sick call usually required two to four hours every morning even though all of us were working. The senior medical officer didn't do much practicing of medicine but all three flight surgeons and our surgeon pitched in most days. When the bulk of patients had been accommodated and those waiting had slowed, several of us could go on to other duties. The Medical Officer of the Day (MOD) always stayed to the end, made sure everything was left ship-shape and that the corpsmen were squared away. (Aren't these navy terms great? and so descriptive?)

Simultaneously to sick call proceeding along one of the flight surgeons would usually be across the starboard passageway in the Aviation Medicine spaces. He would do flight physicals, work with the aviation-specialist corpsmen doing various testing of flight crew, etc. There were nearly two hundred pilots and aircrew aboard so annual flight physicals were an ongoing process. Most of the aircrew had learned it was easier to get their exam while deployed at sea instead of wasting a day doing it onshore at the NAS hospital…. and since we didn't do flight physicals when Indy was making a port call, we kept busy while at sea.

Sick call would normally be completed by 1200 hours at least, just in time for lunch in one of the wardrooms. Meals were served on the carrier every six hours "by the bells" at 0600, 1200, 1800 and Midnight. The wardroom would be open for about an hour. We rarely missed. More on doctoring routines later. Time to examine the routines of flight surgeon duties.

THE FLIGHT SURGEONS'
RESPONSIBILITY

ALL THAT TIME in Pensacola was not spent just so we could practice medicine on the carrier. We had significant and important responsibilities to the airwing and especially its aircrews. Each squadron had a Ready Room (discussed elsewhere) that was a beehive of activity during flight ops and served as a gathering place all the time. The ready room was a relaxed lounge when no flights ops were in progress. Normal social interaction and conversation was ongoing almost all the time ... even at night when perhaps the only ones there were a few duty officers. A movie was shown every evening at 1900. During non-flight ops times a backgammon tournament might be in progress or a card game in one corner. The ready room was the squadron's office, workroom, break room and playroom. It was where the pilots and flight officers became friends, swapped stories, cross-educated one another and lived together like a family.

That is where the flight surgeon's major responsibility lay. We were expected to become an integral part of the family .... of each and all squadrons. We had to live, work and play with everyone as a group and individually. We needed to become friends with everyone, learn their backgrounds, their family situations stateside, their aspirations and goals.... and especially any physical and/or emotional difficulties they might be having that would compromise their performance in carrier aviation.

Stand back and think about it. Every time a pilot straps into a jet plane on the flight deck he may be killed. Carrier aviation is a dangerous occupation. So much can go wrong with disastrous consequences.... a "cold" cat shot, engine malfunction or other mechanical problem, sudden vertigo, syncope from G-forces, a "hung" bomb, a bouncing deck on recovery.... many things can go wrong and some do. All the senior pilots and flight officers have probably lost a friend or several. The younger aircrew have heard about it in enough details to understand the risks.

Flying that bird off and on the carrier in fair weather and calm seas requires a high level of knowledge and technical skill, top level physical coordination and intense concentration. Then multiply that by magnitudes at night and/or with stormy seas. There is no dreaming during carrier landings.

Now stand back and consider the other tension and stress everyone must control. There are expectations and demands from the squadron skipper and other senior officers. There is peer pressure. What if there are also marital problems stateside or a gravely ill child. It can be complicated and complex.... but remember a Naval Aviator can't admit or show any weakness, worry or fear. The macho of the trade demands coolness under stress and acting like everything is a "piece of cake." [I had one fighter squadron skipper who used that term frequently ... then later had a heart attack.]

Balancing all that are several factors protecting the pilots. First, they are well-trained and highly competent or they would not get to the level of carrier aviation. They relish the challenge like an athlete in a competition or a surgeon with a tough case. Secondly each thinks he is invincible ... that the accident will happen to someone else, but not him. The younger ones likely don't fully appreciate the risks because their frontal lobes aren't "there" yet.

So where does Jolly Flight Surgeon fit into the picture? His medical background and in particular the NAMI training has prepared him for all the above. He knows the stress is there under the surface and he is trained to recognize it and to help manage it.

His job responsibility is the health and safety of flight crew. There are multiple areas of application. He gives regular presentations to each squadron about various aspects of aviation physiology. (Fortunately, he can give the same one to each of the squadrons and by the time he has finished the circuit it's usually a slick program.)

One repeated topic is the danger to oneself AND OTHERS to fly with a cold. The congestion of a cold or nasal/sinus allergy compromises Eustachian tube function and can result in severe vertigo, etc. It is not uncommon for a squadron CO or XO to observe congestion, fever or whatever in a pilot and send him to sick bay. He cannot return to flight status without an "up chit" which is a written medical clearance for flight. (More on up chits and down chits later.)

Flight surgeons observe for limps or other musculo-skeletal aberrations in case someone has had a mishap with a ladder or a knee-knocker.

Most important of all is observation for signs and symptoms of emotional stress because that old saw applies, "An ounce of prevention is worth a pound of cure." How does one recognize changes in behavior or manifestations of stress? ... by knowing well the norms for everyone. How does one know the norms? .... by being regular friends, buddies, workmates, etc. with them all. Get to know your aircrew. Become friends through conversation, joke-swapping, playing backgammon with them, watching movies in their ready room, all the rest. The goal is to establish trust so that if a pilot is having a problem, he will confide it with doc.

Alert! Caveat! Fact!!! Flying is a close-knit profession, especially on a navy carrier. Pilots and flight officers will not trust emotionally and psychologically anyone who doesn't fly with them ... who doesn't share the risk ... who doesn't understand the intricacies of the stress... who isn't one of the THERE I WUZ brotherhood.

So, fly we did... in F-4s, A-6s, Fudds, helicopters, A-3s. We were not allowed to fly in RA-5Cs because they were too dangerous in low and slow flight. Only glazed-eyed second and third tour aviators flew them on a carrier. We also didn't fly with our A-4 squadrons because the Skyhawk is a single-seater. With six squadrons for flying, we scheduled regular hops in rotation when flight ops were planned. Two to four hops a week while at sea allowed flying with each squadron on a regular basis.

So that's two pages of preliminary prose to explain what a flight surgeon did in the afternoons. When we weren't flying, we made rounds. It was almost like seeing patients you have in the hospital. You make rounds to see them all. Right after lunch I would visit every ready room if possible. However, it wasn't just a buzz in and buzz out visit. It was more extended. I would sit in a lounge chair and chat with whoever was there and genuinely get to know them. Being a natural extrovert and something of a conversationalist was extremely helpful. It took time but I think most everyone got to know me and trust me to some degree.

Now don't think this was all just for work and responsibility. Yes, it was expected and part of my job .... but it was fun. Naval Aviators and Flight Officers are good people. As a group they are intelligent, motivated, friendly and accepting after they get to know you. It wasn't so hard to become part of the squadron family .... each of the squadron families. The guys are used to turnover of personnel and pretty much accept newcomers at face value. Once I learned the names and faces, had a few chats, flew with them some .... THERE I WUZ ... part of the squadron family .... I was "in."

I had a coffee mug with my name on it hanging in every ready room. Even when in a hurry, pouring half a cup and sitting for a few sips was enough for relaxing and sharing with whoever was in the ready room. I certainly couldn't drink six or eight full cups of coffee in an afternoon although navy people are notorious for drinking lots and lots of coffee. Sometimes I would play backgammon with someone for an hour or more. A lot was just spontaneous. Sometimes I would go in when a briefing was in progress. Just sitting for the presentation was family. Sometimes I would be the presenter. During flight ops those going to fly were in flight suits. If I were scheduled, we briefed for the hops and then went topside to climb into the big bird for up, up and away. It was an exciting life in many ways.

Around 1800 wherever I was (you, know…. THERE I WUZ :) and it was time for chow it was fun and rewarding to eat with some of the flight crew. I tried to rotate rounds so that evening chow would rotate among the squadrons also. We had a corny faux jingle we often used when it was time to go eat. Someone would say, "Jeet?" The response was, "Nah, squeet." That was navy carrier lingo for "Did you eat?" … "No, let's go eat."

I watched a movie most evenings at 1900 in a different ready room, also in an informal rotation which sometimes depended on what movie was showing. After the movie sometimes I would visit another ready room, sometimes go to my room to read or sleep, sometimes something else was going on. They were full days. If flight ops were in progress even more activity occurred and more on that later. During CAP drills (Combat Air Patrol) we would have non-stop flight operations for forty-eight hours or more to test combat readiness of all hands. That would mean little sleep and lots of night rounds everywhere. Sometimes I was scheduled to fly on a night hop as well.

So that is an overview of a flight surgeon's more-or-less typical day on a carrier. Every fourth day when it was my turn to be the MOD there were other activities and responsibilities, about which more later. Remember this was the ROUTINE ROUTINE ROUTINE. There were plenty of out-of-the-box happenings that really made a completely routine day an oxymoron.

TOALES LAVABO POR FAVOR

THERE I WUZ … on the ship with no towels. Well at least I got the "please" right. Here is the story.

After my flight from Rota to *Independence* and my first carrier trap in the COD, the learning curve began.…. layout of the ship, introductions to key personnel, settling into my room. Rank does have its privileges. As the two flight surgeons for the airwing and both lieutenants Al Cohen and I shared a medium-sized compartment. The lower one's rank or rating, the less living space is allotted. Higher ranks had more space. Space was always a consideration on a huge carrier and efficiency was mandatory as is normal on most ships.

Alas! I rapidly discovered that there were no towels. Not knowing that in advance, I had brought none. The ship had very efficient laundry service. Large nylon mesh bags with a huge safety pin were provided. You put <u>everything </u>in it and the whole unopened bag was washed and dried in the bag, then returned to your room. I just had to "make do" until the first port call to buy some towels. Likely I borrowed one from Al but I don't remember that detail. In just a few days we tied up to the pier in Barcelona and my first mission was to find towels.

My knowledge of Spanish at that time was limited. Undoubtedly someone on the ship spoke Spanish and likely they spoke English at the department store in Barcelona, but I didn't know any of that. So, I consulted my handy little translation guidebook and memorized how to ask for "bath towels." It was to be *"Toales lavabo, por favor."* Little did I know that the correct Spanish was *"Toallas de bano."*

After getting some advice and directions … off I went up La Rambla (very wide tree-lined pedestrian boulevard into the city from the pier) to find <u>El Corte Ingles</u> department store which was not too far from La Rambla and the dock. Polite and accommodating salespeople directed me to the towel department. Maybe I was lucky that pronouncing "toales" was about the same as "toallas" and nobody seemed to care that I was asking for "towels wash basin, please."

Finding the right department, I soon discovered that the largest towel available was about half the size of U.S. bath towels. However, a medium towel was better than no towel so I bought some. They were good and faithful towels for the remainder of the cruise. Navy showers are notorious for the need to conserve water so smaller towels fit right in with the program. Eventually I guess those towels went wherever old towels go when no longer needed.

That mission accomplished the next order of business was exploring Barcelona and having lunch. When getting advice from old dogs who knew something of Barcelona several recommendations stood out. First was to explore the old quarter with narrow winding cobblestone streets and good restaurants. It was the original part of the city like the French Quarter is in New Orleans. The Barri Gotic was just off the Rambla and close to the pier. It was interesting sightseeing and my first experience in Spain. In those days I walked and walked everywhere. At twenty-six and in top physical condition from the NAMI efforts in Pensacola, it was the proverbial "piece of cake." I covered large portions of the barrio. Some of the areas close to La Rambla and up further from the dock were in good condition with shops and restaurants. Closer to the pier it was mostly warehouses and not too well kept.

Another embarrassing language glitch occurred during my walking around. I had been reading about Spanish wine and planned to pick up a few bottles. One recommended wine was Federico Paternina "Banda Azul" and I had written down the name to look for it. I stumbled across a small wine shop and went inside to look for it. After browsing and browsing, searching repeatedly among the Spanish red wines, I could not find "Banda Azul." Wines by Federico Paternina were well stocked but nowhere was the Banda Azul. Finally, I approached the clerk who was friendly but spoke no English. I asked if he had Federico Paternina "Banda Azul." He said, "Si." I explained that I had looked and looked but could not find it. He took me over to the Rioja section and pointed to a wine. I scrutinized the label carefully but could not see "Banda Azul" written anywhere on the label. After my continuing puzzlement and frustrated questioning, the now exasperated clerk picked up the bottle and kept running his finger over and tapping a wide diagonal blue band prominently across the center of the label and saying, "Banda Azul, Banda Azul, Banda Azul." Damnation.... Banda Azul was that blue band across the label.... three shades of "cara roja" for me!

By now I was hungry and thirsty. Carrying both "toallas y Banda Azul" I found the suggested restaurant, Los Caracoles. The name means "snails" which is their most famous dish and I can attest that they were delicious. I had a table outside on the sidewalk, under the overhang and mostly in the shade.... it was July. The snails were served piping hot in a brown crockery dish and floating in a wonderfully rich sauce. Accompanied with fresh-baked crusty bread, a small green salad and a bottle of wine .... it was perfect for a hungry young man who has just walked the barrio for a few hours. That bread had a special affinity for the sauce.

At that time, I didn't know much about Spanish wine (obviously!) so at the waiter's suggestion I selected a local rose' which was just delicious with both the snails and the weather. I always thought it was a "perillada" but later learned that "parellada" is a Catalonian white grape, so perhaps that word in my memory was Penedes, the local region that makes lots of inexpensive red, white and rose' wines and it was just the confusion of a novice. The rose' was light, cold and refreshing.... perfect for a thirsty young man ... the whole bottle seemed to be gone much too fast.

THERE I WUZ ... a happy young Naval Flight Surgeon rambling down La Rambla back to the Indy with toallas and Banda Azul rioja in hand and a confident wine-enhanced spring in my stride.

NOTE: <u>Los Caracoles</u> was founded in 1835 by the Bofarull family which for four generations has operated the world-famous restaurant ever since. The original Bofarull name was changed to <u>Los Caracoles</u> for it most famous dish, the snails. I went back later in the cruise at our second port call to Barcelona. The snails were just as good but in cold weather I sat inside and ordered a red wine. On the second visit there was a large charcoal fire behind an open grate on the corner where passersby on the street could absorb the warmth for a minute.

Over forty years later we dined again at <u>Los Caracoles</u> with Betty and Buddy Lipsey right after a red-legged partridge hunt in Toledo, hosted by Tracy and Gonzalo Rodrigues de Castro. The snails were still wonderful. We enjoyed other delectable cuisine and much better wine.

GURIA

A BARCELONA RESTAURANT FOR MEAT AND EYE CANDY

A FEW DAYS before a scheduled port call the anticipation level began to grow. Everyone was excited about having shore leave and visiting a foreign port with its exciting new experiences. People on the Indy who had previously visited any of the ports of call were the best source of information. Virtually everyone recommended GURIA in Barcelona. It was a steak house with excellent steaks and all the trimmings.... but that wasn't why they recommended GURIA.

The main attraction at GURIA was the dozen or so gorgeous women ... the wait staff.

The steaks might satisfy your physical appetite, but the waitstaff would feed your fantasy.

I don't know if it were true or not but the story was that the young ladies were daughters of some of the wealthiest and/or aristocrat families of Spain. They were mostly in their late teens or early twenties and had enrolled to work at Guria for a year or so "to experience the outside real world" away from their sheltered upbringing. After GURIA they would make their debut and become available for marriage and then family. At

GURIA they were carefully chaperoned, apparently living in guarded facilities and totally, completely unavailable. Look, but no touch.

Whatever their origin, background and reasons for being there …. they were simply gorgeous. Their faces and figures were such that they might have been the finalists in a beauty pageant. The black uniforms with white trim that the waitresses wore were stylish and tailored …. and form fitting. Black clothing eliminates shadows and is the traditional color for hiding a figure while white and light-colored clothes show underlying form much more. There was too much form under those black uniforms to hide. Did I say "gorgeous" yet?

[The movie and song *"Pretty Woman"* said, *"… I don't believe you, you're not the truth. No one could look as good as you. Mercy"* …. but the song was wrong …… these women DID!]

Those young ladies were most impressive. They were poised, obviously well-mannered and completely professional at table service. They smiled, spoke perfect English, were friendly and paid attention to every detail of your meal. It was impossible to be completely furtive in the observation and appreciation of the young ladies' beauty … and they knew everyone was admiring them, both men and women patrons … yet they seemed proud and happy with not the slightest hint of embarrassment at being on display as it were…. gorgeous young women.

Oh … the steaks…. so busy describing the eye candy… just forgot the meat. [Don't any of you crude male chauvinist pigs confuse the two.] We had steaks on the ship, but nothing like those at GURIA…. and the wait staff on the Indy was dramatically less appealing. GURIA served huge, high-quality beef steaks of your choice and cooked exactly like you requested. Young sailormen just off a ship have large appetites. I dined and ogled at GURIA three times.

THERE I WUZ …**Yum, Yum**. That describes the steaks, not the wait staff …. well …. maybe both.

THE PSYCHOLOGY OF A CRUISE

IT IS THE same psychology as a vacation, a college course, even a weekend. The psychology is the mental and emotional attitudes and feelings of a beginning, middle and end of the event. Even a one-day event like a picnic or a hunting trip has similar psychological aspects of a beginning, middle and end. You will recognize these considerations.

The Beginning ... There is anticipation beforehand, excitement at the change coming and the adventure in prospect. There may be some remorse at leaving loved ones behind in the case of a cruise. Packing, last minute arrangements stateside, boarding the ship, settling into berthing spaces, et al happen quickly. Some are exhilarated and some are depressed about the cruise.... but the day of sailing arrives. Bands play, flags are flying, families wave goodbye from the dock, lines are cast off and the ship is underway. It is an open-ended prospect. It is <u>forward</u> thinking. Everyone understands that the eight months or so of the cruise will include lots of flight ops, maybe some accidents and deaths, plenty of port calls with new and exotic experiences. <u>Imagination</u> plays the important role. However, one's mindset also is looking backward at things left behind, loved ones, tasks undone, favorite pastimes and maybe some unpleasant things. You are off on the cruise but one foot is still at home in your thinking and feeling.

The Middle ... After a while adjustment into the routines takes your mind and feelings off things at home. A period of homesickness may come and go. The newness of surroundings and activities wears off as regular habit patterns develop around work responsibilities, mealtimes and the other activities. Adjustment leads to <u>routine</u> playing the important role and one thinks less and less about home. The important things like family and other loved ones are ever present in one's emotions, but time and distance have a way of dulling that. The trivial and inconsequential things are completely out of mind.

The End ... The bulk of the cruise is now history. Your thoughts return to home .... what you have missed, what you will enjoy (or dislike) when you get back, etc. Your emotions are less and less about the cruise and more about stateside return. Feelings of <u>completeness</u> and accomplishment start to surround your emotions and thought processes. So, memory and backward thinking about the cruise fade into the recesses of your mind as you shift into the mindset of getting ashore again.

My observation has been that beginnings of cruises, vacations, weekends, college courses, etc. take about 10-15% of lengthy events and the same percentage for endings. However, for short events like weekends or day trips the beginning and end may merge with no middle. The relaxation from a vacation or weekend probably depends on having a significant "middle" psychologically. That is because your mind is thinking what you left behind during the beginning and what you are returning to during the ending. Your emotions follow the same pattern. If you don't have enough "middle" to relax, to purge your mind and emotions, then the change of scene and pace doesn't do much for you.

Mini Beginnings, Middles and Ends ... To complicate it a little, consider that each "at-sea" period on a cruise and each port call all have their own beginning, middle and end.

The at-sea period of about ten days has a day or two of beginning, a day or two of ending and the rest in the middle. During the beginning as your routines are resumed, anticipation occurs again of what is to be accomplished during that segment: Combat Air Patrol (CAP) exercises for 48 hours perhaps, training programs scheduled, etc. The beginning also has some memories of what happened in the port you just left.... just like the thinking and feelings of the "big-beginning" of the whole cruise.

The middle blends with the middles of all the other at-sea middles. All the "mini-middles" combined constitute the bulk of your memory of the whole cruise. The port calls all have individual personalities, but at the end of the cruise they tend to get lumped together in your recall.

The end of the mini-cruise (a.k.a. "at-sea" period) has you thinking about the next port call and what you would like to do upon arrival ...... just like your thinking at the end of the major-length total cruise and you start contemplating things for when you get back stateside.

Port calls have the same psychological beginning, middle and end phases. Shore leave isn't every day so your thinking and feelings revolve around the schedule a great deal. Maybe a week in port allows two or more visits ashore. You have made plans so the beginning phase is back to anticipation, the middle is shorter for shore leave and the end has you thinking about going to sea again.

It might be more appropriate to consider shore leave during port calls as single-day short vacations.... applying the same psychology as for a picnic or fishing trip.... each having its own beginning, middle and end.

Cruise Sections ... The first at-sea segment of a long cruise could be considered "beginning." The last at-sea segment, the "ending." All the rest would be "middle." On a Mediterranean cruise the beginning and end would be the transatlantic crossings while the middle would be the time inside the Straits of Gibraltar.

Shakedown Cruises ... Shorter cruises of just a few weeks for training, proofing repairs from drydock, etc. have lots more "middle" percentagewise because there is less port call time AND the beginning and end phases are shortened psychologically because everyone knows that it is a short cruise and they won't be gone to sea long.

BULKHEADS, HATCHES, LADDERS AND KNEE-KNOCKERS

PASSAGEWAYS, NON-SKID AND GUTTERS

WE ALL KEPT busy on the carrier and it was an active life. Physical fitness was easy to maintain because we walked all over the ship. Even to go eat, use the restroom facilities, make rounds in Ready Rooms or almost anything required walking and usually using ladders to change decks. That was physically taxing for multiple reasons.

1. **Bulkheads** …As you walked along a passageway (or ran for General Quarters calls) there was a thick steel plate bulkhead about every second or third step you took. The strength of the ship depended on these multiple bulkheads which functioned like I-beams. Holes (called hatches) were cut in the steel bulkhead plates at the passageways so you could walk through. That was a physical task because the hatch-holes were not large enough for easy transit. The bottom of the easy ones was about five or six inches above the deck but the top was only about five feet high. So, you had to step over and bend down at the same time. If

you didn't watch out you might bump your head or trip or both. Sprawling out on the steel deck with a banged head is not fun.… and the non-skid painted on the deck could cause abrasions of the hands and even knees through the cloth of your trousers.

2. **Hatches** …To make it worse about every fourth or fifth bulkhead hatch was even smaller and had a hatch cover (like a vertical door, but with offset hinges.) There were rubber gaskets all around the hatch cover and multiple "dog brackets". The screw-mounted "dogs" were around the hatch opening of the bulkhead. This arrangement was so the hatch could be "battened" and dogged tightly all around to make water-tight compartments in the ship during battle stations. Problem.… the bottom of these hatches was about a foot above the deck and really required a major step to get up and over it …. AND head room was less. When running for General Quarters it was like everyone being in a race with low hurdles every third step and a high hurdle after about four or five low hurdles.

3. **Knee-Knockers** …By now you have probably figured why we called bulkheads "knee-knockers." It is likely that there was not a single sailor on the ship who had not banged his knee …. or more usually his shin…. on one of these bulkheads. That was quite common indeed. We regularly saw these scrapes, abrasions and bruises in sickbay and sometimes they were seriously infected.

4. **Making Way**.… It was proper protocol besides expected military courtesy to step aside and "make way" for higher ranked people… especially when going in opposite directions along a passageway or on a ladder. Officers made way for higher ranking officers, enlisted men for chiefs and officers, etc. Except when everyone followed directional rules during the rush to General Quarters, this frequently complicated making progress along passageways. Sometimes people-jams at bulkhead hatches resembled merging traffic on a highway.

5. **Ladders** caused their share of injuries also. Except for the multi-deck escalators for flight crew (See elsewhere.) there were no staircases on the carrier. Transit up or down from one deck to another was via a ladder. They were steel and they were steep. They had narrow foot plates with perforations and blunt knobs to minimize slippage. Slipping on a ladder when in a hurry was common. The only handrail was a rope or chain which you could catch but it was a moving support. We saw scrapes and bruises from the ladder routinely. Occasionally someone would sustain a fracture and I had one sailor with a dislocated shoulder.

6. **Ladders Again** … Fortunately everyone on the ship was young and in relatively good physical condition or the ladders would have been a major problem. The risers were higher than most staircases, the width of the footplate narrower and the steepness of the angle was about halfway between vertical and a standard staircase. Going up was straight forward but going down was the hazard. We didn't turn around and go down backwards like you would on a normal ladder with rungs. We walked down frontward like on a regular staircase EXCEPT the configuration of the ladder made that a feat. Your heel could easily slip off a footplate and catching yourself on the wobbly side ropes/chains was iffy. If you were in a hurry…. LOOKOUT.

7. **Non-Skid** … Now what is synonymous with ships? Water. As Samuel Taylor Coleridge put it in his 1798 *Rime of the Ancient Mariner*, "Water, water, everywhere, And all the boards did shrink. Water, water, everywhere Nor any drop to drink." He was of course referring to the ocean and ships have a way of getting ocean all over, even inside during high seas. This was less of a problem with the huge carrier … but remember cleanliness and maintenance in the navy requires frequent application of water and paint to most surfaces…. to keep them clean and to prevent rust in the constant water and humidity. Sailors didn't earn the nickname "swabbies" for nothing. Wet steel

decks (and even dry ones) are SLIPPERY, especially when the ship is moving around in 'weather' ... meaning not calm. So, the carrier used lots and lots of Non-Skid. Non-Skid is a special paint, navy grey or black, which has a high content of gritty particles, either sand or other. The flight deck, hangar deck, most passageways and about anywhere people would be walking were painted with Non-Skid for safety.

8. **Gutters** ... The main passageways had non-skid painted all along the higher center part and had a gutter on each side. This configuration was so that if water did get in the passageway, it would drain off in the gutters and allow safer tread in the center.

9. **Center Tape** ... When someone was swabbing a passageway, or painting it, or replenishing non-skid ... a tape would be placed down the center and only one side would be done at a time. This was to allow personnel to proceed along the passageway on the unobstructed side at any time.

So, yes, THERE I WUZ ... in the land of bulkheads, hatches, ladders, knee-knockers, passageways, non-skid and gutters .... and fortunately, didn't suffer any significant injury.

THE HORNET'S NEST, THE ANTHILL AND THE POSSUM

CONSIDER THE AIRCRAFT carrier as a combination of a hornets' nest, an anthill and an opossum.

The three analogies are valid:

Hornets' Nest …The 70 to 100 fighter/attack aircraft which can fly out to attack an intruder at any indication of danger are something like hornets in a nest. The hornets go about their daily routines of eating and sleeping, but at any alarm are ready to fly out and sting the threat. One important current fighter/attack plane is named the F/A-18 Hornet and the F/A-18 Super Hornet. The analogy is not new. The collective firepower of a modern carrier packs quite a sting. You don't want to stir up the nest and have the swarm chasing your behind.

Anthill … With five thousand active sailors aboard a carrier the analogy of an anthill is easy. Just like the tunnels and passages of an anthill the ship has intricate spaces and pathways. The human "ants" scurry around with daily activities. Would "busy as a bee" and "beehive" be a better analogy? Perhaps…. but bees do their work outside the hive, ants are both inside and outside the anthill. Draw your own analogies.

Opossum … The carrier is like a mother possum with her pouch full of little ones. The aircraft carrier is a big mother ship and contains multiple smaller boats and vessels… plus some wheeled vehicles. Upon dropping anchor out from a dock, various motor launches (stored stacked in the hangar bay/deck spaces) are hoisted out of the carrier into the water to ferry personnel back and forth between ship and shore.

1. The Admiral's Barge … This is a motor launch, about thirty feet long with interior cabin in polished wood and cushioned seating, usually white above the waterline and black below. It was for the use of the Admiral when he wanted it, but sometimes used as an officers' launch when the Admiral was absent or didn't want it. Capacity for officers was maybe thirty.

2. The Captain's Gig … Like the Admirals Barge, similar in size and capacity… for the Captain's use, but also pressed into service for officer transport. This terminology and names of these two vessels is interesting for a naval history buff.

3. Officers Launches About the same size as the barge and gig, but less posh in décor.

4. Crew Boats … These are larger open vessels, a.k.a. whale boats. They are somewhat larger and wider, have a capacity of maybe 50-70 crew. They weren't so much fun in the rain. The Indy's whaleboats for the crew were uncovered, but some newer ones are covered. You can appreciate the size of the carrier and the hangar bay when you consider all these vessels and the following vehicles stored in one corner while aircraft are everywhere … on the ready, being repaired, engines on blocks, etc….. and that standby nuke plane always ready.

5. Vehicles … Indy had a small collection of vehicles.

The van was the workhorse for errands, pickup of supplies, parts and the like. It could carry personnel also when needed. [See the separate section about the time we sent the van to Davy Jones' locker.]

There were some sedans, presumably for transport of the Admiral, the Captain, VIPs and various designated people.

Observations … A sailor knows the difference between waves and swells. It's a science of its own and both intricate and lengthy. Herewith is an attempt at simplification and how it affected me and the Indy.

Both waves and swells are generated by wind blowing across the water. The higher the velocity of the wind, the larger the wave. Waves are local wind-generated walls of water. Swells are waves that were generated at a distance and then roll along across the ocean. Think in terms of the effect of dropping a pebble into a pond.

Waves generally have tops that curl over and "break" …. think surfers catching a wave. Swells mostly don't have white water tops but just sort of smoothly roll along without much effect from LOCAL wind. If local wind is prominent, swells can have whitewater tops also.

If you think any of this is confusing, get into a discussion of whitewater navy, blue water navy, green water navy and brown water navy.

First the Indy. Weather affected us all the time but it was more for flight ops than for the ship. Indy was large enough that we were never in danger of waves or swells. Even if the ship were pitching, rolling and/or yawing, it affected flight ops, especially recovery of aircraft and their traps… but not so much the ship. Our 280,000 horsepower and our mass kept us going along in even the severest conditions. I have heard that carriers can ride through hurricanes if ever necessary.

Ship to Shore Launch Trips in Heavy Swells … This was an eye-opener! and scary at the first encounter. THERE I WUZ in an officers' launch to go ashore. As we left the ship and motored into the swells, our launch would go down into a trough and then ride back up to the crest. Imagine sitting in a smallish, little craft and looking up to see a wall of water ten or twenty feet over your head. Had it been a wave and curled over you … goodbye. However, the launch just rides up to the top of the swell. Then imagine the launch sitting on top of the swell with its propellers spinning in the air as you crested over into the next trough. It was daunting and scary the first time, but we got accustomed to it …. sort of.

POTPOURRI AFLOAT

ASSORTED HAPPENINGS AND VARIOUS CONSIDERATIONS

THE FOLLOWING ITEMS are mostly short items of interest that do not deserve a chapter of their own but are each worthy of consideration. They are in random order.

Navy Showers ... The classic "navy shower" is:

1. Quickly wet yourself and turn off the water,
2. Soap down all-over including hair
3. Rinse off as rapidly as possible, turn off water.

Obviously, the goal is to use as little water as possible. That is because water supply on navy ships is always limited. Carriers have much more capacity, but there is not unlimited water on carriers, so shower technique is standard procedure. Historic examination would indicate that sailors did not shower at all. Maybe they washed with sea water or maybe didn't wash at all. Even drinking water was in short supply during the days of sail.

There is an old navy joke about hygiene and washing. The chief lines up some sailors and announces, "Men, some of you are starting to smell groaty. I think your underwear needs changing. Jones, you change with Smith. Jackson, you change with Perkins."

The Head … On that subject, ahem, there is that old navy term, "the head," which means the bathroom and the toilet. I am not a navy historian but as I understand it the term also comes from those days of sail. Sailing ships don't sail directly into the wind, but with it or tacking across it. Ships then had bowsprits, often with figureheads. The safest place to relieve oneself of the body's natural unwanted leftovers, was up at the bow, the head. From just a rail, progress added a board with a hole, like an outhouse seat… but the term "head" was ingrained in the sailors' vocabulary … probably for all time. (Incidentally, the toilets on the Indy were stainless steel, not porcelain.)

U.S.S. Saratoga (CVA-60) … The second Forrestal class carrier, *Saratoga,* was launched, commissioned and went to sea. From the very beginning there was a major water shortage. The engineers could not figure out why because all the evaporators were functioning properly. Multiple system checks did not help. The previous *Forrestal* had not had the problem and the following *Ranger* did not, nor did the *Independence*. After five or six years in the fleet Saratoga went into drydock for overhaul, repairs, refitting, et al. That water shortage problem was at the top of the list. It was discovered that during construction the pipefitters had misrouted some pipes and half of the evaporators were pumping their fresh water directly back into the sea.

AND while overhaul was proceeding some of the engineers noted on the blueprints that there was a machine shop in a certain location, but they could not find an entrance to it. Puzzled, they cut a hole in a steel bulkhead where a door into the machine shop should have been. There inside was the machine shop with all its equipment … lathes, drill presses, everything … standing there unused for those five or so years. Someone had welded a solid steel plate where the door was supposed to be.

Ham Radio … We were at sea before the days of cell phones, satellites, the internet and all the modern ways people keep in touch. Of course, Indy was equipped with every state-of-the-art communication system in existence at the time, but they were for official business only. Maybe the Admiral or the Captain sneaked in a personal call now and then, but the rest of us were just not in touch with our families except by mail and if you could afford a telephone call when on shore leave. Ham radio to the rescue. We had several ham radio hobbyists onboard and there was a rig on the far aft port side. Some evenings we would stand in line for a turn at a three-minute call home. The operator would "raise" another hobbyist in your hometown or nearby and they would do a "phone patch" to make the call. It was fun but the long wait in line* was not very efficient. I think I made maybe two or at most three phone calls during the cruise.

*Usually on the ship officers were given head of the line privileges according to rank, but for the phone patch ham radio calls it was first come, first served for enlisted and officers alike. Also, they shut down the operation at a certain time and if you didn't get a turn before that, too bad, your wait was for naught.

Anchors and Chains ... The reference is always to the size of a carrier but rarely do people consider the anchors and anchor chains. Can you imagine the size, weight and strength they had to be to hold the carrier? By now you have surmised that I explored the Indy rather thoroughly. First it was part of my job as "health and safety inspector" every fourth day as MOD. It was also because of curiosity and fascination with it all. Going far forward into the forecastle anchor room was impressive. You couldn't see the anchors themselves from inside the ship, but those chains.... each link was massive and weighed 350 pounds. The chain was 1,440 feet long but you didn't see all of it. The winches were enormous. The anchors each weighed 60,000 pounds ... that is 30 TONS. The chains went out the port and starboard hawseholes to hold the anchors high above the water.

Ever heard the term "drop anchor?" Until you have seen a carrier do it, you "ain't seen nuthin." The chain is disconnected from the capstan/winch and when the last chocking wedge is banged out with a sledgehammer, away she goes. Loud! Fast! The anchor free falls to the distant water and on below to the bottom.... with the chain leaping and clanking all the way.

NOTE: When the Indy was decommissioned in Bremerton, WA and cannibalized for parts, the port anchor and both chains were installed on the *USS George H.W.Bush (CVN-77)*.

Sea Chest ... An interesting thing aboard Indy was that many people "took care of the doc." They saw to it that we had various perks. One such was a steel sea chest issued to me and stenciled with my name, etc. ..... "because I should have one." It was about the size of a footlocker and foldable when not in use. One of the carpenters insisted on making for me a similar sized wooden sea chest. I still have both.

The Gibraltar Bear.... The Bear was a Russian Tupolev TU-95 "Bear" Bomber. As our carriers passed through the Straits of Gibraltar a "Bear" would always be there to scope out our navy, take reconnaissance photos and even hassle the ship a little. The TU-95 was enormous, 151 feet long, swept wings with span of 164 feet, four turboprop engines. (The F-4 Phantom was 63 and 38 feet, respectively.) The Bear had a range of 9,300 miles. The Russians knew when our fleet units were coming and going from the Mediterranean, so would send a Bear to keep tabs. It would not overfly European countries but would fly out into the north Atlantic, down to Gibraltar, then back home.

Of course, we expected the Bear to be there so when spotted on radar, we sent up a couple of F-4 Phantoms. (We had continual radar "eyes" on anything within 200 miles of us.) Our F-4s would "escort" the Bear. If it tried to get too close to us or turned toward us instead of keeping a polite distance, one of the F-4s would fly under its wing tip and pull up to force it to turn off or have a midair collision. We watched all the action in the air. The Phantoms looked so small compared to the Bear, it was like a mosquito pestering the ear of a pig. The Bear would take their photos and turn back for home.

FOD ... The initials meant "foreign object damage" but was used to refer to something that would cause the damage. When a jet engine sucked in a screw, loose piece of metal, small rock, small piece of paper ... almost anything lying out on the flight deck during operations ... damage would occur to the engine. Not only was that expensive to repair but it endangered the lives of flight crew. So FOD, the bad foreign object, that might be lurking in wait on the flight deck was always a concern. To minimize if not eliminate FOD, before any session of flight operations began, the deck crew would do a "FOD Walkdown." Several dozen sailors would line up at the bow, elbow to elbow maybe a foot or two apart and slowly walk to the stern, sort of like a slow broom sweep. They kept eyes constantly on the deck looking for anything, no matter how small, that was loose and might fly into a jet intake.

The Island … Eyes and Ears of the ship and the aircraft. The island was multi-stories high and had many components… ship's bridge with views in every direction, Pri-Fly (Primary Flight Control, like a tower at an airport) where all flight deck activity could be seen, Vulture's Row, the exhaust stacks going up through the middle at the starboard side, etc. All around and above the top few levels were more radar and radio gear than you can imagine. At flight deck level was the Battle Dressing Station where emergency-care corpsmen were stationed during flight ops.…. and where a flight surgeon joined them for General Quarters. The Island was bigger than it looks in photos and there are ladders and passageways connecting everything. There are people on the bridge in the island 24/7/365. There are two bridges, The Admirals Bridge where he can observe and monitor the task force and of course the main Captain's Bridge for controlling the ship. Pri-Fly was responsible for the aircraft on deck and in the air. You could write a book about all the intricacies and technical things going on in the island all the time.

Urinals … Being an all-male crew we had urinals on the Indy in strategic places which added to our efficiency. The newer class carriers do not have urinals because three or four hundred, maybe more, women are in the crew, so the heads are "gender neutral." The modern navy also has a significant number of female pilots and aircrew. Without any personal knowledge my guess would be that the conversation topics and language patterns aboard carriers has changed including in the squadron ready rooms.

Pregnancy … Yep, research has shown that when young men and women are together, sexual activity occurs. The first time that women sailors were permanently assigned to an aircraft carrier was in 1994 aboard the Eisenhower. 415 women (8.4%) of a crew of 4,967 departed Norfolk, VA for a six-months cruise. On return fourteen were reported as having become pregnant during the cruise. Another 24 had been pregnant before departure. That is a 9% pregnancy rate among the female crew.

"Fraternization" onboard is against regulations. However, one couple was removed from the ship for having sex onboard in private spaces but videotaping it and showing it around. The fourteen pregnant women presumably became so while on shore leave. Why not? If male sailors historically have been so promiscuous ashore, why not the ladies? I have no information about STDs among women crew. Maybe current flight surgeons are proficient as gynecologists now also. Does NAMI now include a course on gynecology? Likely the flight surgeons don't need to be obstetricians as pregnant crew are transferred ashore.

Another interesting aspect is that some women sailors have deliberately become pregnant because they didn't want to deploy on a cruise.

More About Women on Carriers … Fast forward twenty-five years. Women make up 19% of personnel in the entire Navy. Not that high a percentage is aboard modern carriers, but a significant number are. Separate berthing and head facilities have been arranged. In a study done in 2019 there were seven female flight officers in one squadron and on February 2, 2019 the first all-female flyover was recorded. It's a different Navy from when I served on the Indy in 1966 …. but then, isn't everything different now? Life always proceeds into new worlds.

Sports … The traditional all male sports on carriers may have changed also. Women athletes are prominent in basketball, ring boxing, wrestling and other sports that are part of carrier life.

Well, that's a lucky thirteen mixed-bag collection of random thoughts, so on to other topics.

HOW TO SIMULATE LIVING IN AN AIRCRAFT CARRIER

THREE DOZEN SUGGESTIONS **from the Author's Experience and Shipmate Stories**

1. Live in a steel dumpster for six months on the curb of a busy street.

2. Rewire and replumb your house so all wires and pipes are exposed. Paint them gray.

3. Add 10-12 inches high thresholds in every doorway and lower the top the same amount.

4. Paint the inside and outside of your house Navy grey every month, needed or not.

5. Have your children scrub the floors twice a day. Four times a day have them empty all trash cans and sweep the driveway whether needed or not.

6. Have a compressor inject air into your main water line periodically to keep some bubbles knocking and fizzing throughout the pipes and so that the water sputters while showering.

7. Insist that everyone turns off the water after soaping and tell them randomly at least twice a week that they used too much

water so no bathing that day. Also randomly turn off the water heater and give an evil chuckle when they gripe about it.

8. Have a seven-year-old give you a haircut with dull-edged and loose-hinged hedge clippers.

9. Run into your children's room when they are asleep and shout "General Quarters, General Quarters" through a megaphone.... and at 0500 daily blow a whistle in their room and shout, "Reveille, reveille, heave out."

10. Post a menu at breakfast announcing steak for dinner but serve creamed chipped beef on a slab (toast) .... a.k.a. "SOS" = s____ -on-a-shingle.... or hot dogs .... or Spam ... or _____.

11. Arrange for a small plane to roll its wheels and bang across your roof periodically.

12. Keep a lawnmower running inside your main room to simulate the carrier noise and fumes. Also put half water and half lube oil in a humidifier and run it on the other end of the house.

13. Before driving out of your driveway line up your family shoulder-to-shoulder and have them slowly walk to the street scrutinizing every inch of the concrete and pick up every leaf, twig, insect, discarded chewing gum or whatever might suck into your carburetor.

14. Raise all beds so close to the ceiling that one must get completely out just to turn over.

15. Buy the cheapest coffee available, keep it opened on a shelf for six months, then let it simmer in the pot for four or five hours before serving.

16. Provide wobbly rocking chairs and barf bags for everyone and insist they rock in them every time a thunderstorm rolls through.

17. Take apart all appliances every month to inspect them, then reassemble.

18. Install a brass bell by the front door and every time your mother-in-law comes or goes ring the bell four times and announce loudly

through a megaphone, "mother-in-law arriving" or "mother-in-law departing."

19. Also destroy all wristwatches and clocks except your own and clang the entry bell every thirty minutes so your family can live "by the bells." Go from one clang up to eight every four hours so that everyone must count the clangs to know what to do next.

20. Every time you leave or return to your house salute the mailbox and request permission from your dog to exit or enter.

21. While you are trying to sleep and/or during meals have the members of a motorcycle gang bang sledgehammers on your roof to simulate launching and recovering aircraft.

22. At mealtime drive the family to McDonald's but park three blocks away. Line up single file and walk slowly to the front door. Time it to get there just at closing time and prearrange for the manager to shout, "Chow is secured." as he locks the door. Take earplugs with you for the moaning and bitching on the way back to your car.

23. Two or three hours after you fall asleep have your spouse shine a flashlight into your eyes and shout, "Sorry, wrong rack."

24. Be sure once a month to have your spouse set off the smoke alarm so you can run into the kitchen and stand by the stove and shout, "Stove manned and ready." After standing there three or four hours shout, "Stove secured." and return to what you were doing.

25. Remove the chairs and put teeter-totters (a.k.a. seesaw) around your dining room table and insist everyone eat their meals seated on one across from someone else.

26. Before going to get gas for your car, have a family meeting several hours ahead and arrange for the fire department and ambulance to meet you at the gas station. Then have the family stand at attention around the gas pumps as you test a fuel sample. Only then can you fill up your gas tank.

27. Inspect all around your car for two hours checking tire pressure, oil level, fuel gauge and all headlights, taillights and turn lights. Keep a detailed log of all readings.

28. When you are sick, go to the bathroom medicine cabinet (a.k.a. household sickbay), give yourself a small packet of APCs ("all-purpose cure" = aspirin, phenacetin, caffeine) and tell yourself to return to your duty station.

29. Put a large tub of water outside of a window. Stand inside and stare at the water for at least four straight hours.

30. If the weather is hot and humid, close all doors and windows, then pull the circuit-breakers on the air-conditioner(s) and all fans. If the weather is frigid, open all doors and windows and turn all fans on high speed.

31. If you serve stuffed cabbage one day, remove the cabbage leaves the next day, grind up the meat, re-bake and call it meatloaf. The third day, grind the meat again and serve as hamburgers. The fourth day, grind up again, chop up the cabbage leaves from day one and serve a delicious cabbage-beef soup.

32. Use only the rinse cycle on your clothes washer, use turpentine instead of detergent, dry the clothes no more than ten minutes then distribute randomly to family members.

33. Now and then put on your best clothes, salute the mailbox, get permission from your dog to leave, walk to the seediest part of town, pay $20. per beer in a trashy bar then walk home in the freezing rain.

34. After ten or twenty years of running your household as above in admirable ship-shape manner, have your twenty-year-old son's best friend come over and tell you what you have been doing wrong. As he takes charge for two years, smile and keep repeating, "Aye, aye, sir."

35. Invite sixty people with poor hygiene and bad habits to live with you for six months.

36. Never sit around and tell yourself how great a life this is when you are really wondering why you did all this in the first place.

That is an even three dozen ways to simulate being on an aircraft carrier. The list could go on for many more pages but by now certainly you have the general idea of what it is like.

Anchors Aweigh .... Go Navy.

V

NAVAL AVIATORS

CAREER PATH OF A
NAVAL AVIATOR

TO BE ACCEPTED as a candidate for flight training to be a Naval Aviator a person first must have a college degree and pass a rigorous physical and psychological examination at the Naval Aerospace Medical Institute (NAMI) in Pensacola, FL. More people get the "NAMI Whammy" than continue into the training program. The "Whammy" is when someone fails an essential qualification and is "busted out" of the program. Those who continue along and successfully complete flight training to earn their Wings of Gold and become a Naval Aviator are then launched into their careers. There are multiple pathways and the goals extend all the way up to squadron commanding officer, CAG (commander of an airwing of multiple squadrons), Captain rank and Captain of an aircraft carrier, Admiral rank and commander of a task force, various large commands like CINCLANT and CINCPAC, Chief of Naval Operations, etc. There are many hurdles along the way and it is a pyramid structure of decreasing numbers to the top.

So, Aaron Aviator graduates in Pensacola and other training centers depending on whether he has chosen AND qualifies for jets or props or helicopters, etc. from the various career choices. Off he goes to the fleet as a junior officer.... Ensign or LTJG in most cases. He may go immediately to a squadron deployed on a carrier or perhaps to a land-based unit. Suppose it is a carrier squadron. He is known as a first tour officer. His performance is recorded by his seniors in fitness reports and his reputation is begun. Success is the norm. Failure results in his first obligated length of tour being his only service as he leaves the Navy, sometimes for a job as a pilot in civil or commercial aviation. Failure could also result in his death. It happens more frequently than anyone hopes.

While on his first tour Aaron Aviator usually gets/earns/acquires a call sign (nickname.... like in the *Top Gun* movie) because no macho aviator wants to key his mike and say, "That's a 'raaje', Aaron." ["raaje" is slang for "roger," meaning "I understand."] The call sign may derive from anything.... his name, behavior, incident... whatever sticks... and the aviator community is quite inventive. Call signs can change as well.

After two to four years of service in the fleet Successful Aaron has probably earned the rank of LT (Lieutenant with two wide stripes/bars ... the equivalent of a Captain in the Army, Air Force and Marines.) "Double A" now rotates to a "desk job" which is usually a training school such as the War College, perhaps getting a master's degree at a regular college.... it varies. Double A continues to fly with some nearby unit and must log a minimum of four hours flight time per month to continue receiving flight pay.

After a year or so of "flying furniture" Double A is likely promoted to LCDR and is assigned to the active fleet again, this time as a second (or third) tour pilot in a senior position and in charge of some division of the squadron such as Maintenance, Ops, etc. Several years of experience earning ensues and Double A establishes a record and reputation of success. He goes next to another desk job with more advanced training schools including training for command. By and by Double A achieves promotion to CDR ... a three stripe Commander.

Aaron "Double A" Aviator is ready to be the XO of a fleet squadron, at least his third tour of active flying. The Executive Officer of a squadron is second in command and as the name implies, he "executes" and makes happen all the functions that the CO leads. XO tours are usually shorter than previous ones, maybe a single year, as Double A is in training to be a Commanding Officer of a squadron, likely a shorter tour also.

Next step-up would-be commander of an air wing composed of perhaps eight or ten squadrons. The traditional moniker is "CAG" for Commander Air Group. (Groups of squadrons, but now designated Wings, so technically he would be the "CAW", but who wants to be called that… even if he squawks a lot?) The CAG has had FAM Hops (training) in all the aircraft types in his wing and rotates flying in them regardless of his previous experience. You know …. the expectation is that a Naval Aviator can "do anything, anytime, anywhere" and do it well. That's not always true, but it is a consistent opinion and attitude within naval aviation communities.

It's a great fantasy that fits with the THERE I WUZ theme! … and that's likely where the famous saying originated, "A Naval Aviator leaves the fleet with great nostalgia, but no regrets." Double A has seen some of his friends get killed, has had some close calls himself and has matured to the level of full realization of the hazards of carrier ops. Also, his reflexes have slowed a bit even though he won't ever, ever admit it. He is "thirtyish" now or pushing it.

By the time Double A leaves the fleet as CAG he may have been promoted to full "bird" Captain with four wide stripes. "Yes, SIR!" Taking his nostalgia and many, many tales and sea stories, he flies a desk again for a while … schools, training, learning … this time in the "Deep Draft" pipeline of the Bluewater Navy. The goal is to be assigned as XO, then CO of an aircraft carrier … but first he must master ship handling. So Double A serves a year or so each as XO and CO of a deep draft navy ship such as a supply ship, a fuel ship or other such. All of these are essential to support carriers and carrier task forces.

If success follows our stalwart Double A, he moves on up the chain of command. Another old navy saying is appropriate here. The best time to leave a command is "when the band is playing and the flags are flying" .… meaning your unit is functioning at a peak level. Double A is now ready to be XO, then Commanding Officer of a supercarrier. He must be good AND lucky AND a political player as well. The pyramid system is in full force at this level of naval careers. Even as skipper of the carrier he and his performance are being scrutinized constantly. The admiral of the carrier task force might designate the carrier as his flagship and be onboard daily. In any case the high-ranking commanders of the entire Navy will be watching and evaluating performance. Double A probably knows a lot of them and maybe flew with some in younger days.

In his forties now and with over twenty years of experience our Successful Double A is promoted to Admiral and moves along up to increasing levels of responsibility as his talents, vacancies, luck and politics allow. From not getting "whammied" at NAMI, in and out of the fleet, ADMIRAL AARON "Double A" AVIATOR is now "Triple A" and a top SEA DOG. Yessir!!!

AVIATOR VIGNETTES

A FEW TALES AND INTERESTING OBSERVATIONS

NAVAL AVIATORS ARE a close-knit group, almost a clan. It is because they have shared the same training, experiences AND harrowing experiences. Mostly Alpha males with Type-A personalities they are achievers, courageous, maintain health, not afraid to make decisions or to express opinions and usually control their emotions.

One example is when a warning light flashes on in the cockpit. It may be "fire" or maybe "hydraulic failure" etc. The competent pilot immediately checks everything, then if he can't find anything wrong with the controls or other observation, he keys his mike and mumbles to his RIO, "Fire warning light, pulling breaker, prob'ly be all right." RIO dutifully responds, "Roger that." (Well what else is there to do?.... crawl out on the wing and shoot a fire extinguisher up the jet intake?)

Naval Aviators are also mostly young men with significant levels of testosterone that influences all the above and an interest in sex. Hmmmm …where did that term "cockpit" originate???

[The title comes to us from "cock," an Old English term for a small boat, and "swain," which means servant. A cockswain is a

boat servant. Over time, this title led to the steering compartment of smaller boats, where the cockswain sat, being called a cockpit.]

Since Freud started the discussion of phallic symbols in dreams and elsewhere at about the same time as airplanes were invented and developed, there has long been a correlation between the two…. and Naval Aviator actions and vocabulary frequently affirm the connection.

(Don't get carried away with that last word. It is not an intentional pun, just a Freudian slip.)

So here are some interesting observations from my association with Naval Aviators.

They have a macho aura that is either natural or they work at maintaining it. Swagger might be a good word, but it's old-fashioned. (More appropriate might be "swigger" since they often enjoy significant amounts of alcoholic beverages.) In a later section is a discussion of the Centurion achievement of 100 traps and the "Flaming Hooker" initiation rite which are somewhat symbolic. Somebody, sometime in the past called a tailhook sparking on the deck at night, a "flaming hooker" and it is part of the macho language now.

One CAG's last name started with a "G." When he initialed something, he used a red pencil (pay attention to that) and extended the horizontal bar on the letter "G" with a little arrow, just like the scientific male symbol. He was a good guy, excellent pilot, good leader, one of the best …. just pointing out that symbolism.

Jet fighter planes are long, have pointed leading nosecones, have a lot of thrust and if the engine pods and/or gear are toward the rear……. well, what do you think?

Just listening to casual conversation in the ready rooms picked up some salty language sometimes with frequent references to exploits from the past or planned. I wonder what has evolved with so many women aviators now and mixed-gender squadrons and ready rooms…. as well as wardroom meals, et al. I have no doubt that the female Naval Aviators can more than hold their own, but the conversations on the ship have probably been moderated.

Frequently stateside single male aviators will pool their resources to rent a house/apartment together to save money. Sometimes that would be called a "bachelor pad" or other such. Aviators' favorite term is "Snake Ranch" …. not to be confused with "cockpit."

When getting low on fuel sometimes pilots key their mike and say, "Let's hit the tanker." There is a certain phallic symbolism in mid-air refueling. The planes are equipped with a long, pointed probe that must be inserted into the drogue basket trailing behind the rear end of the tanker plane. Here is a quote from a Navy fighter pilot glossary……

"And on a black-ass night in the middle of the ocean with critical fuel state, that'll raise the pucker factor. The fuel hose extends some 30 feet aft of the tanker, ending in a padded cone (the Basket–also evocatively known as the "beaver") designed to receive your probe and guide it to a successful coupling. This whole business results in one of the trickiest maneuvers in aviation. Never mind that the basket is dancing around the cockpit (a hit on the cockpit plexiglass could ruin your whole day), the pilot must hold steady until the basket settles down, then add power–if you're lucky, your probe is in the beaver, uh, basket. Thrust drives the probe tip deeper in and completes the coupling. (Enough…this is beginning to resemble an overwrought romance novel.)"

Full throttle with afterburners is called military power and sometimes "balls to the wall."

Remember that old Naval Aviator joke, "There is nothing better in life than a good landing, a good bowel movement and a good orgasm…. a night carrier landing is the only way you can experience all three at the same time."

The first nuclear carrier was Enterprise (CVN-65.) Its nickname was "Big E" and it's call sign was "climax." Here are two more quotes from the same Navy fighter pilot glossary ….

"The control stick in an airplane, which in addition to allowing control of pitch and roll ….

And then there's the flesh-and-bones "Stick".…"

"What's this? Rest? Of course not. The Naval Aviator never rests. He flies, he drinks, he chases poon, and he dreams about flying, drinking, and chasing poon. But he never rests."

For the cognoscenti we shall end with ….

"Penetration … piercing the clouds."

"Helen …. Mini-Helen …. Micro-Helen" [Depends on how long you've been at sea.]

"Mary Ann Barnes" & "Nellie Darling" …. [two aviator bar songs, not to be elucidated here.]

Go Navy…. Go Naval Aviators …. Bravo Zulu …. That's a Rog….

NAVAL AVIATORS AS
INDIVIDUALS

THE MILITARY DEVOTES a great deal of time and training to instill standards of proficiency in its personnel. This is true at virtually every level because success depends on group action where all the individuals in a unit understand their responsibilities and have the training to perform their duties well. Perhaps a pinnacle of this is among Naval Aviators.

We all have seen movies where a busload of newbie recruits arrives at boot camp or some other training facility. A kaleidoscope of individuals starts together. Hairstyles, clothes, personalities, attitudes, behaviors are spread across the spectrum. The goal is to develop uniformity. That's what the word "uniform" means, to wit,

Definition of uniform

1. *having always the same form, manner, or degree: not varying or variable… uniform procedures*
2. *consistent in conduct or opinion … uniform interpretation of rules.*
3. *of the same form with others: conforming to one rule or mode: CONSONANT*
4. *presenting an unvaried appearance of surface, pattern, or color*

When people think of the uniformed services, they generally visualize people in uniform clothing without considering the aspects of uniform behavior, training and experience which are highly more important than just the clothes worn. The clothes just serve to identify the individuals who have come together to accomplish a common goal or mission.

The uniformed services are also known as the armed forces. A friend of mine who is a retired Marine colonel told me once that the mission of Marines is to "break things and kill people." Like it or not, war is violence. All armed forces are "armed" to exert "force."

The Navy, its ships, its airwings, its aircraft, its rockets, missiles and bombs and its personnel are joined together and trained to exert force. Yet even with the common goal of the armed forces, the men and women in the uniformed services are individuals. Each has a different background, each has a different expectation, each has a different life path. A good portion of this book discusses the consistency of performance expected of the individuals and how that is accomplished but let's consider individual personalities.

All the individuals who have earned gold wings and become Naval Aviators have undergone the same rigorous training program, learning how to fly, how to perform, even how to behave. Then each has been required to demonstrate proficiency at all aspects of the profession. The culmination is carrier qualifications where everyone must demonstrate proficiency in performing a highly standardized and rigidly narrow set of skills. It may be a corny cliché, but it is literally "Do or die."

Yet …. each Naval Aviator is an individual. Among them as a group is a panoply of differences. Here are a few examples to demonstrate that Naval Aviators are not just automatons or human robots.

Harvard Law School … One of my pilots was a Yale graduate with a good academic record. He had always wanted to be an attorney, but economics and life situations had led him into naval aviation. He was an accomplished pilot and naval officer with promotions on schedule and a promising career in the Navy in prospect. However, as a few years went by he kept thinking about shifting into the law as originally hoped. We had many discussions about all this, usually while bending elbows somewhere or the other. He and his wife would come to our house for dinner and we would go to theirs. By and by he decided to make the move. He made an appointment with the Dean of the Harvard Law School, then checked out an F-4 and flew from Oceana to Boston. Arriving at the dean's office in dress white uniform he made his case. His Yale academic records and navy experience on his application were impressive as well. Acceptance to law school followed soon thereafter and when his obligated navy tour finished, off he went to Boston to begin law school. Bravo for fulfilling his dreams beyond being a Naval Aviator.

Long Term Investor Thinking #1 … This pilot was single and of course enjoyed the usual behaviors of single aviators when ashore and off duty. However, he had an eye on the future as well. He was interested in stock investments and decided that Toyota Motor Company was the future. Although Toyota was founded in 1933 and played a role in the Japanese war efforts of that era, post war they began exporting automobiles to other countries. They entered the U.S. market in 1957 and by the middle 1960s had established a growth curve. My pilot friend was enthusiastic about Toyota's prospects and touted them frequently, also putting his money where his mouth was by starting a regular investment program. He probably became a multimillionaire. Unfortunately, I didn't follow him and buy Toyota stock at the time.

Long Term Investor Thinking #2 … Another pilot had been a naval officer for a few years before going to flight training. When he earned his wings and began receiving flight pay (hazardous duty pay), he decided that he had been living reasonably well without the flight pay, so why not just save it instead of spending it each payday. So, he socked it away. You can imagine what the eventual value became by investing $200.00 a month from the early 1960s.

Oil Painting and Classical Music … One senior LCDR aviator on his third sea tour was not only a top pilot, but also interested in fine art. We became friends because he had a cousin that I had known at

Tulane Medical School. He invited me to his stateroom a few times to show off some oil paintings he was doing while he listened to classical music. Later after the navy he became interested in photography and had several collections of his work published.

Duplicate Bridge Hobbyist ... One aviator was devoted to duplicate bridge and had won a few competitions. He bemoaned that there were few others on the cruise interested in his hobby but he did organize a foursome from time to time.

Athletes ... Several aviators had been standouts in college athletics before going into the Navy flight training program. There were athletic programs on the carrier but none of the caliber of their background experience.

Academician ... Another aviator planned an academic career after his navy obligation. He was going to get a PhD in literature and be a college professor.

Career Choices ... These were varied. Several individuals planned Navy careers of at least twenty years and if successful, maybe thirty or more. It would depend on if they were promoted to Captain and Admiral. (Remember the pyramid system in the military.)

Others planned to finish their Navy obligations and fly for commercial airlines. There was a long history of military pilots supplying the needs of commercial airlines.

Of course, lots of the pilots were in their early twenties and had not thought further than the excitement and challenges of what they were doing at that time. There were many differences among them. Some were married, some single. Some of the married aviators had children, some not. Some had happy marriages and supportive wives. Some had significant marital difficulties. Each aviator had individual circumstances.

Bottom Line ... (to use the cliché) Naval Aviators all must be the same in the proficiency and exacting skills of carrier flight operations. They either are the same technically and in performance or they leave.... or die. When difficult flight conditions and close calls come along, some are smooth and relaxed in manner, some show their nervousness and apprehension. The veneer of "macho" could hide a lot of worry, fear and self-doubt. The Flight Surgeon's role was to know and understand all the differences of the individuals in a group facade where everyone appeared and behaved all the same.

IN HIS OWN WORDS

[Author's Note: The following "There I Wuz" stories are in one of my Naval Aviator's own words, quoted from his obituary after he died in his eighties. He survived three potentially deadly aircraft accident/incidents while piloting his F-4 Phantom fighter jet.]

#1 (DURING A night landing on an airstrip in Florida) "…my nose wheel simply collapsed and I slid 3-4,000 feet down the runway trailing flames. The centerline tank had ruptured during the slide and a small amount of residual fuel sparked off. After the aircraft came to a stop, my back-seater RIO and I simply climbed down and waited for a ride. The fire had gone out on its own…."

#2 (During his combat tour in Viet Nam flying off the Indy in 1965) "… after our mission and preparing for our trap on the *Independence*, a hydraulic pump failed and that prevented the landing gear from lowering. The ship diverted me to Da Nang for a night landing. I activated my emergency air system to lower the landing gear, but only the left main and the nose wheel came down. So now I was faced with a one wheel up landing. I flew out over the water and dumped my remaining ordnance, returned to Da Nang and asked for landing … it so happened that they had an emergency arresting gear rigged a very short 300 feet from the overrun and wire. I burned my fuel to a low state, made the approach, caught the wire and slid out on two landing gear and an empty bomb rack. My NFO and I opened our canopies as if we did this stuff every day. Everything was cool and there was no fire…."

#3 (On his last combat mission, flying over Laos his F-4 Phantom took enemy fire.) "… We dropped our 250lb fragmentation bombs over the Ho Chi Minh trail and as we were climbing out, my aircraft was hit and decided not to cooperate any longer. The cockpits began filling with smoke so my NFO jettisoned his canopy. With it gone suction pulled flames out from under his seat, so he ejected. Now it gets heavy. The flames came around me and burned my face and hands. I pulled my seat's face curtain to eject but nothing happened. I then pulled the seat's secondary firing handle without results. I next pulled the canopy jettison handle but it wouldn't move. I was not too functional at this time and I thought about the end. But then, the canopy left and the seat operated normally. My chute opened and I could see the trees getting closer. Down I went into the foliage. My chute caught up in the top of a tree and my feet landed on a limb next to the main trunk. I disconnected from my chute and sat down on the limb. I was 80 feet up. I clearly remember the thought, as I looked down, 'this is no time to screw up.' I disconnected and dropped my seat survival pack to the ground, put my gloves on over my burns and skinned down the tree. The limb I had sat on was the lowest limb on the tree. An hour or so later the Air Force sent two helos. The helicopter pilots called the area, 'the land of the 100-foot trees.' We were plucked out of the jungle and taken to a refurbished WWII Japanese hospital … we returned to duty two months later."

ASSORTED AVIATOR ANECDOTES

THESE STORIES ARE all true and happened on my watch. Undoubtedly many more could be told by other flight surgeons. I have heard quite a few, but they aren't my stories to tell.

Stranded on the Shores of Tripoli … When a pilot could not "get aboard," i.e., land on the carrier for various reasons (usually bad weather, low fuel, etc.), he would fly to a designated land-based airfield. This was called a Bingo field and having to land there was called a Bingo. There was a certain negative connotation to having to Bingo. It implied failure even though there was often none involved. There was pride in being able to "get aboard" even with various adverse conditions. We always had a relatively nearby "Bingo" field in the Mediterranean because we were mostly close to some or other airfield on land. In the central Med that was Wheelus Air Force Base on the periphery of Tripoli, Libya. [Remember the Naval Aviator's teasing and joking comment to Air Force pilots: "Anyone can land on a two-mile runway."]

It's interesting that it was the same "shores of Tripoli" where several hundred years ago the Marines had to go take care of business …. and earned the nickname of "leathernecks" there. In 1966 Libya was friendly so the AFB airstrip was a convenient bingo field. The airstrip is still there, but no longer a USAF base. There were not that many times a pilot had to Bingo to the backup landing strip, but occasionally it happened. On this occasion an A-4 pilot had landed there one night and planned to refuel and return to the Indy the next day when our flight operations were in progress.

Problem: He ate something tainted and developed acute staph food poisoning with severe vomiting and diarrhea which ultimately proceeded to dehydration. The pilot probably planned to recover and fly back to Indy but got worse. I don't know why the hospital at Wheelus didn't take care of him, but anyway we sent a plane to (1) pick him up and bring him back to Indy and (2) take another pilot over to fly his A-4 back.

THERE I WUZ ... in sickbay as MOD and they brought in the pilot who was in shock and obtunded. We rapidly started an IV and pushed fluids. Soon the pilot recovered but we kept him for observation until he was stable and back to normal.

Jerusalem and Jordan High Jinks ... Special Services planned a side visit to Jerusalem while we were in port at Beirut. About forty or fifty of us signed up to go. There was a problem getting there because none of the Muslim countries would allow a flight directly into Israel. So, arrangements were made for us to fly to Jordan and then take a bus into Israel. A Jordanian Airlines plane would fly us to Amman, Jordan. The plane was a C-47 and could carry only half of our group. Off they flew. The two pilots were to do an immediate turn around and come back to pick up the second half of us. It was about an hour of flight time each way, two hours round trip. We waited, and waited, and waited, and waited .... no plane and no word. Finally, after four or five hours had elapsed the Jordanian Air C-47 arrived back. We loaded our group and flew on to Amman. Only later did we find out what the problem had been. Both pilots had eaten the same box lunch in Amman and developed severe staph food poisoning with vomiting and diarrhea. They had to wait until recovering before flying back to get the second group. Damn. That staph toxin food poisoning is common around the Med. Had we known about the pilots' problem we might not have flown with them so soon after their illness.

Gout be Damned, I Gotta Go to Nam … One of my pilots was on a promising career track. He was a Naval Academy graduate, an excellent aviator and exemplary officer. He had received early promotions and had flown in several squadrons and served in airwing staff positions. He had deployed several times at sea. However, he realized one day that all his peers had made combat deployments to Viet Nam, but he had not. The Navy officer corps is a pyramid system with smaller and smaller numbers who advance to Captain and Admiral. If he didn't have a Viet Nam combat tour like his peer competitors, he would have no chance.

In the Med he had put on a few pounds and decided to trim up, then volunteer to go on a Viet Nam combat tour. He began a low-carbohydrate diet that was in vogue then. The diet restricts carbohydrate but lots of meat is usually substituted. He came in one day complaining of foot pain. One of his big toe joints was swollen, inflamed and tender. I prescribed treatment and ordered a Uric Acid lab test. The result came back with a significantly elevated level. The aviator had precipitated gout with the semi-starvation diet.

Problem: He would not qualify for a combat tour with gout and that would hamstring his career. Quote/Unquote, "Gout be damned, I gotta go to Nam."

Gout is an inherited disorder of purine metabolism resulting in high levels of uric acid. That causes uric acid crystals to be deposited in joints, kidneys and other places. Untreated and ongoing it can lead to serious problems. The pilot had never had problems until the diet had increased his purine intake and decreased his metabolic management thereof.

We had several long talks. On a normal diet he was not likely to have many problems. We discussed the risks of starvation in a prisoner status triggering the gout again. However, the overriding factor was the importance of his career…. "Gout be damned, I gotta go to Nam." The pilot was not just one of my guys. He was a particular friend and I had flown with him often. There was no way I was going to cripple his career with red flags in his health record.

With careful reading of the health record a physician would probably pick up the episode, but otherwise it would not be obvious. The pilot did go on a combat tour to Viet Nam in the late 1960s. Unfortunately, he was shot down … but survived and was captured by the North Vietnamese. He spent four or five years as a POW in the notorious "Hanoi Hilton" where there was a lot of torture and brutal treatment. He paid a dear price for his patriotism and Navy career. He was released in 1973. I don't know if the gout ever bothered him, but maybe not because prisoner diets don't include much purine-rich food. Although prisoners were undernourished, their scanty nutrition was mostly rice and not absolute starvation.

My pilot friend returned from Viet Nam, received multiple military medals and did progress to Captain. He had several prominent Navy positions. I have heard that he died a few years ago in his eighties. RIP my old friend. You were a steadfast patriot who served your country well.

Navy…Air Force…Navy…Air Force…Navy…
FUH-GEDDA-BOUT-IT …. One pilot on the Indy with us had a most interesting career AND a remarkable episode that is worth the telling. He was a Naval Academy graduate, then decided he wanted to be an Air Force pilot, so transferred services. He was a competent pilot and when the Air Force wanted to send an exchange pilot to a Navy squadron, they sent him.…. maybe because he had been a Naval Academy graduate.

Anyway, THERE HE WUZ flying off and on the carrier in VF-84 flying F-4 Phantom II fighter planes. He was an Air Force Captain which is the same equivalent rank as a LT in the Navy with two wide stripes. This is important for the story. The VF-84 squadron was called the "Jolly Rogers" and the aircraft had a skull-and-crossbones on the tail along with the large NAVY markings on the fuselage. Note that the Navy nomenclature for a fighter squadron is "Fighter Squadron Eighty-four" while Air Force nomenclature would be "Eighty-fourth Fighter Squadron." Also note that air force bases have their name first, ex., Offutt Air Force Base while the navy designation is Naval Air Station Oceana, i.e., name at the end. All this is background.

(That pilot and I had a special connection because he had done a tour at the air force base in my hometown and still owned a home there. I flew with him a few times.)

After the Indy Med cruise, the F-4 squadrons were based at NAS Oceana. Later in 1967 our air force exchange pilot decided to go to the 20th birthday anniversary of the Air Force which was 18 September 1967. I think it was at Offutt Air Force Base in Nebraska. So, he checked out one of the VF-84 F-4 Phantoms and flew to Nebraska. He rolled out on the runway and taxied to the terminal. The Air Force was logging everyone who came to the celebration so they could notify the pilots' hometown newspapers for public relations. So, a young airman was there with clipboard and a questionnaire when the Navy Phantom shut down and the pilot in full flight gear climbed down. The conversation went something like this:

Airman: "Welcome to Offutt Air Force Base, Sir. What is your name, sir?"

Pilot: "Roger Jolly." (fictional)

Airman: (writing all the information on his clipboard) "What is your rank, Sir?"

Response: "Captain."

Airman: (seeing all the Navy markings on the F-4, stiffens with respect at the senior rank.) "Yes, SIR, That's Captain Roger Jolly, United States Navy."

Response: "No, United States Air Force."

Airman: "Uh, yes sir. I see your squadron is the 84th Fighter Squadron."

Response: "No, it's Fighter Squadron 84."

Airman: "Uh, yes sir. From where did you fly today?"

Response: "From the air station at Oceana in Virginia Beach.

Airman: "Yes sir, Oceana Air Force Base."

Response: "No, it's the Naval Air Station Oceana."

By now the airman is getting flustered. Airman: "Let's see, let me get this right. You are in a Navy squadron and a Navy airplane and from a Naval Air Station, but you are an Air Force pilot and an Air Force Captain.... uh …. okay … and Sir where did you graduate college?"

Pilot: "Naval Academy."

Airman: "Thank you, Sir." and walks away muttering FUH-GEDDA-BOUT-IT. [a.k.a. YGBSM]

THE ADMIRAL AND THE CAPTAIN

REAR ADMIRAL GEORGE **P. Koch was Commander of Carrier Division Six** and was aboard with his staff of forty or fifty including officers and enlisted who performed various functions. The ships in a Carrier Division vary, but usually include the carrier, one or two cruisers, a destroyer squadron of two to six ships, sometimes a submarine or two, an oiler, a supply ship, sometimes a munitions replenishment ship, et al. Of course, the Airwing was a vital component of the command. A Carrier Division was also called a Battle Strike Group or Carrier Task Force. The number and kinds of ships varied depending on many factors. The carrier ALWAYS had at least one destroyer escort, sometimes more. Our destroyer escort followed astern and besides its protective function it was considered a "plane guard," always available for rescue of any downed aircrew, man overboard, whatever.

The captains of all the ships plus the CAG of the airwing all reported to Admiral Koch who was responsible for their movements, training, proficiency and battle readiness. The admiral was of course an experienced Naval Aviator who had captained ships, etc. He understood how all in his command functioned.

Admiral Koch had private quarters that were quite spacious and had its own galley for meal preparation. There was a bedroom, a lounge area with dining table at one end and spacious shower/bath unit. There were four or five stewards to cook, serve, clean the spaces and whatever was necessary to "take care of the admiral." (The stewards were mostly from the Philippines. They enlisted in the U.S. Navy and after a period of service earned citizenship.)

How do I know so much about the Admiral's Spaces? Because his wife had a few medical issues. When we were in port, she would come aboard for a few days. Admiral Koch would send word to Sickbay and I would make "house calls" (in this case, "Admiral's Quarters calls") to attend to Mrs. Koch's medical needs. Both Admiral and Mrs. were very cordial and quite appreciative of the medical help.

Piping the Admiral (and Captain) … There is a long-standing Navy tradition that whenever the Admiral or Captain and sometimes VIPs came aboard or left the ship, they would receive a ceremonial "piping." This is called "Manning the Side" and its origin was the need to hoist a bosun's chair in rough seas when ladders could not be safely used. That is no longer necessary but the crewmen are still used and are called "Side Boys." There are normally eight bosun's mates in dress uniforms. That is possible because advance notice is given when the admiral or captain is planning to "arrive" or "depart."

So, when either of these two officers is coming or going, the hangar bay space by the gangway is prepared. An area is roped off using white ropes looped between multiple posts on wide bases. The posts are made from used 5" artillery shell casings that have a wooden bullet-shaped top fitting inserted into the shell casing to simulate an artillery round. The wood is dark and highly polished as are the shell casings. It makes an impressive entry way for the "brass." The side boys stand around at ease until the admiral or captain gets there. On signal they line up to make a corridor, four to a side. The Officer of the Deck and his Bosun are at the head of the gangway and the Bosun has his pipe for the ceremonial. Turning on the 1MC to be heard all over the ship, the Bosun pipes the attention call, double taps the bell twice and announces, "Admiral, arriving." (or departing or Captain arriving/departing whichever is the case.) The side boys and everyone around salutes while the A or C goes by. The marine escort is always there as well. The piping ceremony is traditional, impressive and is a show of respect. It is another example of RHIP .... "Rank Has Its Privilege."

The Lawn in Admiral Koch's Quarters ... One day in port the admiral's stewards were seen coming up the gang and across the hangar bay carrying a set of outdoor metal lawn furniture.

The joke went around that the admiral's spaces were so large he had a lawn and had bought some lawn furniture. The admiral was just like everyone else on the ship when various merchandise for sale in foreign ports caught the eye and were a must-have purchase. Frequently the prices were significantly cheaper than stateside so the goods were a bargain and if you wanted something, it saved you money.

Hence the famous saying we had, ".... going around the world, going broke saving money." We often said that jokingly to someone coming aboard with a conspicuous souvenir they had purchased ashore. The joke had some truth to it.

Captain John P. Fox ... Captain of *USS Independence* ... Likewise Captain Fox was a Naval Aviator who had come through his career with increasing commands and experience. By the time he became the Captain of Indy he knew what he was doing. He had thorough knowledge of naval aviation, the airwing and how it functioned. He also understood handling a deep draft ship. His staff included trained and experienced officers in navigation, communications, operations, supply, weapons, engineering and all things important for carrier operations. It was amazing to see the skill and professionalism in the various areas of expertise.

Captain Fox likely had similar spacious quarters like the Admiral with private galley, Philippine stewards, all the perks. I never made medical "quarters calls" for the Captain, so am speculating about his facilities, but you can be sure they were comfortable and private. We didn't see Captain Fox much because his responsibilities kept him busy.

Executive Officer, Commander Fred Bromley ... We saw CDR Bromley much more for two reasons. First, he flew with some of the squadrons enough to keep his skills honed. Second and most important however was that he and his Marine escort were everywhere. One of his major responsibilities was to be the "eyes and ears" of the Captain. He made rounds of the entire ship regularly, got to know most everyone including lots of enlisted crew, especially the chiefs. CDR Bromley investigated work areas, was concerned with morale, wanted to receive input of all kinds. He was the right man for the job and I expect he eventually "made Admiral."

VI

DOCTOR DUTIES

DISPERSAL OF MEDICAL FACILITIES ON A CARRIER

MEDICAL DEPARTMENT FACILITIES

THE FIGURE BELOW depicts a carrier profile and the location of the main medical department (Sickbay) aboard ship. All current carriers have their medical department several decks below the hangar deck (main deck), between frames 90 and 120. Access is from the port or starboard side. The medical department was located amidships for patient accessibility, surgical procedure stability, and for interior protection from battle damage. In addition to detailing the main medical space the diagram also reveals the six dispersed and peripherally located medical aid stations on aircraft carriers called "battle dressing stations (BDS)". When the ship is in Readiness Condition I (general quarters), and all hands are at "battle stations," the ship is entirely closed. All water-tight doors are secured to enhance the ship's survivability. This can make casualty movement a tedious and difficult process. To avoid unnecessary delays in the primary treatment of injured personnel, the battle dressing stations are manned by physicians, dentists, and corpsmen so that casualties that occur within their areas of responsibility can be given primary emergency care and stabilization until movement to the main sickbay can be accomplished. A major advantage of the battle dressing station concept is that it allows the dispersion of medical personnel and equipment throughout the ship. Should one area of the ship be damaged with a loss of medical assets, there still are more available to carry on the job.

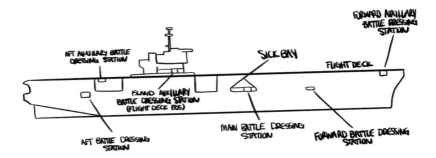

SICK BAY

MY SECONDARY WORK PLACE

THAT MAY SOUND strange for a physician to call the Medical Department of a ship a secondary workplace. Think about it this way. The ship's company Medical Department included two physicians whose sole responsibilities were the care and safety of the crew, i.e., medical care which included preventive care. Sickbay was their primary workspace. On the other hand, the flight surgeons aboard Indy were attached to the Airwing and squadrons, had received specialized training to equip them for airwing duties and that's where their primary responsibilities were. However, while deployed, the airwing was melded with the ship in most ways, including healthcare facilities and practice, so we flight surgeons certainly carried a medical care load in Sick Bay. We were one medical team for the health and safety of all.

The Medical Department of the Indy was called "Sick Bay" by almost everyone. Sick Bay was a complex collection of many things to provide both routine health care and contingency emergency care. Routine care was for both sick and healthy sailors, both enlisted and officers. This section is to describe something of how "Sick Bay" on an aircraft carrier is equipped, staffed and how it operates. (pun intended)

People are primary so let's talk about staffing first. Deployed carriers usually have four physicians…. two ship's company and two flight surgeons onboard with the airwing. The *Independence* on the 1966 Mediterranean Cruise had five physicians because an extra Marine flight surgeon was aboard with the Marine A-4 squadron.

Indy had a Senior Medical Officer (SMO) with a master's degree in public health and the ship also had a four-year-residency-trained general surgeon. The three flight surgeons with the airwing completed our merry band of docs. Collectively we provided whatever medical care was needed, we shared the responsibilities and workload, we rotated work schedules and time off … much like in civilian life with call schedules, et al.

There was a Medical Service Corps officer doing the administrative work … personnel records, supply management et al just like a hospital administrator would do. We had a dental department with several dentists and a small group of dental assistants.

There was a staff of about thirty hospital corpsmen (HM rating) of multiple assorted training, skills and seniority. There was a Chief Petty Officer with significant experience who oversaw the corpsmen and overall care. We had a large contingent of HM First Class Petty Officers who were highly trained and experienced. I don't recall any of the corpsmen being below the level of HM Third Class Petty Officer (E-4) as all of them had important training before being assigned to the fleet. So, we had mostly 1st, 2nd and 3rd class petty officer corpsmen. Besides basic training and knowledge of general health care, many were specialists in one field or another…. x-ray technician, pharmacist's mate, scrub tech, laboratory technician, emergency care technician, nursing care, etc.…. the whole broad range of training and skills needed to provide care on the carrier.

Several corpsmen had special training in Aviation Medicine and had ratings as Aviation Medical Technicians. One bright and efficient corpsman I recall as being exceptional was Red (X). Yes, he had red hair. He was a Third Class but had the savvy of a First Class. He knew optometry, audiology, etc..... all the physical examinations needed for flight physicals. He was competent and always upbeat. The Aviation Medicine spaces were outboard across the starboard passageway and a bit larger than the main treatment room. It held the optical lane for refractions, tonometry and other eye/vision testing .... an important part of flying health. Also, there was a soundproof audiology booth. [Ha, Ha .... nowhere on a carrier is soundproof... but it was insulated and quiet enough for good hearing testing.] This was an important care center and Red kept it running smoothly. It was a pleasure to work with him.

The layout of Sick Bay was efficient. The location was midships below the main deck which was the most stable place on the ship and the most protected spot from any battle damage. The medical spaces were between the main starboard and port passageways and you could access Sickbay from either side easily at several places. There were several lateral passages within Sickbay for easy access to every section.

There was a small registration space with chairs and a desk. It served like a reception/waiting room in a medical office. Of course, another room held health records for everyone onboard. There was a large central treatment room where we held sick call. We had standup writing desks on the side bulkheads and various equipment hung around everywhere. Several treatment tables were available with overhead spotlights, et al. After a crewman registered for sick call, his vital signs would be recorded, his records retrieved and then he would be seen by one of the physicians in the main treatment room. There were several private consultation rooms when needed.

Prescriptions were filled around the corner in the pharmacy by one of the corpsmen pharmacist mates. We had a small lab and Xray unit when studies were needed. The corpsmen were well-trained and I don't recall ever having any problems with these specialized areas. The operating room was adjacent to and adjoining the main treatment room. Surgical lights, cabinets filled with instruments and equipment, sterilizing apparatus, general anesthesia console .... all were there. It was a well-equipped OR suite. The scrub sink was in the Rx Room by the OR door.

Across the lateral passageway from the OR, RX Room, lab and Xray spaces, etc. were various offices: Senior Medical Officer, Surgeon, Medical Service Corp/Admin, Flight Surgeons (we three shared one generous space); a medical library stocked amazingly well with books on every phase of medicine; the pharmacy stock room.

Across the port-side main passageway were spaces outboard .... in about the same position as the Aviation Medicine spaces on starboard. The forward portion was the Senior Medical Officer's living quarters ... roomy, private head, not plush but upscale as befitting a senior Commander ... and he was promoted to full "bird" Captain before the cruise was over. Just aft of his quarters was a padded cell. That's right .... the overhead and all bulkheads were thickly padded. I think this was in case we ever had a screaming-meemy patient with violent inclinations. We had two desks in there and used the space as a private consultation room. [A later section will describe an interesting patient I interviewed there at length.]

In the main center section of Sickbay between the port and starboard main passageways was the hospital section with multiple beds. It was just aft of the reception room/treatment room/OR complex and was connected to the Rx Room so a gurney could be rolled directly to hospital beds without having to use main passageways. Almost unbelievably the Indy had a ninety-bed hospital capability. That was not all lower bunks using floor space, but double decker bunks if required. We never used that 90-bed capacity of course but it was there for battle conditions if ever necessary. In practice we kept about a dozen beds functional, usually having only a handful of "inpatients" .... post-op patients, acute illnesses, injuries, patients needing intravenous therapy, etc. There were facilities with showers, sinks, heads to service the hospital unit and a small galley for specialized diet preparation. The usual nurse's station, parked gurneys, various equipment and accessories were there.

Since we didn't operate but a dozen hospital beds, did all that other capacity go to waste? Nope. No space is wasted on a ship. The Hospital Corpsmen used it as their berthing spaces. It was a perk of their job on the ship …. more privacy, less crowded head facilities, lower bunks for most, snacks from the galley, etc.… and they were close at hand if needed in their job capacities.

Just aft of Sickbay in another lateral passage between port and starboard main passageways were the dental spaces. They were small but efficient with a row of dental chair rooms, some offices, supply room, et al.

Another amazing statistical fact of an aircraft carrier Sick Bay is that it has a 4,000-unit Blood Bank. Again, you read that right …. four thousand units of blood. (chuckle and smile) ….

The four thousand units were "on the hoof." Every crewman on the ship, officers and enlisted, could be sent down to Sickbay to donate a unit of blood if necessary and each would have been happy to do it. In battle or disaster situations all hands go to the rescue of others and giving a needed unit of blood would be part of that. We had everyone's blood type on file, had complete typing and crossmatching capability and so could have requested donors according to what types of blood were needed.

Another interesting thing we had in the Operating Room was a supply of cylinders of cyclopropane. That might not be significant for a layperson, but it was an incredible hazard unrealized by the Captain of the ship and the other senior officers. Cyclopropane is a great anesthetic gas which is gentle on mucous membranes, has a pleasant induction and rapid recovery with few side effects. However, it is HIGHLY EXPLOSIVE. Al Cohen, MD (my roommate flight surgeon) received some special anesthesia training before the cruise and recommended AGAINST having cyclopropane onboard for anesthesia because of the danger. Plenty of other agents were on hand and we never used the cyclopropane. Al had a dispute about it with the Senior Medical Officer, but the SMO insisted we bring it onboard and stock it "just in case." Just in case indeed! Just in case that cyclopropane had sparked and exploded it would have blown a hole in the bottom of the carrier and we would have gone to Davey Jones' locker in a hurry. That's why we never used it and kept it tucked as safely away as possible.

Senior Medical Officer … [Herewith called "No Name SMO" for reasons that will be obvious.]

Our SMO was a Commander with three full stripes of rank…. and he was not only proud of it but insisted everyone else be impressed with it also. The other four physicians didn't have a lot of respect for SMO for multiple reasons. He didn't help with patient care and we decided that might be because he wasn't very accomplished as a physician. That's a polite way to express our opinion of him as a physician. He never took a turn "on call" and he was picky about military protocol and administrative details. That master's degree in public health had given him an attitude of "knowing everything" about health and sanitation on the ship. One of the corpsmen was assigned to health and sanitation inspections, reports, remedies, et al.

SMO "rode" him constantly. The poor corpsman came to me several times just to talk and get some emotional relief from the constant needling by SMO. [The corpsman and I made an "end-run" in Beirut with a food poisoning outbreak which will be detailed in another section.]

When SMO received his promotion to Captain, it caused another "flap." SMO had spacious private quarters with private head facilities…. but it contained a standard navy steel bunk. SMO found out that the Commanding-Officer-Captain of the Indy, who was also a four-stripe "bird" Captain, had a real wooden double-size bed in his quarters. SMO insisted that he was now a full four-stripe Captain and by god he was going to have a real bed also. The stewards took hell until they found and brought a bed to SMO's quarters.

Wrap Up … It is highly appropriate to finish this section on Sickbay with a huge upbeat compliment to Navy Medicine. The Medical Department on the Indy was well-designed, well-equipped and efficiently operated. The cadre of hospital corpsmen as a group were very well-trained, competent, proficient, skilled and knowledgeable. They were motivated, worked well together as a team, took good care of their patients and much more. It was a genuine pleasure working with them and they deserve highest compliments for a job well done.

Here's hoping they all enjoyed smooth sailing and following seas thereafter.

DECKPLAN ... LAYOUT DIAGRAM OF SICKBAY

BELOW DEPICTS THE basic layout of our Indy medical department, showing the location of the various treatment and supporting spaces. Each carrier may have mild modification of this layout based on the arrival of new medical equipment or the proposed long-term needs of the department. One exception to this typical layout is the Enterprise-class carrier, which has two separate wards and a specific area for sick call screening. Nimitz-class uses either the ward or the physical examination area for sick call screening and schedules all physical examinations, eye, and ENT clinics after sick call is secured. The advantages of the Nimitz-class layout are size, privacy, and complete access control. Other notable features of the Nimitz-class carrier are the spacious surgical suite and the intensive care unit (ICU).

USS INDEPENDENCE SICKBAY

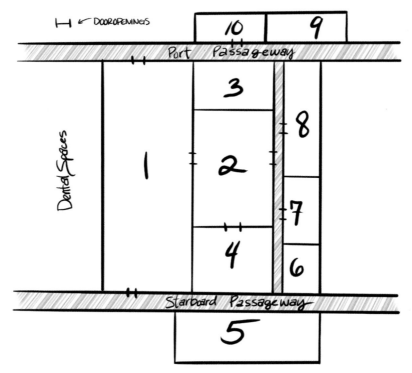

1. HOSPITAL BEDS + SUPPORT FACILITIES
2. MAIN OUTPATIENT SICKBAY
3. OPERATING ROOM
4. RECIEVING SPACES/ADMIN
5. AVIATION MEDICINE SPACES
6. PHARMACY
7. FLIGHT SURGEONS OFFICE + MEDICAL LIBRARY
8. MEDICAL RECORDS
9. SENIOR MEDICAL OFFICERS QUARTERS
10. PADDED CELL

MOD

MEDICAL OFFICER OF THE DAY

EVERY FOURTH DAY we each took a turn as Medical Officer of the Day (MOD.) It was like the call schedule at a hospital so was nothing new. We rotated MOD at sea from segment to segment and had a separate rotation schedule for when we were in port. It didn't matter so much when we were at sea but made some difference in port so that shore leave was equal.

At sea we mostly shared the medical workload at sick call and the afternoon flight surgeon activities. We never scheduled flights on a day we were the MOD. It's hard to give emergency medical care when you are a hundred miles away in the sky. Of course, we swapped days around as is usual with rotations.

If we were in port the MOD stayed on the ship. The other three went ashore except that one of us had to stay reasonably close and in touch through the Shore Patrol as second doctor backup to return rapidly if needed. That never happened during the cruise. The other two were essentially untethered to tour inland or do about anything they chose.

I don't recall what shore leave the various other officers rotated, but enlisted men had shore leave one day out of four. The operational capability of the ship was paramount. Enough crew, both officers and enlisted, always remained onboard to enable immediate departure and action if required. [In the South China Sea and Gulf of Tonkin carriers would stay on station with active combat flight ops for a month or more, then rotate out for R & R somewhere.]

When in port our MOD duties were a little different. We mostly held sick call alone. Usually there were few sailors reporting. Some were ashore and the others were carrying the workloads with reduced personnel. Of course, we were on call for twenty-four hours for any medical emergencies. They were rare on the ship but it was not uncommon for an injury to occur ashore. In the afternoons there were no flight physicals nor other aviation duties and of course no flight ops. The squadron ready rooms had reduced personnel as well. So even though we were onboard as MOD and the only physician, there was plenty of down time for relaxation.

In port or at sea the MOD had certain responsibilities. We were Officer in Charge (OIC) of the Medical Department. That meant supervising the hospital corpsmen in our team who were still onboard in port and always onboard at sea. We also assumed responsibility for the health and safety of the entire ship. That didn't involve a huge workload and mostly it was interesting and fun. It was almost like making rounds at a hospital. In effect we "made rounds" of the ship.

There was a formal checklist of duties, but it was informal in practice. No one was picky if your rounds were not perfect, not even the senior medical officer who was a little picky. The MOD was expected to tour the ship generally and observe for "health and safety." The list included the engine room, the electronics centers, radar spaces, berthing spaces, lounges, heads, passageways, the brig, the mess decks and wardrooms.... virtually anywhere and everywhere on the ship. Of course, we didn't visit every place every day. What our tour of the ship was intended to do was see if everything were clean and safe. We walked lots of the passageways to observe that they had no accumulated dirt or debris, that their surfaces were dry, non-skid well-maintained and no obstructions blocking them. We would duck into spaces here and there and just look around. This mostly only involved just walking around and observing, then later filing the MOD report …. a check-the-boxes form. It was rare to find a discrepancy. The most common was some snack wrapper or discarded food. Mentioning it was enough to get it cleaned up and no report was necessary. People got used to us looking and didn't want anything amiss on the reports.

Inspection of the brig was mandatory. Health and safety of the prisoners was an important concern… First to be sure they were not being abused by the Marine guards (They never were.), Second that the brig spaces were clean, healthy and safe (They always were… and cleaner than other spaces on the ship because the Marines had the inmates polish and shine everything.) [See details in Brig section.] Third was to have a private conversation with each prisoner to allow him to express any grievances, concerns, etc……. and at the same time for us as physicians to observe for any signs of malnutrition, dehydration, skin problems, abuse, illness, psychological health, etc., etc. (There were rarely any problems and those only minor.) It was never necessary for me to remove a prisoner to sickbay hospitalization or some major intervention. Sometimes a prescription was required for medications in the brig. Some of the inmates had terms of imprisonment long enough that we developed personally friendly terms with them …. sort of the usual doctor-patient relationship. Also recall that a different MOD made the brig inspection each day on a four-day rotation. So, we kept good watch on the health and safety in the brig from the perspectives of multiple observers. We also got to know the Marine guard detachment well.

The Goat Locker … The Chiefs' Mess refers to the group of Chiefs at every level who are serving on the carrier. It is not just the dining area, which is Chiefs' Mess without "the." [This is like "wardroom" and "the wardroom" which have two different connotations: respectively, the physical spaces and the collective group of officers on the ship. A wardroom on a ship is the officers' lounge and dining area.]

The Chiefs' Lounge and Dining Area is known as the "Goat Locker." Over the entrance to the Chiefs' Goat Locker on the carrier was a motto sign/emblem which read, "Chiefs…. The Backbone of the Navy." There is a huge truth in that! … about which more later. It is off limits to anyone except chiefs…. and this includes officers and even the commanding officer of the ship unless they are specifically invited. The MOD did not inspect the Goat Locker.

Enlisted Mess Decks … This was a major inspection requirement because any food service place is a hazard for unsanitary conditions. Spilled food not cleaned up; trays and cutlery not properly washed; kettles, pots, grills, et al accumulating detritus; personnel not using sanitary techniques; et al … the list was long. In a crew of thousands and 15-17,000 meals a day being served all this was incredibly important. A single sailor returning from shore leave with an infectious disease could infect hundreds of others. The crowded berthing spaces, the showers and heads, the food service areas and the cooking areas were prime spots for disease spread. In the Mediterranean infectious hepatitis was a constant worry. Common colds, Influenza and other viruses lurked among the shipboard population and ashore. We had a few cases of chicken pox on the cruise including one varicella pneumonitis.

The Chief-in-Charge … Please refer to the section on CHOW TIME. It details the professionalism and careers of those in the enlisted Culinary Specialist (CS) rating. By the time a CS "striker" advances to Chief Petty Officer he has had voluminous experience in food service. He has been to professional training programs in management, accounting, inventory, purchasing and supply chains, cooking including high-end culinary training, sanitation and more. He is a genuine professional in every aspect of food service and the culinary arts. If the Chief has advanced to Senior Chief or Master Chief and oversees the food service on a carrier, for both enlisted and officer crew … everyone …. you can bet your bippy he knows what he is doing and has a lot of savvy about it.

The "duty chief" on any day on the enlisted mess decks was one of several senior (or master) chiefs who rotated head-man-for-the-day responsibility similarly to how we physicians rotated MOD. Whoever it was that day knew that the MOD would be along for inspection, usually late in the evening before bedtime ... for several reasons. First the MOD had movie time with its squadron camaraderie duties.... and for a while after. Second was the walk-around of the ship unless that had been done in the afternoon earlier. Next was the inspection of the brig which took some time because it was much more than just a look-see.

The fourth and main reason for a later inspection of the Enlisted Mess Decks was because the MOD was getting hungry and it was about the same time as MidRats. Without question MidRats on the enlisted mess decks was better than in the wardroom.

The **"Duty-Chief-of-the-Day"** (shall I coin a term? ... DCOD) kept an eye out for the MOD. He recognized you immediately when you arrived. There was no slipping in for a clandestine inspection. The DCOD would come over immediately to greet you and chat. DCOD would invite MOD to have a good look around to be sure everything was shipshape, clean and sanitary, that the food was wholesome, nutritious and served properly, et al. ...... "and by the way, Doc, would you like some fried chicken? or a nice rib-eye? We can cook it up in a jiffy. How about some fresh baked bread right out of the oven? Would you prefer to check out the serving line and select a few things to see how delicious our food preparation is?"

You get the idea. Inspecting the Enlisted Mess Decks was a great way to top off the day of being MOD. The mess decks usually had sterling reports and any discrepancies noted were just mentioned to the DCOD and taken care of without need for writeup.

THERE I WUZ... eating fried chicken or a steak with fresh bread from the oven and thinking to myself, "Life on a carrier as a flight surgeon is a great way to serve your country."

AMAZING SPACE

"HOW SWEET THE sound???" ... of motors, vibrations, thumps, conversation, background hum, clanking, squeals and so many more. The carrier is a floating noise machine. However, there are many, many spaces aboard which are relatively quiet or particularly noisy. I don't think anywhere on a carrier is ever actually quiet. Even our "soundproof" booth in Aviation Medicine that we used for testing hearing was not soundproof. It was quiet but you could hear and feel some noise and vibrations. At least it was quiet enough for audiometric testing. Probably that was the quietest space on the ship.

Certainly, the loudest was the flight deck during flight operations. That's why everyone was required to wear those mickey-mouse ear protectors. Why not just ear plugs? .... because then you could not tell when a sailor was wearing them. On one occasion the Air Boss who had a microphone and flight deck speaker that could be heard over the roar, stopped flight operations because a sailor was not wearing his mickey-mouse ear protectors. The Air Boss told the sailor to get off the deck and get his protectors.

That was important because loud noise damages the hair cells in the inner ear causing permanent hearing loss. There is a scale of Damage Risk Criteria (DRC) which indicates the likelihood of hearing damage at various decibel levels and how long the exposure that could cause the damage. We had a Sound Level Meter in the Aviation Medicine department of sickbay and used it to measure sound levels all over the ship. It was part of our health and safety function.

So, from time to time, we went around to all the spaces in the ship and measured the ambient noise levels. Without getting technical, under 85 decibels of continuous noise was considered safe. The higher the decibels of exposure, the shorter the time that would cause damage. If personnel were exposed to sustained noise for periods of time that exceeded safe limits for either decibels or time, ear protection was required. We knew where the noisy spaces were and part of our inspection was to be sure crewmen were wearing ear protection during exposure. Mostly everyone was cooperative and wanted to protect hearing. Our reports logged sound levels and if crew were wearing protection.

The engine room was noisy, the radar center was quiet. People didn't' talk much in either… in the engine because you couldn't be heard well, in radar because it might disturb the concentration of the air traffic controllers.

No further discussion is needed. We had a good industrial-grade hearing protection program, monitored it regularly and I don't recall any cases of hearing loss from life on the carrier.

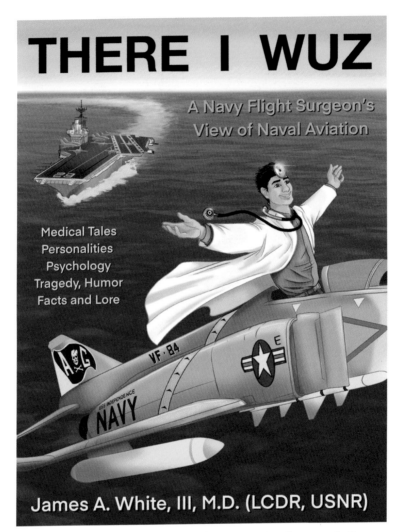

THERE I WUZ

A Navy Flight Surgeon's
View of Naval Aviation

Medical Tales
Personalities
Psychology
Tragedy, Humor
Facts and Lore

VF-84

USS INDEPENDENCE

NAVY

James A. White, III, M.D. (LCDR, USNR)

Cover artwork and design by the author's granddaughter, Reade Spivey.

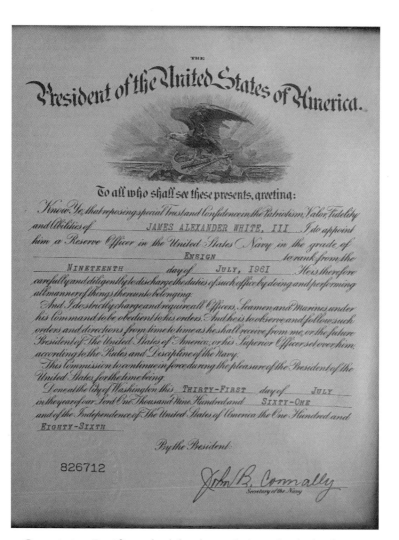

THE

President of the United States of America.

To all who shall see these presents, greeting:

Know Ye, that reposing special Trust and Confidence in the Patriotism, Valor, Fidelity and Abilities of _____ JAMES ALEXANDER WHITE, III _____ I do appoint him a Reserve Officer in the United States Navy in the grade of _____ ENSIGN _____ to rank from the _____ NINETEENTH _____ day of _____ JULY, 1961 _____ He is therefore carefully and diligently to discharge the duties of such office by doing and performing all manner of things thereunto belonging.

And I do strictly charge and require all Officers, Seamen and Marines under his command to be obedient to his orders. And he is to observe and follow such orders and directions from time to time as he shall receive from me, or the future President of The United States of America, or his Superior Officer set over him, according to the Rules and Discipline of the Navy.

This Commission to continue in force during the pleasure of the President of the United States for the time being.

Done at the City of Washington this _____ THIRTY-FIRST _____ day of _____ JULY _____ in the year of our Lord One Thousand Nine Hundred and _____ SIXTY-ONE _____ and of the Independence of The United States of America the One Hundred and _____ EIGHTY-SIXTH _____

By the President:

826712

John B. Connally
Secretary of the Navy

Commission Certificate, backdated to include medical school years.

The author as an Ensign Senior Medical Student Extern in 1963 at the Oakland Naval Hospital (Oak Knoll) in Oakland, CA."

The author (L) and his medical school roommate and lifelong friend, Art Lochridge M.D., in Service Dress Blue uniforms in Pensacola in 1966.

The Bayshore Apartments in Warrington, FL where the author's daughter
Elizabeth was born while the author was at NAMI in NAS Pensacola.

T-34 Mentor, used for Primary Flight Training
for Student Naval Aviators in 1966.

The author and his wife Virginia after the outdoor
NAMI graduation ceremony in Pensacola.

The author and Virginia at the indoor reception after graduation.

The author in Formal Dress Blue uniform and Virginia at the
celebration Formal Ball of Student Flight Surgeon Class 112.

The Indy plaque with construction and commissioning dates.

Ready Room coffee mugs personalized with call sign "Doc" and squadron logos.

From a dusty old box half a century later here are the author's orange flight suit [same one used in "Cat Eyes" chapter], parachute harness, anti-gravity suit, oxygen mask, poopy-suit flight gloves, thigh pad and NATOPS F4J manual. (The flight helmet is in another dusty old box somewhere.)

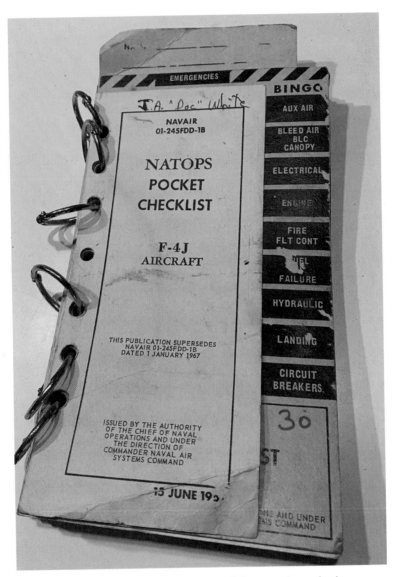

Enlargement of NATOPS manual showing the author's call sign. "Doc" is likely used for many flight surgeons by many squadrons in the Navy and Marines.

Art Lochridge in Viet Nam flying with his Marine helicopter squadron. Note flak jacket and two sidearms.

F-4 and A-6 models from the author's collection.

U.S.S. Independence (CVA-62)

8 Jan. 1966
2:00 A.M.

Hi love,
    Very late ↑ and I'm very tired,
but wanted to drop you a quick note.
    We are having carrier qualifications
now. About 30 new pilots and RIO's
(Radar Intercept Officers — back seat in F-4)
came over from U.S. because there is
no available carrier on the East coast.
They each need 10 day and 6 night
landings. They have flown the Phantom
before in the training program +
practiced carrier landing techniques,
but this is first time on the
carrier. It gets pretty "hairy" at
times, but so far, so good.

Front page of a letter to Virginia from Indy. 1966 date should have been 1967.

8 are all finished (8 pilots of 18.)

Anyway, flight ops went until 12:30 AM tonight + I passed out "flight rations" afterward: little 2 oz. bottles of 100 proof brandy. So, very little sleep tonight. Same tomorrow, too. C'est la vie.

Hope all is well there. I'm thinking about you! 3 weeks

Much much love to you both.

Jeeves, G.-A.

Dr. J. A. White, III LT MC
CVW-7 Staff
FPO New York, N. Y. 09501

8¢
U.S. AIR MAIL

Mrs. Virginia H. White
25 De Peyster Avenue
Tenafly
New Jersey 07670

VIA AIR MAIL

Back page of the letter with envelope at bottom.

Back in Virginia Beach in spring 1967.

Poignant and typical Navy occurrence as ships and crew sail off to sea: the author's two-year old daughter and her grandmother watching from the oceanfront as the carrier sailed away for a shakedown cruise in Spring 1968.

Author's calling card with Indy sign and three challenge coins.

The infamous putty knife and screwdriver which were in the author's hands for many hours of labor to repair the house at 8208 Oceanfront.

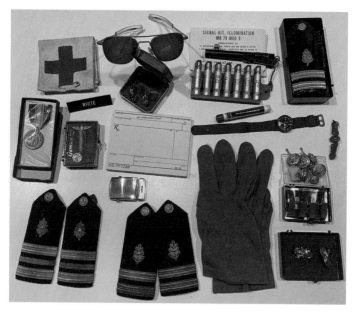

Author's collection of insignia: rank pins from ENS, LT, LCDR, shoulder boards, medals/ribbons, assorted medical memorabilia, survival items, et al … from that dusty old box.

At the National Naval Aviation Museum, NAS Pensacola in October 2019… holding VF-41 "Black Aces" squadron cap with Black Aces aircraft tail through front window.

In the Cubi Point Officers Club 'Plaque Bar' Café at the museum in Pensacola. All the Cubi memorabilia were shipped from the Philippines to recreate the atmosphere and preserve the history of forty years of WestPac cruises.

Gene Berry reminiscing in an F-4 Phantom cockpit at the museum in Pensacola. (Did you know that when you cut the wings off an F-4, the cockpit shrinks?)

The Blue Angels at Sherman Field, NAS Pensacola.

VII

CARRIER LIFE

CHOW TIME

FEEDING THE FLIGHT FORCES OF THE FLEET

"A busy sailor is a happy sailor" …. IF HE IS WELL-FED!

JUST IMAGINE FOUR or five thousand active young men working sometimes around the clock…. Do you suppose they might eat a lot of food? It is almost mind-boggling. This won't be a definitive discussion of the food service on an aircraft carrier, nor its supply chain, but just some observations from living and working on the *U.S.S. Independence (CVA-62* for the better part of a year. An aircraft carrier is a small city unto itself. Although combat aircraft operations are the reason for being …. all the other functions of a community must be there to support that.

The carrier has avenues and streets (called passages), staircases (called ladders), rooms (called spaces), etc. The terminology and lingo are amazing. As for citizens it has policemen, firemen, electricians, plumbers, laborers, technicians, barbers, dentists, doctors, nurses, lab techs, machinists, carpenters, mechanics, photographers, writers, pharmacists, cooks, radio and radar operators, repairmen …. the list might consume this whole page. A carrier is indeed a small city at sea …

AND EVERYONE EATS, not just "three squares a day," but almost around the clock.

That's easy to understand when you know the carrier never sleeps. It operates 24/7/365 virtually for its entire lifespan of about fifty years. People come and go, the ship can be at sea or in port, but always people work in shifts with some on duty while others sleep, eat, etc., etc.

It takes a lot of food and a lot of food preparation to feed the crew. Just for an example to lend perspective, the crew of a carrier eats 1,600 pounds of chicken, 160 gallons of milk, 30 cases of cereal, 350 pounds of lettuce, ETC....... EVERY DAY. A supply ship must replenish food stores about every 7-10 days and it delivers 400,000 to one million pounds of food each time. That's a minimum of about ten pounds per day per crewmember.

[The reality is that the range and operational limits of a modern nuclear carrier is not its fuel but its food supply. The Indy had to resupply fuel as well as food.]

So, let's describe the basics about food service on a carrier. The Navy, as all military, is organized as a hierarchy. The range goes from the Senior Officer Present Afloat (SOPA) to the beginning seaman. Officers included an Admiral sometimes, Captain of the ship, etc. to Ensigns and Warrant Officers.... both ship's company and airwing totaling probably three or four hundred in the officer ranks. The remaining crew was four thousand plus enlisted men with Senior Chief Petty Officers (chiefs) to First Class Petty Officers and on down the line in the enlisted rates. The food is served in different venues according to rank but it is well-known that the enlisted men have better food than the officers .... as will be explained below.

Everyone on active duty receives base pay, a food allowance, a housing allowance, special pay sometimes (flight/hazardous duty pay, professional pay, et al.), sometimes certain incentive pay, bonuses and the like. How the food allowance is handled is different for officers and enlisted. The food allowance is called the Basic Allowance for Subsistence or **BAS**. (Remember the Navy way is special names, abbreviations and lingo.) In 1966 the BAS for officers was $48.66 per month. It was the same whether you were single or married, with or without other dependents. I don't know what the BAS for enlisted was at that time. *

Partly that is because BAS was paid directly in cash to officers who then purchased their own food whereas the BAS for enlisted was paid to the Enlisted Mess in lump sum calculated according to head count aboard.

In 2020 the BAS for officers is $256.68 per month and for enlisted $372.71 per month. If the same ratio difference existed in 1966, then enlisted would have received $70.56 per month. That illustrates two things: inflation and that enlisted eat better than officers as mentioned.

Enlisted Mess Decks …Food service on the Indy was basically four meals a day: breakfast, lunch, dinner and "Mid Rats" …. the lingo for Midnight Rations. That said, remember that shifts and watches were ongoing so people worked, slept and ate on differing schedules. In practice the enlisted mess decks were serving food probably twenty hours a day and you could get food those other hours when required. Food was offered in service lines like a cafeteria and a crewman would go along with a steel tray and select what was wanted. There was no real limit on quantity and it was all you cared to eat … but waste was out. The protocol was to take all you want and eat all you take, then go back for seconds if still hungry.

The ship had freezers and refrigerators (called "Reefers" onboard), storerooms, etc. Over 15,000 meals a day were prepared by over a hundred cooks in multiple galleys and served by additional personnel in multiple mess deck locations. Efficient food service was a goal because time waiting in line was time away from a duty station.

There was usually a good variety of fresh vegetables and fruit, lots of meat of all kinds, pasta, potatoes, cakes, pies and other desserts; eggs, bacon, sausage, ham, toast, sweet rolls, juices, cereal et al for breakfast …. really a well-thought-out varied offering. There was an onboard bakery that produced fresh bread of all kinds daily. Menus were planned in twenty-one-day cycles and there was a maximum of variety as much as possible. Every port call allowed topping up of the fresh fruits and vegetables. The ship had ample stores of dried and canned goods for use if necessary, when fresh and frozen were not available.

There would be theme meals illustrating perhaps the cuisine of an upcoming port of call. There would be Italian night, Greek night, etc..... steak night, taco night, spaghetti night, chili night, etc. Soups and salads were always available. Holiday meals followed traditional patterns such as Thanksgiving's turkey, dressing, cranberry sauce, et al. At MidRats there was a grill and sailors could get hamburgers, cheeseburgers, hot dogs, sandwiches of multiple kinds and various short orders with all the trimmings ... in addition to what was available in the serving line.

With all that food being cooked, served and eaten there was considerable cleanup involved and a goodly number of sailors took care of that. Washing pots and pans, serving trays, glassware, silverware, etc. was important and disposing of garbage.

Some of the cooks and food service people were genuine professionals who made an entire career of that occupation. They have the designation of Culinary Specialist (CS.) They receive special training, go to genuine cooking schools and get high-end culinary training and experience. They rotate between sea and shore duty, but always in cooking and food service duties. As they advance up the ranks in their chosen specialty field, their knowledge and skills just get better and better. On the ship they supervise and often prepare personally the food for the Captain's private table, for the Admiral when aboard and the officers' wardrooms. They prepare and supervise cuisine for high-ranking officers during shore rotations. Some advance even to cooking in the White House for the President. Fleet wide competition among the carriers and other ships was ongoing and awards given for the best food service.

Bottom Line: A well-fed crew is a happy crew and the Indy crew ate well.

Chiefs' Mess and First-Class Mess ... The Chief Petty Officers of E-7, E-8, E-9 rank had their own private mess and it was well-known as the best food on the ship. The First-Class Petty Officers of E-6 rank also had a private mess which was a cut above the general crew mess decks and second only to the Chiefs' Mess.

It's easy to understand why the food in the Chiefs' Mess was so good. Remember that the bosses for all the food served on the ship were the senior CS chefs who had the most training and experience in the culinary arts …. and they were also chiefs themselves. They had full control over all the food supplies, logistics, preparation et al and made sure the Chiefs' Mess was tops.

Remember that all BAS (food allowances) for the entire enlisted crew was paid in a lump sum to the enlisted mess. It was the monthly budget for food. Cash didn't exchange hands. It was accounting records of income, supplies purchased, inventories, etc….. all on paper. The CS career included training in all the aspects of management. So, the CS chiefs knew firsthand what was in stock and were able to draw the best and prepare the best for their fellow chiefs….and had the skills to make it special.

Likewise, the First-Class Petty Officers in the CS rating had an inside track on the food supplies and significant training and experience of their own…. so, they could take care of fellow first-class petty officers (E-6) in their private mess.

Bottom line: The Chiefs' Mess had personal service from the professional chefs aboard who only supervised the Wardroom food, but personally prepared the cuisine for the chiefs and the senior officers.

Officers' Wardrooms … The wardroom on a navy ship is where the officers dine, have meetings and relax. They use it as a private lounge and a dining room. Movies are shown in the evenings. There were two wardrooms on the *Independence*. Both were significantly large areas to accommodate the large number of officers onboard. Each had different design, décor, atmosphere and served a different purpose as discussed below. Adjoining the wardroom is always a galley and scullery serviced by stewards who are now trained Culinary Specialists (see above.) They prepare and serve the meals.

Main Wardroom (a.k.a. Main Deck Ship's Company

Wardroom) … was always open at sea or in port. It had dark wood-paneled walls, carpet, comfortable furnishings, real silver knives, forks and spoons, top quality dishes, elegant glassware, white linen tablecloths and napkins, even some navy art on the walls. Except for the Admiral's Quarters and the Captain's Quarters it was the most elegant area of the ship and the only place that wasn't steel and utility.

As on any navy ship there were certain traditions, etiquette and rules for the main deck wardroom. Officers had to be dressed in the uniform of the day…. no casual attire and especially no flight suits allowed. In navy wardrooms officers may not discuss politics, religion, sex or work issues. They should not perform work nor meet with a subordinate in the wardroom. At mealtime, an officer asks permission from the senior officer present before taking a seat at the dining table…. and if leaving before the whole group and presiding officer are leaving, he asks permission to be excused. The senior and presiding officer was the Executive Officer of the ship, not the captain who had his own private quarters with dining facilities, chef and stewards.

Most of the airwing officers did not dine much in the main wardroom but used the auxiliary wardroom (see below.) However, as physicians we provided medical care for all hands onboard and became better acquainted with the ship's company officers. So, we ate more in the main wardroom. It was part of our job to get to know and be friendly with all officers…. AND the food was decidedly better in the main wardroom. Also, as physicians our routines and responsibilities allowed reasonable control of our schedules so that we could arrange to eat at the proper times. Since menus were posted in advance, if we saw something that appealed to the palate, we could be sure to be there.

Mealtimes were at fixed hours. Everyone was seated together and served at the table by stewards in white jackets. There were multiple tables and with so many officers on the carrier people could eat in shifts with some time variance during the meal hours. The pace of meals was more relaxed and lengthier in the main wardroom. Breakfast was informal, dinner in the evening much more formal and traditional, lunch was in between.

One interesting feature in the main wardroom always intrigued me. Coffee is ubiquitous on a carrier and probably all navy ships. There was a pot or large urn of coffee available most everywhere there were workspaces. The main wardroom also had such an urn but at breakfast, lunch or dinner the stewards would fill large real silver coffee pots and place them on the tables. The coffee pots were unique. They had wide bases (historically important to provide stability in rough seas…. like a ship's decanter) and they had a straight handle sticking out on the side from the pouring spout rather than a loop handle at the back as on most pitchers.

The handle was a tradition from when spaces were smaller and there wasn't much elbow room with people seated closely together. The tradition and current etiquette required that you did not pour your own coffee. You grasped the side handle with knuckles up, keeping your elbows by your side and then pouring a cup for your neighbor either next to you or across the table as well. Your neighbor would pour your cup. A full pot had a bit of heft for that backhanded technique but we were all fit young men so it was another "piece of cake" situation.

The main wardroom was the site of occasional formal all-officers meals. These were usually when in port and we would be entertaining local naval officers and other officials from the country we were visiting. Dress whites or dress blues would be the uniform for the occasion.

The main wardroom contained the Mid Rats Grill for officers which was just off the main wardroom dining and lounge area. It was to the left of the entrance and adjacent to the galley, tucked back behind a bulkhead out of sight but easily accessible.

"The Wardroom" … With a "the" before "wardroom" the term referred to the people, not the physical spaces. "The Wardroom" meant the total of the officers onboard the ship. Food service was managed completely differently than for the enlisted chow as described above. The protocol was as follows:

1. Each officer received his BAS paid directly to him with monthly pay.

2. "The Wardroom" had shares, one for each officer aboard.

3. The chief steward would do a formal inventory every day of all foodstuffs and supplies on hand in "The Wardroom" larder. The total value of inventory on hand would be divided by the number of officers in "The Wardroom" to determine the value of a share.

4. On checking aboard the ship for duty each officer would "buy in" to "The Wardroom" by paying for a share as calculated at the last inventory (the day before.)

5. On leaving duty from the ship each officer would receive payment of the value of a share.

6. Share values went up and down depending on replenishment purchases and consumption depletions. Exactly accurate records were kept.

7. The officers ate all their breakfast, lunch and dinner meals and food consumed in one of the two wardroom sites and shared collectively the costs thereof.

8. Every month the chief steward would calculate the total cost of the food served to "The Wardroom" officers. He would divide by the number of shares (officer members of the mess) and present each officer with a bill for the proportionate share of that month's consumption.

9. Additional food purchased at the Mid Rats Grill were not included. You signed a "chit" for whatever you ate at Midrats, like a charge account, and it was added to your bill each month.

The Auxiliary Wardroom ... When the airwing was deployed aboard and the carrier sailed off to sea, a second auxiliary wardroom was opened to accommodate the large number of additional officers. There were more officers in the airwing than in ship's company because of all the pilots and flight officers. (A small example was the Medical Department. Ship's company was one surgeon and the senior medical officer. Our airwing brought three flight surgeons.)

The auxiliary wardroom was also known as the aviation wardroom or airwing wardroom. Any officer could eat in either wardroom but there were distinct differences between the two in food and food service, in attire, in décor, in ambiance including noise level. Whereas the Main Wardroom was on the main deck amidships in the quietest and most stable location, the auxiliary wardroom was on an "O" level deck just under the forward end of the flight deck equipment deck. If you were eating there during flight operations, every time the catapult fired off an aircraft the entire wardroom would shake and vibrate with a loud hiss and thump. We got used to it, but it was very disconcerting and discomfiting at first and to newcomers. It's kind of hard to have a conversation and enjoy a meal with that noise and vibration constantly banging away.

Without flight ops it was calm enough but there was no carpet and wood paneling. It was all steel, plain, utilitarian, metal/Formica tables, no linen, steel tableware, etc. Food was served cafeteria style on a tray. The food was plentiful and good, but less imaginative than the main wardroom, less far up the culinary ladder, but second helpings were easier if you were hungry.

However, there were several other good reasons to eat in the auxiliary wardroom. First it was a lot faster to just go down the serving line, carry your own tray, then just eat and leave. Second you could eat in a flight suit or any casual or work clothes. If you wanted to eat before you went ashore in civilian clothes, or after you returned, this was the only place.

Third there were no formalities of permission from the senior officer. Fourth, while politics, religion and sex were supposed to be left out of conversation, work conversation was common. An awful lot of THERE I WUZ stories were told here.... particularly the scary ones you might have just experienced. Talking about close calls and mishaps was an important release and tension-relieving mechanism .... even psychologically therapeutic in many ways.

Fifth, the hours of service were longer and less rigid for starting times. If they were open, you could eat.... often when the main wardroom was not available. Sixth, there was more space. The main wardroom could get crowded but that rarely happened in the auxiliary wardroom.

There was no financial incentive between eating in one or the other wardroom because all expenses of food in both was grouped into the bookkeeping for the daily inventory and share calculation.

So, that's a synopsis of "Chow Time" and feeding the crew on the *U.S.S. Independence* in 1966.

SAILORS ASHORE

THE GOOD, THE BAD AND THE UGLY

YOU MUST ADMIT .... it's a little frustrating for young adult men to be crammed together in restricted space, without alcohol, without women, for long periods of time, expected to follow strict rules ... when to eat, shower, work, sleep ... and even how to do it.

It is no wonder that shore leave is a relief valve that is important, even necessary, for smooth functioning aboard a navy ship. Of course, each sailor is different and each behaves differently when ashore. Here following are some descriptions of happenings by sailors ashore.... some good, some bad, some ugly.

Drinking ... The old saying, "acting like a drunken sailor," didn't just come into the vernacular without some justification. Enjoying some alcoholic beverages is routine for most sailors on shore leave unless one is a teetotaler. [Remember that no alcoholic beverages are permitted on U.S. Navy ships.] The vendors ashore know that and there are numerous venues close to the docks designed to cater to sailors' thirst.

Although drinking patterns differ with individuals at any age, there is some correlation with age. The <u>older sailors... 25 years old and up</u>....

are less likely to abuse alcohol ashore. First, their frontal lobes have developed. Second, most are in their second (or more) sea duty tour. That means several things besides being more mature: 1) The newness of wild shore leave has worn off, maybe they had some previous untoward experiences. 2) Eighteen-to-twenty-year-old sailors who couldn't adjust to life aboard a ship with all its limitations, don't re-enlist. 3) The older sailors have advanced to petty officers and chiefs, who are not only more mature, but are leaders, role models and desirous of setting good examples for the younger guys. 4) The "older" sailors are more likely to be married, have children and a more responsible attitude toward life. 5) The older guys are likely proceeding with a career in the Navy and don't want aberrant behavior ashore to blot their record and prevent promotion and advancement.

Most sailors go ashore, "have a few," eat a good meal or two, maybe sightsee a little, maybe shop for local souvenirs ... then return to the ship happy, satisfied, relaxed and ready to return to routine work and life onboard. Call this "the good."

Now let's describe some examples of "the bad" and "the ugly." Most everybody knows the difference between a "happy drunk" and a "belligerent drunk." The happy drunks don't cause much trouble but might just go to sleep (a.k.a. pass out) from excessive consumption. We regularly had the shore patrol (SP) bring heavily drunk and limp sailors down to sickbay for observation. It wasn't safe to just put them in their regular berth because there was a small risk that they might stop breathing. We always had a group of "on duty" corpsmen, available and ready for true medical emergencies. We received the drunk sailors, did a physical examination including sensorium testing, vital signs, etc. to be sure the problem was just alcohol excess. We usually "laid them out" on the deck in the aviation medicine spaces for observation until they sobered up. We checked on the drunks regularly until they were recovered and could walk out on their own.

It was not uncommon for a drunken sailor to vomit all over the deck and/or himself. The rule was that such a sailor had to clean up his own mess. He had to stay in sickbay until recovered enough to do so. That of course served two purposes. First the corpsmen shouldn't have to routinely clean up the vomitus of drunken sailors. Second the miscreant sailor perhaps learned to understand the consequences of his alcohol excesses. Call this "the bad."

So much for the happy drunks which were the majority. From time to time the shore patrol would bring in a belligerent drunk. Usually, they would be in handcuffs with several stalwart SPs to control them. Most had bruises from fights ashore, some had lacerations and even occasionally one had a fracture. We of course attended their medical needs first. Then we had to keep them until sobered up just like the other happy drunks.

Problem ... Belligerent drunks want to fight. The shore patrol couldn't just stay until they sobered. Corpsmen are not equipped nor trained to restrain belligerent drunks, nor should they be exposed to risk of harm themselves from the belligerent drunk. Since the alcohol was a depressant, medical sedation was contraindicated.

Solution ... Restraint in a safe, humane way.

The Clamshell Litter ... In sickbay we had a special litter or stretcher that was designed to transfer a sick or injured person from one ship to another via a cable stretched from ship to ship across open water. With a regular litter there was a risk of the patient sliding out and into the water. The clamshell litter solved that problem and eliminated the risk. It looked a little like an Egyptian mummy case made of wire over a steel frame.... maybe even like a coffin made of wire. It was roomy enough for a patient wrapped in lots of blankets for warmth and even an outer water repellant sheet to keep dry from rain and waves. After a patient was placed in the Clamshell, firm latches kept it closed securely during transfer from ship to ship.

Belligerent drunks were secure in the clamshell. It was sort of like a private awfully close quarters jail cell. Shore Patrol helped us secure them there. We could easily observe them and they could do no harm .... to us nor themselves .... like slugging a bulkhead and fracturing their hand.

[We saw occasional "boxer's fractures" of the fifth metacarpal from just that behavior.] Fortunately, we never had more bellicose drunks than we had clamshells. Call this "the ugly."

Sex ... Drinking was one void in the young men's shipboard life. Sex was another. Sailors on shore leave are not just thirsty for alcoholic beverages. They are also thirsty for female companionship. The vendors in port very well know that also and attempt to supply the demand. Sailor partakers of feminine delights ashore usually returned to the ship happy. Call that "the good." However, sometimes they were not happy for long. Call that "the bad."

After every port call, we began to have sailors show up in sick call with urethritis. That is the medical name of the diagnosis, a.k.a. gonorrhea. The sailors called it "the clap." Gonorrhea is one of many Sexually Transmitted Infections (STI's) [also STD's = sexually transmitted diseases] that we saw on the ship from "activity" ashore. There are basically two kinds of urethritis: gonococcal and non-gonococcal. The difference is determined by microscopic examination of urethral discharge.

There is a misnomer that is common even among medical professionals. Gonorrhea or gonococcal urethritis is properly called GCU, but non-gonococcal urethritis is commonly but erroneously called NSU = non-specific urethritis. It should be called by its correct name, NGU = non-gonococcal urethritis. Be that as it may, "the clap" was common in sickbay after port calls.

Call that "the bad."

Fortunately, both GCU and NGU are usually easily cured with antibiotics. If untreated, some complications can occur such as prostatitis, cystitis, epidydimo-orchitis and even reactive arthritis. The worst complication of all is "taking it home to mama." In women complications are much more serious and often don't demonstrate many symptoms. Call that "the ugly." .... and that doesn't even consider the psychosocial/marital complications that ensue at home.

Urethritis was not the only STI we diagnosed in sickbay. Others included syphilis of course, chancroid, lymphogranuloma venereum (LGV) [caused by chlamydia], crabs (a genital insect infestation [pubic lice] …. that itches!!), genital warts from human papilloma virus (HPV), genital herpes … we saw it all. Fortunately, we had full laboratory facilities for accurate diagnosis and a full-spectrum pharmacy for treatment.

SIDE NOTE: There was a double standard of sorts in the Navy. Having an STD in your health records didn't seem to affect enlisted careers much, but in officer's health records, STDs adversely affected their fitness reports, promotions and careers. "Good ole doc" in sickbay seemed to understand that and many an officer's health records were "doctored" (pun intended) or perhaps a better expression would be "fogged." STDs were jokingly called, **"Officers Colds."** Medical professionals could interpret the chart, lab results, et al and understand all the facts of history, but others probably not. Call this "bad AND good."

SIDE NOTE #2: The flight surgeon who "saved my bacon" was lifelong friend Gene Berry, M.D. He was deployed on the *USS Roosevelt (CV-42)* in combat operations in Viet Nam, where he earned a Navy Air Medal. At one time for a period of over a month, maybe it was six weeks the "Rosey" was on the line with combat operations. For R & R the Rosey sailed into U.S. Naval Base Subic Bay in the Philippines. Adjacent is Olongapo, Philippines where all those sailors on shore leave could find whatever activity suited their pent-up desires. By and by after Rosey went back to sea, all those urethritis cases started showing up in sickbay. Gene was observant enough to know that over five hundred cases (including officer's colds) in a crew of 4,000 was an exceptional prevalence. He gathered all the medical information, did statistical analysis, then wrote and published a paper about it. Bravo, Gene.

DOUBLE-UGLY "FULL HOUSE" … Back to the Independence on its Med Cruise in 1966. It was common to see sailors in sickbay who had more than one STD. Urethritis was common, but so were crabs and skin disorders. Syphilis was not rare. We considered syphilis and gonorrhea as the two most dangerous and most needing complete treatment and cure. The others were important but not the major problems of the first two. Somehow, we developed a term for multiple STDs. If a sailor had both gonorrhea and syphilis and three (or more) of the other 'minor' STDs (see above) …. we called it a FULL HOUSE. It was a double-ugly price to pay for some rollicking frivolity ashore.

More "Good, Bad and Ugly" of Sailors Ashore … There were lots of good things sailors enjoyed.

1. Exotic and different restaurants, meals and foods were in every port city. Emphasize that word 'different' because even if a sailor ate perhaps a steak, it was different from the steak served onboard. Even common foods like potatoes and favorite vegetables were prepared and seasoned differently. [My favorite example was the steak at GURIA in Barcelona.]

2. Shopping was fun. There were all kinds of local handicrafts, clothing, toys, trinkets, et al. A whole section elsewhere is devoted to souvenir shopping in the Mediterranean.

3. There were side trips planned to famous cities and some sailors enjoyed visits to Paris, Munich, Rome, Florence, Venice, Jerusalem and others that were distant from port cities. These will be discussed in other sections also.

4. A special visit to Argostoli Bay in Greece deserves mention and a separate section.

SIDE NOTE #3: My cousin Graham Kramer served aboard Indy for three or four years during the early sixties. He was the Assistant Tours Officer during Med deployments and managed the books of the Recreation Fund of the ship. Graham's favorite reminiscences are the side trips in which he was involved. When Indy and her support ships entered any port in the Mediterranean, a huge strain was placed upon that city because of the large numbers of sailors going ashore in a relatively small geographic area. To diffuse this somewhat the Recreation

Fund sponsored tours to get as many sailors as possible doing their R & R in other areas. Graham enjoyed the planning and execution of these tours to Paris, Rome, the French Alps, the Holy Land and many more.... always in the spirit of ensuring the tours were of top quality. He had to plan and check out transportation, hotels, special discount arrangements, meals, museums, sightseeing, etc. before sending a group of sailors. All his advance planning trip expenses were covered by the Navy. Graham always has a "cat-ate-the-canary" grin on his face when he describes his Indy navy service.

All the above two sections would certainly be called "the good."

AWOL (a.k.a. UA) ... Absent Without Leave and Unauthorized Absence are similar terms for basically the same behavior. A sailor who didn't report back to the ship at the end of his shore leave was considered AWOL or UA. His name, description, available details, etc. would be given to the Shore Patrol who would go searching for him. In many cases the sailor would just be passed out or asleep somewhere and didn't get back to the dock to go aboard or take the boat back to the ship at anchor. When found he would be escorted back to the ship and all was well with perhaps an admonition or two. Occasionally a sailor would be AWOL for several days.... unilaterally extending his one-day shore leave. Likely more than an admonition resulted. There was always a worry that some foul play had occurred and that the sailor might be hurt or dead. Even though AWOL/UA sailors were "in trouble" to varying degrees, there was at least some relief whenever one was found safe and healthy. Call this "the bad."

On one occasion when we were in Palma de Mallorca (Spanish Balearic Islands) a sailor just disappeared. Now there is a fine line between AWOL/UA and desertion. Desertion is when there is no intent of ever coming back. The common term is "jumping ship." That one sailor in Palma just disappeared without a trace with no inkling of where he might be or if he were safe. The Shore Patrol always contacted the local police and authorities when looking for someone. Cooperation was at the highest level and the local police with their contacts, communications, vehicles, et al were a boon. A week went by. Foul play was feared. Finally, just before the ship was to sail and leave the sailor (or his remains) behind, the local authorities found him holed up on the back side of the island about fifty miles away. The word was that his intent was to desert. I have no idea what happened to the sailor but expect it was not a pleasant ending. Call that "the ugly."

Wimpy's Cliff and the Jammed Legs ... We were still in Palma when I received a frantic radio message from the Shore Patrol. THERE I WUZ ... the MOD with the usual core group of corpsmen and we were ready for medical emergencies. We had been receiving the usual contingent of drunks and a few other sailors with injuries.

The frantic call said for us to "get ready" because a sailor had fallen off the cliff at Wimpy's and jammed both his legs up into his abdomen. Wimpy's was a unit of the hamburger chain and lots of sailors went there for food. It was located on a steep road up the mountain behind the harbor. It was outboard of the road and indeed at the top of a cliff. We prepared for the worst including emergency surgery. Our surgeon Al Taquino was notified for possible surgery. I don't recall if he was aboard or ashore. If the latter, he would have been recalled to the ship.

By and by the injured sailor arrived and he was stable. Neither leg had been "jammed into his abdomen," but one ankle was injured. Turned out he had fallen off a ledge or wall on the side of Wimpy's and not off the cliff. X-rays showed that he had a Cotton's fracture of the ankle. That is a serious injury because it can lead to an unstable ankle. Essentially it is a "trimalleolar" fracture where all three stabilizing bones are broken... the medial malleolus, lateral malleolus and the posterior articular surface of the distal tibia.

We splinted the ankle, gave him appropriate pain medications and arranged for him to be transported to the naval hospital in Naples where orthopedic surgery was available. That was probably the end of his navy days. The whole episode reminded me of that childhood game when children sit in a circle and whisper a story around mouth to ear. The story was always grossly distorted at the end. Call this "the ugly."

EVENINGS AFTER DINNER

CATWALK STROLLS, MOVIES AND MIDRATS

CATWALK STROLLS …DINNER every evening on the carrier was at 1800 hours (6:00 PM for landlubbers) except when in a Spanish port when we went to "Spanish Hours" and dinner was at 1900. Movies started at 1900 (or 2000 in Spain). That almost always left half an hour or so between eating and the movie. From the beginning I made it a routine practice to go out on the catwalk after dinner every evening, usually forward of the island on the starboard side about halfway to the bow.

The catwalk is an outdoor passageway on the perimeter and outer edge of the flight deck, although not on the entire perimeter. The catwalk deck is about five feet lower than the surface of the flight deck to allow personnel to be at flight deck level, but to be protected from jet blast and other problems if necessary. It also allowed additional ingress and egress from the flight deck to the interior of the ship. Standing in the catwalk your head was above the surface level of the flight deck but you could easily duck below it if necessary. During flight ops lots of the deck crew would duck into the catwalks during launches and recoveries for safety.

The catwalk was about three feet wide and had a solid steel plate outer side wall that was about four feet high or a little more. Outboard of that was a steel net extending maybe four feet from the catwalk wall. It was a safety net because the flight deck and catwalk were nearly twenty stories above the waterline.

THERE I WUZ … strolling on the catwalk after dinner. It served multiple purposes. It was fresh air on the vast expanse of sea and sky. There was always a breeze, if not naturally, certainly from the forward motion of the ship. It was quieter than the interior of the carrier. There was solitude which can be a rarity and a valuable commodity on the carrier.

Sometimes there was a beautiful sunset. Sometimes it was still daylight, sometimes dark, sometimes overcast, sometimes raining. I mostly skipped the catwalk stroll when it was raining except for light drizzle or misty conditions. If the sky were clear during daylight, the cloud formations could be spectacular. If a clear night, the stars were brilliant and amazing. The moon was special on its own as the phases cycled.

The postprandial catwalk strolls also allowed dinner to settle and the opportunity to stretch the legs a little. These little private respites lasted about twenty to thirty minutes before returning to the bustle inside the carrier.

Movie Time … It is a long tradition in the navy to show a movie after the evening meal except during certain conditions. On the carrier there were always lots of movies going at the same time because of the large crew and the many different work areas. Maybe twenty or thirty movies would be shown every night. Each squadron ready room, the wardrooms, the hangar deck workspaces, enlisted lounges and wherever people were not on duty would show a movie. The various films would be swapped around each day so each location had a different movie each night. Films would make the circuit so from time to time our stash of movies would be swapped with those of a supply ship at sea or someone in port so that mostly there were always new movies in the pipeline.

The movies available were mostly recent releases and not just old movies. The schedule of movies would be posted daily showing what was playing and where. As flight surgeons and medical officers overseeing health and safety everywhere we were welcomed virtually anywhere on the ship and wherever a movie was shown. So, we had a wide choice and could see a movie more than once if desired. It was also part of my job. Going to the various ready rooms every evening for a movie using a somewhat random rotation allowed more friendliness and camaraderie with the flight crews. Except during flight ops most all would gather for the movie and afterwards there was a valuable half hour or so to hang out and chat, etc. Sometimes a backgammon (Acey-Deucey) tournament would proceed or a card game. Since my role was to be part of the squadron family, the evening movie time was perfect for gathering and being with all hands to that purpose.

Thunderball Women ...One interesting evolution happened around the movies. The fourth James Bond movie, *Thunderball*, was released in 1965. It was new, had a lot of action and some amazing gadgetry that appealed to the fantasies of active young men ...... AND the opening credits were shown over an extended sequence of nude women swimming underwater in subdued lighting. Mostly only silhouettes could be seen but enough female form and figure pulchritude was displayed to attract a large crowd wherever *Thunderball* was being shown that evening. It was sensational for our large group of young men with no exposure to the opposite sex for the extended times at sea. People made sure to be there for the opening sequence wherever it was being shown and then left for another movie elsewhere.

The squadron ready rooms might have had a hundred officers from other squadrons standing around. In the hangar deck locations, there might have been five hundred or more watching that sequence of nude women swimming underwater. The whoops, hollers and ongoing outspoken commentary was almost more interesting than the movie! Remember that sailors are notorious for salty language! I didn't keep count but probably watched that swim-fest twenty or more times. Yippee.

MidRats … After the movie and camaraderie in a ready room it was probably pushing 2200 or 2300 hours. It was time for a "Jeet?" "Nah, squeet." Active men of that age get hungry again after four or five hours from a meal. I don't remember specifically but I think the MidRats were open in the Main Wardroom from 2300 to 0100 hours. The variety of food available was quite remarkable.

Full breakfasts were offered: eggs, pancakes or waffles, bacon, sausage, toast, sweet rolls, juice, coffee, milk, etc. Keep in mind that some officers worked the night shifts, might have just awakened and wanted breakfast foods before going on duty. Some regular meat dishes, veggies, soups, salads and the like were available … maybe leftovers from previous meals.

There was a large grill and multiple stewards/cooks to fix about what you wanted. I preferred the short-order offerings: hamburgers, cheeseburgers, hot dogs, grilled cheese sandwiches, BLT sandwiches, ham or ham-and-cheese sandwiches, roast beef or turkey sandwiches, pizza, potato salad, macaroni and cheese, French fries, potato chips, pickles, olives, etc., etc., etc. …. it really was a fun time and place to eat. On request the chef would cook a steak for you. Recall that we signed a chit and later paid for all the food we ate at MidRats.

After that it was usually time to retreat to the room, maybe read a little or write letters and then get some sack time. After an active and busy day, it was never hard to sleep even with the noise, vibrations and other "hum" that is virtually constant on a carrier.

The Afternoons of a Flight Surgeon … (This is a 'lagniappe' to the title of this piece.)

That old saying, "A busy sailor is a happy sailor" applies to officers and flight surgeons as well. Up early, breakfast, sick call, lunch and then the afternoon activities.

Afternoons were quite variable. Occasionally a minor surgical procedure would be scheduled. Sometimes aviation physicals would consume the afternoon along with discussions and teaching sessions with our hospital corpsmen. Sometimes it would be ready room rounds in the afternoon or flying with one of the squadrons.…. F-4s, A-6s, E-2s, Helo, A-3 occasionally.

Flights were usually scheduled for the afternoons, sometimes at night, but rarely in the mornings because of the sick call load.

Not infrequently I would present a "health and safety" educational program for one of the squadrons. The ready room was always filled because the squadron required mandatory attendance for all flight officers. Bulletins, notices and assorted info would be circulated with a rubber stamp that said, "Read and Initial." This insured that every officer "got the word" and then there was no excuse for non-attendance or non-compliance. That was more important for the military mission communications than for just a flight surgeon's lecture.

So, whatever the afternoon's activities were, it was rare to miss dinner at 1800. Then after dinner followed the sequences as detailed above …. we stayed busy.

CARRIER AIRWING
SEVEN (CVW-7)

ORGANIZATION, SQUADRONS, AIRCRAFT, OBSERVATIONS

A CARRIER AIR wing is the "action arm" of an aircraft carrier. The ship is large so it can float enough deck for aircraft to launch and land. Although the airwing can operate from land-based airfields, it needs the carrier to get to where its effectiveness is needed. Onboard the airwing personnel are about half the total crew on the carrier. The proportion of officers in the air wing is higher because most all flight crew are officers.

CAG and Staff ... The commander of the airwing is a CAW, but when first begun these units were called Carrier Air Groups, so CAG was the moniker and it sounds much better than CAW when addressing him. Just like the ship has department heads who each report directly to the Captain, the CAG has a Deputy Commander and a staff of senior officers with expertise and experience in their various functional areas: Operations, Weapons, Maintenance, Intelligence, Landing Signal Officers (LSO) and Flight Surgeons. Sometimes there are a few more. The CAG himself reports directly to the Captain of the Carrier as one of the department heads.

CVW-7 ... was a small group of officers with a small group of enlisted for administrative work and detail completion. Each of the staff officer specialists worked with their respective specialist officer in each squadron and served as advisors and liaison back to the CAG. The two Flight Surgeons also worked with all the squadrons. The staff officers and flight surgeons flew with all the squadrons. Flight surgeons were "back seaters," but the staff aviators were mostly "checked out" in all the aircraft types and qualified to fly them.

The Squadrons ... There were two fighter squadrons flying F-4 Phantoms. There were three attack squadrons: one Navy A-6 squadron, one Navy A-4 squadron and one Marine A-4 squadron. There was a reconnaissance squadron flying the RA-5C, an early warning squadron flying the E-1, the A-3 squadron for radar airborne vectoring and the helicopter squadron. The E-1 and Helicopter "squadrons" were each detachments of a larger parent squadron stateside. In all we had nine squadron units with about 160-200 Officers and about 2,000 Enlisted among them.

Chief Petty Officers (CPO) ...The Chief Petty Officers deserve special mention because they truly are the experts in their various fields. They have all the training, the experience and the maturity to lead effective teams of younger, less-experienced sailors. There is an old Navy saying that chiefs are the "Backbone of the Navy" .... and it's true. Bravo for the CPOs.

Each squadron had a senior experienced aviator officer responsible for the same areas in their squadron: operations, maintenance, weapons, intelligence, etc. .... and the CPOs in those areas knew how to do it and get it done. Here are the squadrons assigned to our CVW-7 airwing deployed on the Independence for the 1966 Mediterranean Cruise.

Fighter Squadrons ... CVW-7 had two F-4 Phantom squadrons:

VF-84 ... The "Jolly Rogers" with a 'Skull and Crossbones' logo; and
VF-41 ... The "Black Aces" with an 'Ace of Spades' as its logo.

Each of these two squadrons had about 20 to 25 officers, half pilots and half RIOs (Radar Intercept Officers.) The pilots of course were Naval Aviators and flew the planes. The RIO or "back seater" was responsible for radar monitoring, navigation and target identification, additional visualization, radio communications and various tasks to assist the pilot. There were about fifteen F-4 Phantoms in each squadron.

At one time fighter pilots flew fighter planes "by the seat of the pants" and fired bullets with visual aim. No longer. Modern combat aircraft are flying weapons platforms. Electronics systems manage many functions including identifying targets, radar guidance of missiles to the target and more.

Each squadron had a Commanding Officer (CO a.k.a. "skipper") and his Executive Officer (XO) as second in command. Both were senior officers with a lot of fleet experience … that famous "been there, done that." Officers assigned to operations, maintenance, weapons, etc. worked with the chiefs and other enlisted to accomplish those phases of the operation. There were 200 or so enlisted men in each squadron with the various skills needed to "keep'em flying."

Attack Squadrons … CVW-7 had three: one A-6 Intruder and two A-4 Skyhawk squadrons (one was a Marine squadron assigned to the airwing.)

VA-75 … The "Sunday Punchers" whose logo was a boxing glove bomb with wings and headed down. The A-6 Intruder cockpit was side-by-side rather than front-and-back like the F-4s. Instead of a RIO flight officer the non-pilot flight officer was a Bombardier/Navigator (B/N) with obvious responsibilities. There were about the same 20-25 officers and the several hundred enlisted men for maintenance, weapons, fueling, electronics repairs, parachute packing, et al. It was fun flying in A-6s because you could see more including the pilot flying the Intruder. There were about the same number of aircraft as in the fighter squadrons.

VA-86 … The "Sidewinders" whose logo was a top hat and cane with a rattlesnake coiled around it and "Atkron 86" at the bottom. The A-4 was an interesting aircraft. It was designed as a one-way nuclear bomber. It would deliver the nuke with a loft technique then an Immelmann maneuver and fly back from whence it came to escape the blast. There wasn't enough fuel for a return flight so the pilot was to eject, parachute and survive/return as best he could. The A-4 Skyhawk was a single-seater, subsonic aircraft but it was quite maneuverable. At one time it was used as the "bogie" enemy aircraft for training at "Top Gun" school. With external fuel tanks it was often used as an airborne tanker for inflight refueling. The squadron had about the same fifteen or so aircraft, but fewer officers, all pilots and of course the enlisted professionals for support.

VMA-324 ... The "Vagabonds" whose logo was a shield with crossed swords and a fanged wolf in the center. They flew the same A-4 Skyhawks as VA-86 and had about the same complement of aircraft, pilots and support folks. One difference of VMA-324 was that they brought along their own Flight Surgeon, Gene Purvis, M.D. who is discussed elsewhere.

RVAH-1 ... The "Smoking Tigers" whose logo was a seated tiger holding a long cigar and blowing a smoke cloud overhead with a wide grin. Their aircraft was the RA-5C Vigilante which was a Mach-Two heavy bomber when designed and then converted to photo reconnaissance. RVAH-1 had only 3-4 aircraft and a correspondingly smaller contingent of officers and enlisted. The plane had a crew of two and was high performance at speed but a notorious and dangerous "dog" when low and slow. For that reason, we flight surgeons were not allowed to fly in it. They launched only one aircraft at a time. All the pilots in the squadron were senior, experienced second and third fleet tour officers who had seen significant numbers of their friends killed in the bird. They always seemed a little glassy eyed to me and somewhat distant.

VAW-12, Detachment 62 ... The "Batmen" whose logo was a black bat in the center flying over a carrier in the distant background with a crescent moon in the left sky and a lightning-bolt cloud on the right. Their aircraft was the E-1B Tracer with the large radar dome on top ... so it was fondly known as the Willy Fudd or "Fudd" and as the

Stoof with a Roof. It had two 9-cylinder radial combustion engines with three-bladed propellers. It was manned by two flight officers and two radar controllers. The plane and its mission are described elsewhere. The detachment had about six aircraft and the appropriate number of officers and enlisted. Their flights were usually double cycles of three hours.

VQ-2 ... Originally "Batmen," changed to "Sandeman" and the logo was a black silhouette man in a long Spanish cape and flat brim hat. (It was the silhouette logo of the Sandeman sherry company which was close to their Rota, Spain home base.) They flew the EA-3B Skywarrior aircraft, originally a bomber but modified for its electronic countermeasures mission. The plane had a "fat" body and was sometimes called a "whale." VQ-3 had only 2-3 planes. The EA-3B had a crew of six, three or four officers and two or three enlisted. On 3 November 1966, an EA-3B flew into the water and we lost all six crewmen. (See elsewhere.)

HC-2 ... Our helicopter detachment was based in Jacksonville, Florida. They were known as the "Fleet Angels" and their logo was a halo with wings in the center with day and night sky background showing two lightning bolts. It obviously symbolized rescue day or night in all weather. Their mission was rescue of downed aircrew. When flight ops began, their helo was first in the air and last to recover. They had 3-4 helicopters and eight or ten flight officers with the necessary maintenance, repair and support personnel.

NOTE: In case you didn't notice, "V" in a squadron name/number designates fixed wing and "H" means rotary wing.

EYES IN THE SKY ....
CYCLES IN THE AIR

WITH ALL THE size and power that is an aircraft carrier it is vulnerable to attack. Lots of preventive measures are ongoing. Radar provides constant surveillance even when at anchor or moored to a pier. A submarine or two usually accompany a carrier for underwater protection. The destroyers and cruisers in the battle group defend against surface attack and all have radar monitoring as well to extend the outreach distance. All that is surface based or underwater but the carrier has its own resources with its aircraft...... both for surveillance and for defense.

Grumman E-1 Tracer Airborne Early Warning Aircraft ... Indy had a detachment (Det-62) from VAW-12 the parent squadron that supplied other carriers as well. They flew an interesting aircraft designed for putting radar surveillance up high in the air and at a distance from the carrier. Hmmm ... I wonder if that's why it was called an "airborne early warning aircraft?" The E-1's original designation was WF so it picked up the nickname Willy Fudd from the cartoon character. It was propeller driven and had a huge radar dome mounted on top giving it a distinctive appearance. That led to another nickname, "Stoof with a Roof" ... a takeoff from the previous S-2F aircraft which was called a "stoof" for obvious reasons. Interestingly the COD plane for onboard delivery of supplies, mail and passengers was a C-1 and about the same configuration without the radar dome. Aren't these navy slang terms wonderful?

Another oddity of the E-1 Fudd was the different wing folding system. The S-2F and the C-1 wings folded upwards, but with the radar dome the E-1 wings had to fold backwards under the dome.

Anyway, Fudds were launched early in the flight operations cycle and with plenty of range and fuel they could stay longer in the air … for two or three cycles (see below.) Fudds not only provided early warning surveillance but they also helped monitor aircraft to enhance the air controllers onboard the carrier.

Douglas EA-3B Skywarrior … This was a much larger electronics warfare aircraft and was nicknamed the "whale" because of its size. It had a crew of six, two pilots and four operating the radar and jamming equipment in the body of the plane. This aircraft could also be modified to serve as a tanker for in-air refueling. It also had long legs.

Combat Air Patrol (CAP) … This was another way the carrier protected itself. In the movie *Top Gun,* you may recall that the fighters encountered MIGs headed toward the carrier and their job was to stop them. The carrier's fighter planes serve that function and it is called Combat Air Patrol or CAP. The F-4 Phantom fighters were launched and flew on station at about two hundred miles from the carrier at all four corners. Since their fuel is limited, the fighters had to be relieved about every few hours. The test of combat readiness was to maintain CAP for forty-eight or seventy-two hours non-stop day and night. It was a strain on everyone, but necessary.

Flight Cycles … From many years' experience and development, the Indy used the standard carrier flight cycles for carrier operations. The timing of a cycle was mostly based on the fuel capacity of the shortest-range aircraft. On our cruise that was the F-4 Phantom. Although the range and fuel capacity were more than an hour and a half, safety required a cushion (1) not to land F-4s at the very last of their fuel and (2) to allow for some possible bolters and extended flight time.

So, the standard flight cycles were one and a half hours. The helicopter was launched first for safety in case a pilot needed to be rescued from the water.... and the helo was the last to land at the end of a cycle.

First the fully fueled aircraft would be launched. The carrier would "turn into the wind" and all four catapults would alternate launching so that each one could recycle for another aircraft in about a minute, meaning the carrier could launch a plane every fifteen seconds. It was an amazing spectacle to watch as planes would be lined up in readiness, start engines, then on signal when their turn came, taxi to the catapult, hook up and fire off into the sky. It was even more amazing when you were in one of the aircraft.

After an hour and a half another launch sequence would occur, then recovery of the first cycle aircraft would commence. Only one plane at a time could trap back onboard. Intervals were spaced for safety and a clear deck was essential. If one plane were somehow unable to get away from the angled deck, a "fouled deck" would be called and the next plane in the landing pattern would be waved off to go around and make its approach in turn.

The fighters would be recovered first due to fuel limitations. Then the attack A-4s and A-6s, finally the propeller driven planes. The planes with "long legs" (more fuel, more range, more time in the air) would often fly for two cycles or three hours, sometimes even 3 cycles and 4 ½ hours.

More about CAP ... This was the real test of the airwing and ship's proficiency. Maintaining continuous flight operations for that 48–72-hour interval was a strain on everyone. It was not just the flight crews who had to fly repeated hops and try to catch some sleep and food when they weren't in the air. It was also the maintenance crews keeping the aircraft functional and safe, sometimes changing engines, a landing gear, whatever. it was the deck crews refueling aircraft, moving them around including on elevators, manning the catapults, the arresting gear, mess decks and wardrooms keeping food available, ship operations, radar controllers et al, etc., etc. EVERYTHING WAS NONSTOP. It was the ultimate beehive, anthill, hornets' nest analogy.

THERE I WUZ .... Participating in CAP must be one of the most amazing and exhilarating experiences of my life. Go Navy.

READY ROOM REMINISCENCES

EACH SQUADRON OF an airwing is a unit with its own small-group identity. Each squadron has its own ready room both on the carrier and ashore at the Naval Air Station. The layout of ready rooms on the carrier and at the NAS are similar, but the décor is individual. Squadron logos abound. The artwork, bulletin boards et al depend on the imagination and talents of the members. For the purposes of this section, I will relate mostly the common elements found and remembered in general.

Coffee Mugs ... Sailors drink a lot of coffee. Some of that is perhaps from boredom, some to counter lack of restful sleep, some habit. Whatever .... each ready room has a coffee pot going most all the time. I don't recall that the coffee was particularly good, nor was it bad. Behind the coffee pot and station ... or maybe to the side ... was a board on the bulkhead (wall for you landlubbers.) The board had rows of hooks to hold coffee mugs. Each member of the squadron had his own mug, mostly the same size and shape, mostly with the squadron logo on one side and the members individual name glazed onto the other side. This back side was where individuality was expressed, call signs instead of names, anything someone wanted.

All this had several practical reasons. It was sanitary as everyone used only his own cup. It eliminated the need to wash cups, a simple rinse was sufficient. That saved ship's water and labor. Expressing individuality on the cups was also important.

As a roving airwing staff officer and particularly as a flight surgeon I was considered a member and at home in all the ready rooms. So, I had a bunch of coffee cups, one for each mug board. They still bring back fond memories of when THERE I WUZ.

Classroom Setup Semi-Lounge Chairs …. You have seen these in movies. Each ready room has display boards behind a podium. Arrayed in rows facing the podium are multiple padded, semi-reclining individual chairs with arms. They are designed for comfort but also for attentive participation in various functions: pre-flight briefings, training lectures, evening movies, et al. No one had an assigned seat, but just took an open one. The chairs were large enough to be comfortable in full flight gear which was bulky.

Main door and side door(s) … There were some real normal-looking doors, all metal, on the ship and not just hatches. Each ready room had the main entrance usually behind the chairs so you could come in and pick a seat without disturbing any formal proceedings. If no presentations were in progress, lights were usually brighter (except for movies) and people would be lounging around in various activities. There was always at least one side door, sometimes several and these might be hatch style. The actual shape of the ready room on the ship was dependent on the ship spaces and passageways. The doors could be closed when privacy was important.

The Desk and Duty Officer …Each ready room and squadron had a large steel desk that was the business center. One of the officers was always on duty, not necessarily behind the desk, but in the ready room prepared to receive alerts, notify the squadron members in case of action commands, take and relay messages, etc., etc.

The desk was also where the scheduling log was kept. If I wanted to fly, the duty officer would open the flight log, see what and when hops were scheduled and who was to pilot the aircraft, etc. Then he could pencil me in for the hop. If it were an F-4 Phantom, the RIO would not fly that hop. If an A-6 Intruder, the Bombardier-Navigator (B/N) would skip the flight. A-4s were single seaters so no flying for me in them.

Bulletin Boards, Log Boards, Landing Score Tally Boards …
There were several different boards hanging around. Announcements,
flight schedules, the tally board with each pilot's name and landing
scores, etc. were all posted and kept current. Communication was vital
and it was efficiently done. The "read and initial" clipboard was an
important element. When some notice or information was important,
it was easy to see who had read it and who had not.

Backgammon (Acey-Deucey) and Card Games … During down
times flight crew could play backgammon as there was a board in most
every ready room. There were tournaments sometimes. Card games were
in progress sometimes, but I don't recall any gambling for money. Likely
it was not allowed. This was a good way to enhance friendships when
schedules permitted.

Stencils … It was amazing how many things had a stencil spray-
painted on them. ID numbers, directions for use, whatever…. and that
was all over the ship.

Escalators … This was remarkably interesting. Mostly the ship
had only steep ladders to get up or down to change decks. [There were
the huge external elevators for moving aircraft back and forth from
flight deck to hangar deck, but these were not for personnel use except
if going along when a plane was moved.] The escalators were for use of
flight crew in getting from ready rooms to the flight deck. The ready
rooms were multiple levels below and all that flight gear was quite heavy.
Climbing ladders in full flight gear would exhaust even the strongest.
The escalators were LONG and high (three or four times longer that
standard escalators in buildings) because they had to span multiple
decks. After preflight briefings pilots and flight officers would take
the escalator from the ready room to the O-3 deck (top deck below the
flight deck) then climb one ladder to the flight deck. A stroll over to
the aircraft, walk around the aircraft to inspect and check everything
for safety, climb aboard, "light the fires" on signal ["*Start your engines*"
called by the Air Boss.], then taxi to the catapult hookup, recheck all
controls and gauges, salute the yellow shirt and whoosh …. into the air.

FLIGHT DECK FACTS

DANGER, RISK, SUCCESS, FAILURE, PRECISION, PRECAUTIONS

CARRIER OPERATIONS ON the open flight deck are possibly the most hazardous of all occupations, both for flight crew and deck crew. Here is an abstract from a Naval Safety Center report:

Abstract

*A comprehensive review of injuries sustained by personnel working on naval flight decks between January 1977 and December 1991 was conducted using database records maintained at the U.S. Naval Safety Center, Norfolk, VA. Data included all fatalities, permanent total disabilities, permanent partial disabilities, and major injuries resulting in 5 or more lost workdays. Injuries were coded using ICD-9-CM codes for analysis. A total of 918 flight deck personnel were reported injured during this 15-yr period, including **43 fatalities, 5 permanent total disabilities, 42 permanent partial disabilities, and 828 major injuries. Of the non-fatalities, a plethora of fractures, traumatic amputations, major lacerations, dislocations, contusions, concussions, burns, crushing*** *injuries, sprains, and strains were reported. Nearly all naval platforms with a flight deck reported an injury. While an average of 51 injuries per 100,000 aircraft recoveries were reported annually on aircraft carriers from 1977-86, a marked reduction to a rate of roughly 30 injuries was observed annually from 1987-90. What makes injuries sustained on the flight deck particularly disconcerting is that* **over 90% can be attributed to human causal factors.**

The Naval Aviation Safety Center does a commendable job in promoting safety and as this report shows, it is incredibly important. I contributed in a small way by writing a medical safety article for their monthly APPROACH magazine one summer during two-weeks reserve active duty.

Those statistics above are for flight deck injuries only and do not include flight crews. Between 1948 and 1988 a total of 12,000 aircraft and 8,500 lives were lost. Those figures include combat loses, but they are a tiny fraction of the total. That calculates to 300 aircraft and 212 lives per year over the forty-year span. Safety has improved greatly since 1948. However, during the eight-month Med Cruise on the Indy in 1966 we lost two aircraft and eight flight crew.... and that was one carrier in less than a year. Do your own math. It is a dangerous occupation. Why so dangerous?

Deck Area ... Although the flight deck is a relatively large area of four acres, the landing zone on the angled deck is about the size of a football field, 317 feet long to be exact.... and space where your tailhook can "catch a wire" for a safe trap is much shorter than that.

Motion of the Deck .... Previously discussed were the three main movements of the ship that make a moving target out of that landing zone: pitch, roll and yaw. There are three other movements that contribute to the difficulties:

4) <u>Surge</u> ... forward and backward movement of the ship, i.e., faster, then slower, caused by wave surge resistance.

5) <u>Sway</u> ... the whole ship slipping side to side, also from wave action.

6) <u>Heave</u> ... the ship moving up and down without much pitch, roll and yaw.

Do the math on that one for the possible combinations of the six ship movements.... and the varying degree of each ... the possibilities are amazing. Bottom line is that every landing and trap is different.

One interesting analogy is that a carrier landing is like "landing on a five-story building in an earthquake." Landing on a carrier is about as harrowing a job as man has ever thought up.

Jet blast, Props and Rotors ... The power behind jet engines at full throttle can sweep a person overboard in an instant. That's one reason why a rescue helicopter is always in the air during flight ops and a "plane guard" destroyer always close at hand. If not overboard, jet blast can slam you into the island or another aircraft. Beware jet blast.

The jet intake can suck you into the spinning jet engine blades as well.

The blades of propellors and rotors are not easily seen because of their motion and that is even worse at night. The blades can chop an arm, decapitate a sailor or shred him to ribbons in a moment. Be alert or pay the consequences.

Fire ... Remember a carrier is a combat ship and the deck is loaded with a profusion of bombs, rockets, bullets, fuel and other fire and/or explosion hazards. In 1967 on the *Forrestal* a Zuni rocket mounted on an F-4 Phantom had an electrical anomaly causing it to fire off on deck and hit an external fuel tank on an A-4 Skyhawk. The ensuing explosions and fire killed 134 navy personnel and injured 161 others.

Yet for all the risks, hazards, danger and disastrous events hundreds of thousands of launches and recoveries are successful and even considered routine. Safety protocols are strictly followed for plane movements, mounting armaments and refueling aircraft. Bravo for the amazing performance of navy men and women both in the air and on the deck of that hazardous workplace.

CATAPULTS

CONSIDER THIS. YOU have a 55,000-pound jet fighter loaded with 16,000 pounds of armaments for a total of over 70,000 pounds. That is 35 tons of motionless dead weight on the deck of an aircraft carrier that is just over a thousand feet long. How do you get it flying to target? Answer: a catapult launch. (The history of aircraft catapults is beyond the scope of this discussion.) On the *Independence* we used four steam catapults which were quite effective.

Fueled, armed with ordinance, pilot and RIO aboard, tail pointed sideways off the edge, the Air Boss called "Light your engines" from the island flight tower and we powered up using the "huffer" to force air through the engine to start rotation. When our turn to launch came, we taxied out to the start of the catapult track and turned starboard for hookup. The shuttle had come back into position from the last launch and our Phantom was attached to it with the bridle cable. Now we were ready to go and had gathered those thousand eyes from the deck, from radar control, from the tower and from television screens all over the ship.

The catapult track was 276 feet long and had a stroke of 253 feet. The goal was to accelerate the aircraft over the length of the track from zero speed to flying speed. Safe flying speed for an F-4 Phantom was

130 knots. (That's about 150 miles per hour.) Think about that.... zero to 150 in 253 feet and you can appreciate the power of those steam catapults.

Full power with afterburners, signals and wham.... the acceleration was amazing. The forces tried to push you backwards into the seat .... but because so many male studly eyes were watching it was considered macho to lean forward into the cat shot else you might be considered a weakling wimp. From the roar of engines and activity on deck, suddenly in seconds you were airborne and it was eerily quiet. Also, from the sudden lack of catapult acceleration forces you felt almost weightless for a moment.

With a heavy load of armament, it was not uncommon for a plane to dip below the level of the flight deck for a moment before it accelerated into a climb with better flying speed. If the catapult failed for some reason (which was called a "cold cat shot") you likely just crashed into the water for lack of flight speed. Those thousand eyes were always worried, like circusgoers watching high-wire performers without a net. If a plane dipped off the cat a little, that was common.... but if the dip was exaggerated and the plane got unusually close to the water, then recovered and flew off, sometimes there was an audible low cheer or happy sigh among those watching.

The catapult made a loud hissing sound from the steam power, then a huge thump as the piston-in-water brake at the end stopped it. The entire ship shuddered and vibrated every time the catapult fired and rammed that brake at the end of the track. No matter where in the ship you might be that thump, vibration and sound was unmistakable. We became used to it, even expecting it while eating, sleeping, treating patients, walking the passageways or whatever.

I have speculated if the mass inertia of the plane converted so suddenly to kinetic energy might have affected the ship's motion, but the ship was so large its mass probably prevented any effect on it. The carrier always "turned into the wind" for launches and recoveries both to eliminate any cross wind but mainly to add the wind over the deck speed to the flying speed of the launching or landing aircraft.

Newer *Ford* class carriers now use electromagnetic catapult systems. They give less shock to the aircraft and are much quieter. There is less maintenance and I believe they are safer.

GEAR .... THREE KINDS
AND COUNTING

THREE KINDS OF gear are essential in carrier aviation: Flight, Landing and Arresting.

Flight Gear ... This describes the full complement of clothing and equipment worn by an aviator when mounting and flying off and on the carrier. One normally just thinks of a flight suit but "flight gear" is so much more. Of course, an aircrewman(woman) wears a flight suit. It can be khaki .... or bright orange for better visualization in a dark ocean. The flight suit has many pockets, most with zippers to secure contents. There are even pockets on the arms and legs which were easier to access during flight. The mundane items might be chewing gum, breath fresheners, Chapstick, antacids, whatever. The pockets contain most anything the pilot wants in them. (In combat situations they also included sidearms and ammunition, knives, food supplies and other "gear" for survival on land if needed.... there was always a worry that too much weight would result in exceeding the limits of the ejection seat if required.) Presumably, the pilot has underwear and not infrequently long johns and extra layers... except when wearing a "poopy suit" when no underwear might be a good idea. (More on that elsewhere.)

Beyond the flight suit there is a host of other "gear." The anti-gravity or G-suit (described elsewhere) is worn over the flight suit. Steel-toed boots are mandatory and flight gloves. The aviation helmet is a biggie part of the equipment. The helmets start plain white but most have colorful designs and squadron logos painted on them. The helmet has a multi-position sliding visor (including a sun-glare shield), earpieces, various strange-looking attachments and fittings.... and plenty of padding inside. The oxygen mask with hose is essential and it attaches to both sides of the helmet with metal fittings and adjustable straps to insure a snug fit. The microphone is inside the mask with communication system hookups included.

The parachute and ejection seat harness are also essential. Made with heavy wide nylon webbing to withstand considerable stress the harness straps around your butt, both legs, around the hips, over the shoulders and around the chest. You don't want to be slipping out when ejecting or hanging from a parachute. When seated in the cockpit the fittings on your harness are attached to shoulder clips and a lap belt. The parachute is thus secured to you and is between you and the ejection seat frame. The shoulder straps have inertia reels allowing movement (just like modern automobile seat belts) which pull back and lock on ejection. The seat also has leg attachments and arm shields to prevent flailing limbs on ejection.

Then there is the "knee pad" which is secured over your thigh with an elastic strap around your leg. This contains a note pad and a secured pen or pencil for writing something in flight. Is that enough? "Flight gear" means lots more than just the suit.... and the weight is not inconsiderable. Strength and fitness are essential for flight crew.

(Some lines of apparel and clothing use the lingo term "gear" to mean about anything you can wear so if a pilot wears all the above, then gear is the right word.)

Landing Gear ... A macho, in-the-know aviator doesn't refer to the those rolling things under the aircraft as wheels. They are the gear.... and if you MUST ... landing gear when you are trying to distinguish from other gear. Of course, aircraft landing gear is more than just the wheels. It is the struts, hydraulic pistons, braces, brakes, fuselage plate, etc. In modern aviation, especially in high-performance navy aircraft, all the gear must be rapidly retractable for streamlined flight and it is only lowered for takeoff and landing. Landing gear is also take-off gear but not referred to as such. In checklist preparation before landing, the call is always "Gear down and <u>locked</u>" which is an especially important consideration. So much for landing gear.

Arresting Gear ... So, you have this 55,000-pound machine flying in at 130 knots (150mph) to land on the carrier. How do you stop it? Brakes won't do it like on a long landing strip ashore. Again, the history of arresting gear is not in the scope of this discussion. Modern supercarriers use arresting cables and a tailhook on the aircraft. The tailhook is retractable during flight and lowered when time to land.

The Indy had four arresting cables but new Ford class carriers only have three. The huge woven steel cables had considerable tensile strength. You can imagine the strength needed to catch ("arrest") that hurtling 55,000-pound mass flying at that speed and bring it to a stop on the angled deck which is maybe 400 feet from fantail to leading edge.

Each end of the cable is attached to a hydraulic damping system below decks to absorb the kinetic energy. When the tailhook engages the "wire" (as they are called by the savvy), the cable is pulled out rapidly as it absorbs the energy, but not too far since it must stop the plane before the end of the deck. A hook runner makes sure the wire is away from the tailhook so the jet can taxi away to clear the deck for the next pilot in the landing pattern to make his trap.

The cables are held a few inches above the surface of the deck so the tailhook dragging along the surface will catch it. The supports are metal arched springs that will mash flat if something rolls over it…. namely an aircraft wheel.

Tailhooks are large strong steel rods with a scoop-looking end that slides along the deck to engage the cable. There is hydraulic pressure to hold the hook down but even so sometimes the hooks bounces, known as a hook skip, and the plane flies off the forward end of the angled deck…. or the pilot misses the cables altogether. That is called a "bolter" and the pilot must fly around for another approach and attempt to land.

At night, the metal against metal of the hook and deck at speed shoots sparks in every direction. That is called a "flaming hooker" and there is a drink named after it. More about that later.

There is an independent non-governmental fraternal organization, the Tailhook Association (of mostly current and former carrier aviators) which is dedicated to supporting carrier aviation… history, traditions, et al and which provides various scholarships and makes other philanthropic contributions. They have conventions, etc. and talk about when …. THERE I WUZ.

THE MEATBALL

"ON GLIDE PATH …. on glide path …. on glide path …. add power ….
add power …. on glide path …. a little high …. on glide path …. add
power …. ADD POWER …. **WAVE OFF! WAVE OFF!**"

Such might be the continuing radio transmission of the Landing
Signal Officer (LSO) on an aircraft carrier when an aircraft was in the
approach to the angled deck and flying down the glide path to a trap
(landing) with his tailhook catching an arresting gear cable (wire.) In
this case the pilot was not staying precisely on the glide path all the way
down and the LSO shouted for him to add full throttle and "go around"
for another try.

LOW AND SLOW is disaster on carrier landings. Low and slow
leads to a ramp strike … which means you fly into the fantail (rear)
of the carrier …. goodbye aircraft and goodbye pilot. Sometimes only
your tailhook scrapes across the round-down (curved edge at the very
rear of the flight deck) and you safely land. You were low and slow, but
not fatally so.

The most hazardous part of aircraft carrier flight operations is
landing a fast-flying hunk of steel with wings … on a larger and slower
hunk of steel that may be pitching (aft end bouncing up and down),
rolling (deck not staying horizontally level) and/or yawing (moving side

to side in the water.) What if it is at night, in the rain, with a lot of wind? You get the idea.

Train, train, train ... practice, practice, practice. Pilots must develop their flying skills to an extremely high level of precision. After learning basic flying and then doing many, many "touch and goes" practicing precise touchdown at the specific point, then student aviators "go to the carrier" and practice actual carrier landings. Only after demonstrating that high level of proficiency do they get their Wings of Gold and graduate as a Naval Aviator.

Historically the first planes used at sea were float planes launched off a standard ship, landed on the water, then hoisted back on the ship with a crane. [Modern aircraft carriers still have a crane, called a "Tilly," which is on wheels, can pick up an aircraft and move it out of the way or pitch it over the side if necessary.]

As naval aviation developed and flat surfaces were added to ships (origin of name "flattop") then landings on the ships were begun. Various techniques were developed and continually improved for stopping (arresting) the aircraft on landing. It has been an ongoing process for a century. Many accidents, including fatal ones, have spurred innovation and improvement. The voluminous history of all this is fascinating reading, however this discussion will just survey some of the highlights and mostly discuss how it was done on the *Independence* in the 1960s.

THERE I WUZ ... on both sides of carrier landings.... frequently in the aircraft along for a hot ride or on the ship watching many, many, many landings ... from Vulture's Row, from Ready Room or other TV screens, on radar screens .... and when not physically watching, hearing the THUMP and squealing of the trap as the plane hit the deck and hooked an arresting cable.

Every landing on the Indy was important to me. If in the aircraft, of course my health and safety were at stake. If not in the aircraft, one of my pilots and his flight officer(s) was there equally at risk. Additionally, it was beneficial to have watched each approach and landing so they could be discussed later with some knowledge and understanding. When a landing was "hairy," i.e., non-routine, close call, etc., it was even more important to have seen it. (More on this later.)

LSO ... So back to history a little. Why that term "Wave Off" when the LSO wanted a pilot not to land and go around the flight pattern and try again? Initially the pilot LSO on deck would use signal flags one in each hand to signal the landing pilot. (This is just like modern airport runway staff who direct taxiing aircraft in airports with lighted wands in both hands.)

In the early days of naval aviation there was no radar, no radio. Communication from the ship to the pilot was with flags in each hand, held out sideways like wings. Later they used painted wood or steel paddles in each hand. Tilting the arms would indicate if aircraft wings were tilted. Other signals had other meanings and the WAVE OFF derived from the flag signal used. The LSO is still sometimes referred to as "Paddles." [Navy monikers can be confusing at first.]

Fast forward to radar, radio and voice communications. Immediate moment-to-moment appraisal of the flight approach is communicated to the pilot ... for safety and to improve his landing. The Landing Signal Officers are senior aviators with plenty of experience and who have been to special training schools to learn about their job as LSO. [Currently the LSO school is at NAS Oceana in Virginia Beach, VA.]

The LSO workstation position during flight ops is on the port side of the angled deck ... in the catwalk .... so, he can see everything, but duck if necessary. The LSO station is at about where the glide slope touches the deck and where the airplane is supposed to catch a wire.... so, the LSO is looking directly up the slope at the aircraft to easily see if the pilot deviates either too high or too low, off to one side or anything else unusual. Usually there are three or more on duty as communication is vital. Radar screens are watched by the assistants. LSO eyes are always on the plane and the LSO has a hand-held control with which he can flash bright red Wave Off Lights at the same time he calls Wave Off on the radio if necessary.

The Meatball ... At approximately the same position as the LSO station is the Fresnel Lens system which produces "The Meatball." The Fresnel lens takes a bright light source which is radiating in many directions and collimates the light waves into parallel beams. The powerful beam is projected up into the sky at an angle of about 3.5 degrees.to produce the glide slope down which the pilot flies to touchdown. Current carriers have a stack of ten light cells while the Indy only had five. The current system is named the Improved Fresnel Lens Optical Landing System (IFLOLS) [Do not think those initials could mean, "If Laughing Out Loud Sometimes," because landing on a carrier is not an amusing proposition. There is however an old Naval Aviator joke that is appropriate here:

"The three best things in life are a good landing, a good orgasm and a good bowel movement. A night carrier landing is one of the few opportunities in life where you get to experience all three at the same time."

Back to the Fresnel Lens, the Meatball and the glide slope. The four top light beams are yellow, the bottom beam is red. Think about the five beams being stacked one on top of another in a vertical column.... shining up into the sky like light through a vertical window. Running across the light system is a horizontal row of green lights which are called datum lights. So, there is a wide but focused beam projected into the sky that the pilot sees when he is in the glide slope. The light that the pilot sees becomes round in appearance when he first sees it at about a mile and a half from the ship.... hence the term "meatball."

If he sees a yellow "meatball" lined up with the green datum lights, that means he is in one of the top four beams, but if he sees a red meatball, he is in the bottom beam and too low. The goal is to fly the plane down the glide slope seeing a yellow meatball across the datum lights all the way to touchdown.

Planes are launched every fifteen seconds (one a minute from each of the four catapults) but only one at a time can be recovered. The airplanes fly a racetrack holding pattern above the carrier (like civilian aircraft at an airport when landing is delayed.) Vectored by radar each plane is directed when the deck is clear for the next trap. The pilot makes a 180 degree turn from the downwind leg to fly around to be directly behind the carrier. In daytime that is at about three-quarters of a nautical mile. At night, the aircraft approaches the ship straight on from about ten miles out. Once lined up and flying straight to the ship the pilot can see the meatball about as soon as he makes his turn in daytime and at about a mile and a half at night.

At this point the pilot radios to the ship, "Call the Ball," meaning he sees it and is lined up for the final approach which is about 15 to 18 seconds of flight and is called the "groove." With flaps and gear down, aircraft trimmed and feet on the rudder pedals the pilot must concentrate intense attention to flying the glide slope down, i.e., staying in one of the yellow Fresnel Lens beams as he descends to the deck. The pilot has left hand on the throttle and right hand on the stick (yoke) to adjust as required.

With eyes on the meatball pilots develop a scan pattern in which they move their eyes constantly to check three main things about their aircraft: airspeed, altitude and angle of attack. About every third or fourth scan they check lineup with the centerline of the angle deck. Adding power, thus speed, increases lift and increases altitude. Decreasing power slows the aircraft, decreases lift and lowers altitude. The angle of attack affects lift also, but importantly the aircraft must be somewhat nose up so the tailhook at the rear is the first thing to contact the deck and hopefully catch one of the arresting cables.

The radar monitors and the LSO with direct vision both day and night keep close tabs on whether the aircraft in in the glide path. That's what that opening line was all about.... the LSO telling the pilot how he is doing moment to moment with instructions for corrections needed to stay in the glide slope to the deck.

Automatic Power Control (APC) ... Just before I rotated out of active duty in the fleet a new system was introduced. The radar systems vectored incoming aircraft on the glide slope in the approach pattern and if a plane were too low the APC would add power. The pilot could be hands-off the throttle and the APC would add the right amount of power to maintain "on glide path." [Fast forward to the time of writing this book …. pilotless, unmanned aircraft are being landed on aircraft carriers using only radar, TV and sensors within the airplane.]

Fresnel Lens Fluctuations … When the seas are calm and the ship is stable, a perfect approach down the glide slope results in about a 14-foot clearance between the tailhook and the round-down. With a bouncing ship that's an entirely different situation. The LSO can increase or decrease the angle of the glide slope about half a degree up or down depending on the motion of the ship. Remember that the carrier always "turns into the wind" to have the wind blowing straight across the deck fore to aft …. which helps catapult launches and landings. The wind across the deck allows the minimum safe flying speed of the aircraft to be less relative to the ship's motion. With an F-4 Phantom at air speed of 130 knots but a 30-knot wind across the deck, the difference between ship and plane would only be 100 knots at touchdown and arrest.

What does the Fresnel Lens system do with a bouncing ship? Good question. Does it flip all over the sky? That would make it impossible to find and fly down to the ship. The Fresnel Lens light system is mounted on a floating carriage which is controlled by a gyroscope to hold the beam steady in the sky. In effect the gyroscope holds the glide slope beam in a constant fixed position as it adjusts for every movement of the ship.

Denouement of an Approach and Trap … So, Aaron Aviator (a.k.a. Double A) has flown a perfect approach, solid in the groove and smooth touchdown …. he immediately adds full military power which includes afterburners. This is in case his tailhook does not engage and he needs flying speed power if he finds himself flying off the forward end of the angled deck. If his tailhook catches a wire, it will stop him even with full power and it pulls him slightly backward. At that point he pulls back power. If the hook still holds the cable, a crewman separates it. The pilot then revs a little and taxis to the designated spot, usually forward (if not simultaneous launching in progress), but aft and to starboard of the angled deck also sometimes. He could even go to the starboard elevator, shut down and have the plane taken to the hangar deck.

Scoring Traps ... If there is a perfect approach and catching the No. 3 or No. 4 wire, that is a ten-point score. Scores go on down depending on other factors. A complete miss for a "go around" or a wave-off is called a Bolter. (See squadron competition on scoring elsewhere.)

Hook Skip ... Sometimes everything is perfect but the tailhook misses the arresting cable. The tailhook protrudes down and is spring-loaded to keep downward pressure on the deck at contact, but sometimes it bounces and that is called a hook-skip. Dang.... perfect approach and touchdown and the hook missed.

The Barrier ... If a tailhook breaks or malfunctions, there is another backup arresting mechanism. Two stanchions come up out of the deck with a net stretched between them. It is called the barrier, is made of steel net and looks a little like a huge tennis net. In an emergency it is used to catch the plane.

Weather Sweat ... Sometimes during flight ops it would be raining like crazy and/or there would be the high seas of swells and waves and/or pitch-black night and/or pitching deck, rolling deck, yawing deck and any combination .... and sometimes all of that at the same time. In those situations, it wasn't just wet outside on the flight deck and in the air. It was wet inside from all the sweat exuded by everyone. The worry was almost a universal "all hands" evolution. Everybody was worried. Those old navy macho, disclaimers of nonchalance, "No sweat" or "Piece of Cake" were nowhere to be heard. Most of the worry was unspoken, but the tension was palpable. As bolters became increasingly frequent, the more the tension and sweat. Eyes stayed glued to radar screens and TV monitors all over the ship. We listened intently to the radio transmissions between pilot and LSO and radar controller. When a trap was successful and the aircrew was safely aboard, there was an audible sigh of relief.

The Tanker ... When an aircraft or several were getting low on fuel, a tanker would be launched. This was another airplane fitted with one or more external fuel tanks and a drogue at the end of a hose for inflight refueling. Of course, now the tanker was in the air and had to get back aboard also. In the open sea too far from land to reach an airstrip, there were only two results…. get back aboard or eject and let the plane crash into the sea…. and hope you were picked up by the helo or destroyer escort.

Bingo … No, we didn't play bingo in the ready rooms. Bingo was a bad word. If the ship were close enough to solid land, a "bingo field" was always selected and briefed in the ready room during preflight planning. If too many bolters occurred, or an aircraft's tailhook was non-functional, or there was a landing gear problem …. or for any reason really that the pilot could not get back aboard, he could call a bingo and go land on the designated "bingo field" …. the solid airstrip ashore. The ship could instruct him to bingo as well. It didn't happen often but when it did, it was important. Fortunately, in the Mediterranean we were nearly always close enough to land to have a bingo field if needed. The open ocean is another story.

Declaration… Please consider this a declaration by the author that there is indeed some truth to that Naval Aviator joke related above. Yep, vouching for its veracity because THERE I WUZ.

VULTURE'S ROW

PSYCHOLOGICALLY LIKE WATCHING HIGHWIRE PERFORMERS WITHOUT A NET

WHEN FLIGHT OPERATIONS were in progress a thousand eyes or more watched every catapult launch and every approach and trap. The people on the flight deck of course were working to assist and assure safety. The radar technicians and officers were watching from the bowels of the ship ... both on their radar screens and on television screens. Every ready room, wardroom and most everywhere else had TV screens. They showed flight ops while going on and at other times had announcements and occasional programs. So, people watched and there may have been two thousand eyes on the aircraft coming and going.... especially in rough weather.

The Air Boss from his tower vantage point in the island and the officers on the bridge, also on the island, all had unobstructed views of everything including their own radar and TV monitors.

However, if you wanted the best observation spot, it was Vulture's Row. About halfway up the island at the very aft part there was an outdoor deck, like the catwalk, but larger. The space could accommodate at least twenty or thirty people and frequently there would be a dozen or more watching flight ops. The height above the flight deck and the island position away from the angled deck approach glide path provided an element of safety not present on the flight deck itself.

Vulture's Row was outdoors so you could not only see, but also hear, feel and smell all the action. The combination of the ship's fuel oil from the stacks, the JP-5 exhaust from aircraft and spilled on the deck sometimes ... plus an ocean salt-air breeze... was an intriguing odor. Combined with the other sensory inputs it was an exciting place to be.

The name derived from the psychological thrill of watching people do any dangerous and hazardous activity. Intellectually and deep in their feelings of course everyone hoped for and always worked diligently for safety. However, Vulture's Row gathered its observers because there was that emotional "what if some disaster happened" in people and they wanted to witness it. Psychologically that is like watching highwire performers with no net and in some ways like watching public hangings, horror movies and murder mysteries. Risk and fear both give one an adrenalin rush whether you are at risk or just watching someone else who is.

Watching flight ops from Vulture's Row was second only to being in the aircraft yourself.... which is covered in more detail on other pages.

So, of course, THERE I WUZ on Vulture's Row watching flight ops and especially approaches and traps. Sometimes I had an 8mm camera in hand taking movies of everything. Besides that adrenalin thrill I was also fact-gathering as I recognized the planes, observed the approaches and watched the flight crews climb down from their big steel birds. Sometimes it was valuable information, sometimes not .... but always exciting.

VII

MARINES AT SEA

THE MARINE DETACHMENT

MOST PEOPLE DON'T think about Marines on an aircraft carrier. They forget that the U.S. Marine Corps is part of the U.S. Navy. They forget that the Marines were founded on 10 November 1775 to have armed infantry on navy ships with the capacity and intent to go ashore and fight various enemies. For over two centuries Marines have served on ships and on land with a highly distinguished record. Such was the case on *U.S.S Independence* on the 1966 Med Cruise.

We had a detachment of about 60-70 Marines, maybe it was more, maybe less.

Why were they there? We had no intention of mounting an amphibious assault. Our power and combat effectiveness were by air attack. Our Marine detachment was there for security and in a police role. Here is a synopsis of the various duties performed by the Marines:

1. **Personal Escort Guards** .... The Captain of the carrier, the Executive Officer and the Task Force Admiral (when aboard) had a Marine guard escort 24/7/365. If they were asleep, the Marine was just outside the hatch of their quarters. If they were on the bridge, their Marine was unobtrusively nearby. If they walked anywhere on the ship, their Marine escort followed dutifully. The Marines wore sidearms and were prepared to

use them if need arose. Undoubtedly the Marines had regular four-hour duty watches just like so many others onboard. They rotated "by the bells."

2.   **Nuclear-armed Ready Plane Guards** .... The hangar deck had a "Ready Plane" in one corner 24/7/365 whether at sea or in port... with a Marine guard close at hand. The aircraft was armed with a nuclear weapon and completely fueled and ready for launch at any time. There was a stanchion-and-rope perimeter around the plane and you better not try to get within it. The quietly efficient Marine even eyed you with suspicion if you stopped to look. The pilot(s) was in the ready room, in flight gear and prebriefed on the potential target. Around the clock enough personnel were ready for immediate launch within thirty minutes of receiving the order. (As a newbie, at first, I wondered why there always seemed to be a couple of guys in full flight gear lounging around one of the ready rooms when NO flight operations were in progress.) Even with the ship at anchor or tied to a pier the plane could launch by cranking up the power of the catapult. Remember the Indy was a war ship and Viet Nam fighting was concurrent even though in the Mediterranean it often seemed like a peace-time cruise in the Navy. (Also remember that I had worked my fanny off at NAMI in Pensacola to be there rather than in Viet Nam.)

The Ready Plane was guarded by a Marine with automatic weapon, sidearm and radio. Likely the whole detachment would have been there rapidly upon radio summons.

3.   **The Brig** .... One of the other important duties of the Marines was operating the brig. Never underestimate the potential for fighting and other miscreant behavior among thousands of young men living and working together in cramped quarters, without women, alcohol, sports or other tension-relieving activities. Sometimes basketball games, volleyball, boxing matches and the like were conducted on the hangar deck during down time but

it was irregular and didn't include everyone. There was a movie every evening everywhere around the ship. (More on that later.)

Also remember the large percentage of the crew under the age of twenty-five which is about when the frontal lobe completes its development. Frontal lobe maturity brings more emotional maturity and self-control which is sometimes in short supply among the 18–25-year-old male population.

Here is where that old navy saying applies, "A busy sailor is a happy sailor." Centuries of experience and the wisdom of senior sailors, both enlisted and officers, understands that too much leisure on a ship can lead to discontent and aggression. So, the military work schedules pretty much keep everyone busy all the time except when they are eating, sleeping, watching a movie, attending to personal requirements (a.k.a. triple-S.), etc. With sleep often difficult from noise, vibration, cramped quarters disturbances, etc. it is easy to become sleep deprived with resultant irritability, etc.

So, among our few thousands of young sailors there were always a few who became involved in unacceptable behavior. They would be arrested and taken before the "Captain's Mast." (See section thereon.) If after a hearing of the facts a sailor was not acquitted, some form of "non-judicial" punishment could be ordered. (Sailors are no longer lashed to the mast of a sailing ship and whipped.) Punishments on the Indy could be loss of pay, reduction in rank, etc..... or a few days in the brig, including even "bread and water" for up to three days.

That's where the Marines came in. They ran the brig which had cells with bars, controlled spaces and locked entrance. At least two Marines and sometimes more were there 24/7. Additional details are in another section.

4. **Nukes and Gold** .... There was an obscure locked vault-like door in one of the inner passageways which always had a Marine guard...again with automatic weapon, sidearm and radio. It

wasn't much discussed and you weren't supposed to ask, but the scuttlebutt was that the spaces contained our nuclear weapons and about six million dollars in gold bullion. The nukes were there for obvious reasons. The gold was in case some foreign monetary need arose. Neither the nukes nor the gold was ever confirmed or denied. I think it was classified information .... just like the flank (top) speed of the carrier which is lots more than admitted. Anyway, whatever was in that locked compartment was guarded by a Marine 24/7.

5. **IOIC** .... The Information and Operational Intelligence Center was off limits to anyone without "top secret clearance AND a need to know." It was where all the secrets were kept, strategic, tactical, charts, targets, et al. There was a locked door with a one-way window beside it and an armed Marine guard on duty behind it. He could see you but you couldn't see him.

THE BRIG

OUR MARINE DETACHMENT served as the guards in the brig on Indy. There were always at least two Marines there. The shifts rotated by the bells like everything else. Sailors were confined to the brig for several reasons…. fighting, theft, dereliction of duty, failure to follow navy procedures such as cleanliness, respect for seniors and others. There were about a dozen barred and locked cells, a central space, the guard station from which every corner could be observed. Even the shower and toilet facilities were open and observable by the guards. There was always observation and scrutiny of every prisoner. The entire brig unit had a strong locked door at the entrance as well so no one could bolt and run out from the central space.

Usually, a problem with a sailor would be presented at a "Captain's Mast" which was a hearing of the facts and accusations and where the sailor would have a chance to defend his actions or explain a situation. A senior line officer would conduct the hearings but usually not the actual captain of Indy despite the traditional name…. which was derived from days of sailing ships when the captain would hear grievances at the main mast daily.

The rules of the UCMJ (Uniform Code of Military Justice) were followed. The UCMJ is federal law. The sailor could be acquitted or assigned various punishments commensurate with the infraction. Punishments might be reprimand, partial forfeiture of pay, confinement to the brig for 3-30 days, including a sentence of only bread and water (B&W) for up to three days in most cases, removal from the ship, recommendation for dishonorable discharge... whatever. There were almost always three to six sailors in the brig, sometimes more.

There was no physical punishment but the Marines kept the prisoners busy ALL THE TIME. There was NO leisure. Every activity was on a tight schedule. Sleep was certain hours, reveille at a given time, Triple-S on a schedule, shoeshine time, write a letter home time, exercise time, mealtime.... everything on a rigid schedule. The Marines even had a procedure for the occasional period when something else wasn't happening. It was called "Shine the Deck." Each prisoner would be given two pieces of cloth about a footlong and six inches wide. One would be placed under each shoe. The prisoner would be required to shuffle his feet back and forth for whatever length of time was necessary and literally shine the deck... which had an almost mirror-like finish.

My familiarity with the brig and its protocol was because the MOD (Medical Officer of the Day) was required to inspect the brig daily, usually after the evening meal or after the movie but anytime was okay and surprise visits were encouraged. The medical staff was responsible for health and safety throughout the ship but the MOD had responsibility for the prisoners in the brig each day. So, I would go every fourth day. Each prisoner was given an opportunity to talk with the MOD in private, out of earshot of the guards, so he could relate any health problems, abuse issues or whatever. The MOD was his outside appeal if he were being mistreated. I never had anyone complain of abuse or mistreatment. They were not happy sailors, but they were cared for and the rules were followed ... albeit meticulously and rigidly.

VMA-324

THE MARINE ATTACK Squadron 324 (V = fixed wing, M = marine, A = attack) was deployed with us on the Indy for the Med Cruise. That was an anomaly for several reasons. First, although Marine Aviators have the same training as Naval Aviators, including carrier landings and launches, their squadrons are infrequently deployed on aircraft carriers going to the Mediterranean, especially during the Viet Nam era when their firepower was needed to support regular land-based Marines. Secondly, we already had one A-4 Skyhawk squadron in Carrier Airwing Seven (CVW-7) [You should be getting the hang of these designation initials by now] and so the Marines were an "extra" squadron or maybe substituted for a Navy squadron.

The third anomaly was that VMA-324 provided an extra flight surgeon onboard. Normally a deployed airwing has two flight surgeons attached to its staff to serve all the squadrons and who also supplement the two ship's company physicians for non-aviation normal medical care. However Marine squadrons mostly each have their own flight surgeon. (That's one of the reasons so many of my NAMI class of docs were assigned to the Marines.) The VMA-324 flight surgeon was Gene Purvis who had an interesting background. He had been a Marine before going to medical school. When he graduated with his M.D. and resumed his military career, he arranged to retain his status as a Marine officer rather than becoming a naval officer and naval flight surgeon. That was very unusual and he may have been the only Marine Flight Surgeon in the Corps.

It was good to have Gene with us. First, he was a great guy .... bright, perceptive, competent, friendly and open .... and willing to carry his workload and more. Besides taking care of his squadron he helped with sick call and the health care needs of everybody onboard. It also gave us an extra physician in the rotation of Medical Officer of the Day (MOD) ... a rotation just like a call schedule for most physicians at hospitals and group practices. Our senior medical officer did not deign to take a position in the rotation nor help much with other medical care. With the ship's board-eligible surgeon Al Taquino and the three flight surgeons that allowed us to be MOD every fourth day instead of every third.

On one of my first days aboard *Independence,* I was walking forward along the port main deck passageway when suddenly a red-headed aviator in an orange flight suit came walking the opposite way. It was Steve Bratton from Arkansas who had been an SAE fraternity brother at Tulane undergraduate. Small world department. Steve was a Marine Aviator with VMA-324 and it was fun to hang out some with him all through the cruise. He also was a good introduction to the Marine squadron during my "FAM" (familiarization) period onboard. The Marines were very welcoming and rapidly included me in their group. I think the Corps has a longstanding liking for physicians.

VMA-324 had the usual squadron complement of a dozen or so A-4 Skyhawks, 20-25 aviators and a few hundred enlisted support personnel for maintenance, weapons, admin, etc. so we had a significant Marine presence in addition to the ship's company security Marines.

IX

POTPOURRI AFLOAT

ODDS AND ENDS

SHELL CASINGS ... Recall those posts used for a white rope corridor when piping in the Captain or Admiral. From time to time the Indy had target practice with its five-inch guns. Those shell casings were impressive when polished. They were about three feet high. I obtained two and planned to polish them and fit wooden tips on them like on the Indy. Alas, I stowed them under the house in NOLA, then became much too busy to worry about them. A few years later they had rusted beyond consideration. They may still be under that house.

Helo Rescue Training (while ashore) ... One day at Oceana a group of us went to the Little Creek Amphibious Base in our flight suits and went out in Chesapeake Bay for practicing helicopter rescue techniques. It was fun going out in one of those large "ducks" that drive on land then go right out in the water to function like a boat.... amphibious indeed. About three or four of us at a time jumped off into the water about thirty yards apart. The "angel" helo flew to one after another and hovered to let down the "horseshoe" collar on a cable for plucking us out of the water. We had been versed in the technique of slipping into it and hooking both arms over it as we were lifted into the helicopter. The helo took our group to shore, then went back out for the next group. Check that training exercise off our list of annual requirements.

Sea Lawyers ... There are always a few sailors who know all the regulations and try to "skate" around them. They use technicalities to get out of doing work. They are often argumentative and usually irritate everyone around them.

Sea Stories ... a.k.a. "nautical fiction." Some of the stories sailors tell are true, some are complete fabrications. There is fun in the telling and in the listening. Lots of sea stories are told by seasoned "sea dogs" to younger newbies who are struggling to learn. Some of the tales are true enough to have value and some are total BS. Seeing a twitch of a smile or a twinkle in the eye can be a clue to the veracity of the sea dog's sea story.

Old Salt ... an experienced seasoned sailor, like sea dogs.

Salty Language ... a.k.a. foul language. Sailors are notorious for this. It was especially true with an all-male crew where few seemed offended at some of the foul words, language and metaphors uttered by sailors.... and the nightly parade of drunks returning from shore leave seemed to have mastered the art. (See "Bosun's Incident" for a <u>mild</u> example.)

Slang, Lingo, Abbreviations and other Navy Language Patterns .... Yes, "navy speak" is a language all its own. It is far too extensive to elaborate here but the internet is filled with Glossaries, Lingo Lists and assorted examples of how sailors think, talk and communicate. At first exposure it's like a foreign language, but you get into the swing of it and learn more and more until you understand most of it (emphasize most, not all.) Lots of it comes from centuries of seafaring tradition, especially naval history and terminology. It's a fascinating and amusing field which is highly recommended to interested parties. Try looking up "Navy Fighter Pilot's Lingo" by H. Paul "Viking" Lillebo. It will keep you laughing while explaining a lot of important aspects of naval aviation and carrier operations.

IN VINO VERITAS

EXCEPTIONS TO THE RULES ON A DRY SHIP

SOME NAVIES ALLOW alcoholic beverages on their military ships, even issuing daily rations, but by long tradition U.S. Navy ships have been "dry." That certainly was the case with Indy, but there were exceptions. The Indy had a large stash of beer in 24/12oz can cases somewhere in the hold. I know this because we broke it out and consumed a bunch of it on the beach in Argostoli Bay, Greece. (See separate section.)

We also had a goodly supply of whiskey and brandy in the sickbay pharmacy. It was there "for medicinal purposes." [A little-known fact is that lots of hospitals keep whiskey, brandy, etc. in their pharmacies for the same reason.] The bourbon was in fifth size bottles (25.6 oz.) and brandy was in little two-ounce bottles (like on airlines), ten bottles in a cardboard carton. The brands were unknown with nondescript labels and the quality matched... not particularly good .... except they contained alcohol. That was their purpose for being there. The physicians and especially the flight surgeons could write a prescription for a "fifth" of bourbon and/or a ten-pack of brandy.

There were lots of hazardous situations on the carrier, the most frequent being flight ops. When a pilot had a close call and was exhibiting excessive anxiety and/or distress behavior we would issue one or two (sometimes more) little bottles of brandy to calm the nerves. Sometimes a ration of bourbon whiskey was indicated. Al Cohen and I kept a small supply of both options in our room. Sometimes we would just issue the brandy or whiskey (we refilled the empty 2-oz brandy bottles with bourbon to dispense if that were the preferred choice of the recipient.) The stressed-out flight crew would then retreat to their room, imbibe and get some sleep. It was a form of sedative.... administered for medicinal purposes.

Sometimes we would invite the pilot, RIO, B/N and/or other flight crew to our room, sometimes one, sometimes several. We would supply whatever they reasonably needed to relax .... even sometimes helping them to their room and putting them to bed. One of the reasons for having them in the room was to allow an opportunity for them to talk about the experience, to tell the THERE I WUZ story. In the privacy of our room a pilot could talk freely just like going to a physician to share confidential medical information. They couldn't discuss fear, anxiety, etc. in the ready room surrounded by peers, but they could "open up" in our room, sharing confidential feelings. Sometimes the invitation to our room was to keep the "medicinal purposes" out of public knowledge and "on the quiet."

The whiskey and brandy relaxed them enough for "In Vino Veritas" .... translated, "in wine there is truth" .... and alcohol is notorious for loosening the tongue and having people speak things they wouldn't say if completely sober. We were practicing a little psychotherapy while we were bartending. Don't a lot of bartenders do that routinely ashore?

We didn't ordinarily carry around the little 2-oz. bottles but sometimes in hazardous conditions for flight ops we would slip a couple into our pocket. Many times, the pilots et al would not ask for whiskey/ brandy because aviation macho just doesn't condone any sign of less than calm perfection.... but they usually seemed quite happy when offered and gladly accepted. When not flying ourselves, we watched flight ops most of the time they were in progress, so we knew when close calls and stressful situations occurred … and who the aircrew were.

We never flew at the same time so one of us was "on duty" while the other was in the air. Gene Purvis, our Marine flight surgeon made it two on the ship when one was flying. Since TV screens all over the ship showed flight ops, we could be in a squadron ready room "hanging out," in the radar center or even in sickbay, the wardroom, almost anywhere.

We discovered an interesting phenomenon. We had a small sink in our room for washup, brushing teeth, shaving, etc. To prevent ever having a faucet left on and overflow the sink, maybe flowing into the passageway, etc. …. all the faucets had spring loaded controls. You pushed down to get water and automatically the push-knob moved back gradually to cutoff.

Anyone who has served on a navy ship probably remembers that the water lines often had air in them. Even taking a shower the water would often sputter a little from the showerhead.

We discovered that if you partially depressed the push-knob on the sink with just the right technique, you could accentuate the bubbly air escape. The result was almost soda water, even if imagination helped that diagnosis. So…. we could fix a bourbon and soda or a brandy and soda as well as straight shots and plain whiskey and water. We felt so sophisticated.

NOTE: Occasionally there were others besides flight crew who benefitted from "medicinal use" alcoholic sedation. Once in a while sailors had to don wet suits and SCUBA gear to go under the ship to fix something. They came back blue with cold and shivering … fitting use for our medications. If some machinery malfunctioned, the sailors involved might need our help for calming their nerves. Jet blast, falls, close calls and other flight deck encounters were not uncommon. We were careful of the need but were not stingy with our offers for brandy or bourbon. Even working outdoors in bad weather, rain and/or cold rendered some sailors in need of libation.

Smuggling Wine … This one I can admit after the fact. That summer of 1963 at Oak Knoll Naval Hospital and the internship in San Francisco had introduced me to good wine with many trips to the California wine country, sipping at winery tasting rooms, et al. I had brought along several books about wine. Wine was a growing interest that eventually became a passion and more. Previously related was the Tale of the Banda Azul in Barcelona. I was exploring European wines and learning more and more. Sometimes I would find a wine or two that just needed buying. What to do?

I had one of those Samsonite hard-shell black briefcases. It was a perfect fit for up to five regular size bottles of wine. It happened that there was a perfect wine cellar/storage space in my room. Each officer on board had a steel locker, desk, closet and drawer combination unit. If you pulled out the bottom drawer there was a void space between the deck and the bottom of the drawer that was about four inches or so. A bottle of wine fit in there perfectly.

Now that was important because officers had the privilege of stewards coming into their rooms several times a week to get the nylon mesh-net laundry bag, deliver clean laundry back, empty trash cans, etc. We had to keep our bourbon and brandy supply out of sight and I had found a perfect place to hide a few bottles of wine.

So, I began picking up a few bottles of wine in various ports of call and bringing them back aboard in my hard-shell briefcase. There was a double rationale operating here. I was smuggling wine aboard, but also had the privilege of providing alcoholic beverages for medicinal purposes. Going up the gangway, saluting the flag and then "Requesting permission to come aboard, Sir" while carrying a case stocked with wine was always something of a "flutter." The OOD of course had the right and authority to search anyone boarding the ship, refusing to accept them, to arrest someone .... and the Bosun had a sidearm.

On the other hand, the OOD recognized my medical insignia and after a while they knew me and I knew most of them. It was never a problem and permission was always promptly granted. I don't think the OOD cared what was in the briefcase and even if he had known it was wine, he probably wouldn't have cared. My rationale was that if ever stopped, inspected, "busted" or whatever, the wine was "for medicinal purposes." That was according to the rules and I don't think anything would have come of it if challenged.

In practice, we provided more bourbon and brandy for medicinal purposes than I had smuggled wine …. and I never served any of the wine.

Surprise …. by the end of the cruise, I had stashed one hundred bottles of wine under my desk/closet/drawer console. The most difficult part was getting it off the ship at the pier in Norfolk on return. I had to do it before the ship went into drydock. I could only carry so much, even as a healthy, fit young 27-year-old. It took many trips from dockside automobile, up the gang, into the bowels of the ship including ladders! … get a load, back to the ladders, gangway and to the car. It was good exercise.

Over the next year and a half, we drank along on the special bottles…. mostly when entertaining someone. For daily wine, the NAS Oceana Navy Exchange had a well-stocked wine department with a good selection of reasonably priced wines. By June of 1968 when packing for the move to New Orleans there were exactly twelve bottles left, mostly the very most special. Eventually we drank them all with relish and fond memories of their provenance.

IN VINO VERITAS

X

PORTS OF CALL

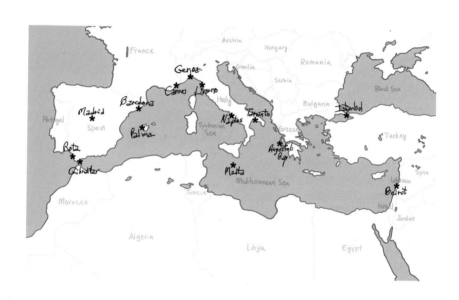

PORTS OF CALL ... SIGHTSEEING AND SOUVENIRS

"I joined the Navy, to see the world....
and what did I see? ...."

I SAW THE SEA. That is the finish phrase of the song, but in fact on the Med Cruise we were in port probably thirty to forty percent of the eight months. I think that was more than usual and there were several reasons: (1) Some of our crew, both officers and enlisted, had served on the previous Indy cruise to combat in Viet Nam. (2) The costs of operations in port were significantly less than at sea. (Fuel costs for both ship and aircraft, plus others.) (3) The med cruise was a public relations cruise to some extent to bolster good will during the Viet Nam combat. We received foreign national visitors and we also supported official reciprocal visits with foreign dignitaries and VIPs both military and civilian. (4) The Navy understood that morale and work efficiency were enhanced by shore leave for crew.

So here is a synopsis of the ports we visited (listed in the approximate order of the cruise) with the local sightseeing opportunities and some of the most common souvenirs purchased by the crewmen. Overall, we had marvelous port calls and educational opportunities.

1. **Cannes, France (First Visit)** … The French Riviera conjures fantasies of beaches and beautiful women. It was July and they were there in abundance … in bikinis … and the sailors were fascinated. The photographer's mates took photos of little else. Of course, there were plentiful bars, casinos and sidewalk cafes that also filled with sailors on shore leave. Souvenirs: bikinis for the lady back stateside, perfumes, exotic canned goods. Side Trips: Paris

2. **Barcelona, Spain (First Visit)** … From the statue of Christopher Columbus who sailed from here in 1492, up the Rambla for a casual stroll, interesting architecture including that of Antoni Gaudi, Spanish cuisine, flamenco dancers, bullfights, lots to see and do here. Souvenir: always postcards to send stateside, castanets, *banderillas*, matador hats, Spanish folding fans, clothing, exotic foods.

3. **Naples (First Visit)** … This is the home port of the Sixth Fleet and we entertained dignitaries both foreign and U.S. plus a Change of Command ceremony as Captain Fox relieved Captain Kennedy. Mount Vesuvius and Pompeii were popular sightseeing locales. Italian food was popular, pasta, *spinachi al burro*, many more. Souvenirs: Cameo shell jewelry, statuettes of Vesuvius, postcards of wall drawings in Pompeii. Side Trips: Rome.

4. **Istanbul** … Through the Dardanelles, the Sea of Marmara and to a pier in the Bosporus. The Hagia Sophia and Blue Mosques with their minarets dominate the skyline. Interesting police patrols of three… one each Army, Navy, Air Force. Exotic street food including tiny grills, doner kebab, raki, Fez headgear, the Golden Horn, crowded cemeteries, shoeshine men everywhere. Souvenirs: a myriad of things from the extensive booths and stalls in the Grand Bazaar…. evil eye pendants, puzzle rings, wire fish perfume holders, jewelry, small rugs, the list is endless.

5. **Valletta, Malta** ... a big rock island south of Sicily in the middle Mediterranean. Valetta was an interesting port with prominent old stone fortresses; evidence of great wealth in the past; lots of barren countryside out of the city, subterranean caves dating back to 4,000 BC for tours. Souvenirs: not too many. Side trips: none. Cuisine: not interesting.

6. **Taranto, Italy** ... Located in the instep of the Italian boot configuration, traditional fleet location. Unfortunately, it was a filthy city ... garbage in the streets, downtrodden and rundown buildings and be careful not to step in dog-do. Oh well, it was shore leave.

7. **Beirut, Lebanon** ... Exotic from every perspective, different culture, mix of modern and old architecture; strong dark coffee in little cups with "mud" settling in the bottom, arak, Fleet Canteen setup in Phoenix Hotel (see separate article.) Souvenirs: brass coffee tables, camel saddles, handheld coffee grinders, inlaid wooden trinket boxes, pistachio nuts, artisanal clothing and fabric with real gold threads. Side Trip: Jerusalem (see separate article.)

8. **Argostoli Bay, Greece** ... See separate article.

9. **Naples (Second Visit)** ... See above but no Change of Command ceremony. Had foreign nationals onboard when the Arab Incident occurred (See separate article.)

10. **Genoa, Italy** ... A prominent port city on the west side of Italy, tucked under the Alps. Lots of side trips: Munich for beer, oompah band music, lederhosen and dirndls; Venice for canals and gondolas, pigeons in San Marco square; skiing in the Alps. Great Piedmont wines such as Barolo, Barbaresco, Gattinara; game dishes in restaurants, white truffles, cheeses.

11. **Palma de Mallorca, Spain** ... A beautiful city at the top of the expansive Bay of Palma. Green hills inland, lots of nightclubs in the city with shows, music, bars aplenty. Famous for beach life, but too cold on our visit. Only side trips were inland tours.

Food like Barcelona, souvenirs not unusual. (See separate article for medical incident.) We didn't go ashore but as some point on the cruise we went into Polensa Bay on the north opposite side of Mallorca.

12. **Cannes, France (Second Visit)** ... No bikinis at Christmas. Rather cold except for the interior of bars. Some went skiing in the French Alps. (See separate article "The Gleaming Bastard.")

13. **Livorno, Italy** ... Midway on west coast of Italy. Gateway to Florence (see separate article), Pisa, Tuscan hillsides with vineyards and olive trees. Good Italian wines, Chianti, Brunello, etc.

14. **Barcelona (Second Visit)** ... Formal "Dining In" at the Avenida Palace Hotel (See separate article) also twice more to Guria (see article.) For sightseeing, see 2. above and another separate article for other activities in Barcelona.

ISTANBUL

WALKING WORRY AND TURKISH INTERROGATION

I HAD MADE a habit of walking a great deal during port calls. It was a good way to get a feel for the city. The fresh air and open spaces were welcome. There was plenty of open space in the ocean but mostly we worked inside the ship except for flight time and catwalk interludes. So walk I did and poked into some interesting places. Nowhere did it feel unsafe except for some of the back places in Istanbul. My sense of direction was good and I always had maps so getting lost was not likely. With all the ladders on the ship fitness was peak, so off I would go.

One day in Istanbul I took a dolmus (shared taxi) into the Golden Horn area. Indy was moored on the Bosporus a fair distance east and a little far to walk. After crossing the Golden Horn, I left the dolmus and it was an easy walk to Topkapi museum, Hagia Sophia and the Blue Mosque. It was amazing to see men carrying huge and heavy loads on their backs all over the city.

After a fruitful morning I went back to the Horn for a grilled fish lunch at a street cart on the pier. Everywhere you went in Istanbul there were men walking around with little water tanks on their backs, a few metal cups and a hose coming from the bottom of the tank for filling them. They were selling drinking water. Not for me.... a little hazardous. Bottled beer was safer.

Walking again I started up the west side of the Horn. On a previous visit I had enjoyed dinner at a famous restaurant at the top of the Horn. The cemeteries on the way up are crowded with tight body density and have the most interesting headstones. A great many stones had Fez hats carved on them at the top indicating an old cemetery because wearing a Fez was outlawed by Kemal Ataturk decades ago as he brought Turkey into the modern world after World War One.

It was starting to be late afternoon so I headed back to the center. Perhaps I had walked a little too far inland or perhaps I was just in the wrong neighborhood but the sun was starting to set and people were giving me the most suspicious looks. Obviously, I was an American and maybe they didn't like me being where I was. Probably I wasn't in danger but that tickle-on-the-back-of-the-neck apprehension was getting my attention. My pace quickened as I walked down out of the narrow darkening streets to the base of the Horn to take a dolmus back out to the ship.

Turkish Interrogation ... Blap, blap ("scream") Blap, Blap ("rapid shouting in Turkish"), Blap... On arrival back at the Indy, there was a remarkable scene. The action was in a small wooden building, little more than a shack. It was out in the expanse of the dock and was used by the Shore Patrol as headquarters. Inland from the "shack" in an open space was a large circular rope corral containing several hundred rundown-looking local men. Surrounding the rope corral were about fifty Turkish soldiers and sailors and airmen. Istanbul police patrols are in threes, one each from the military branches. The Turkish military police were armed and facing the corral to guard the prisoners. Off to one side were about fifty or sixty of us from the ship, both officers and enlisted. I joined the group to observe what in hell was going on.

Someone explained what had happened. These Turkish prisoners were all shoeshine "boys" in the corral. They were all grown men, no boys in the lot. They worked all over Istanbul, mostly downtown and near the mosques where the tourists strolled around every day. They each carried a small wooden box with a footrest on top. Shoe polish, rags and brushes were inside the boxes. We had seen them and some of us had purchased shines. After negotiating a customer for a shoeshine, the shine-man would put his box down, retrieve the materials from inside and the customer would put his foot on the footrest. First one shoe then the other would be shined and the fee collected. Business was probably booming with the ship in town and so many sailors on shore leave.... all wanting a good shine for military uniform standards.

Apparently, what had happened was that a shoeshine man had held a razor blade to the Achilles tendon above the heel of a sailor getting a shine ... then demanded money or else he would cut the tendon.

SIDE NOTE: That's interesting because the medical/anatomical name of the tendon came from the mythology of Greek warrior Achilles getting shot with an arrow in his only vulnerable spot, his heel.... and that occurred in nearly this same place in the world several thousand years BC in the ancient city of Troy whose location on the Dardanelles is now part of modern Turkey. What goes around comes around, a.k.a. history repeats.

So, the Indy sailor reported the incident to our Shore Patrol who reported it to their companion local military police. The Turkish triad patrols had rounded up every shoeshine man in the city and brought them to the dock for interrogation to find out "who dun it." They were taking the shoe-shiners into the shack one at a time. We could hear the loud strokes, probably with a blunt instrument or leather strap ... and the screams of the victim of the moment. Blap, blap, blap.

We stood watching and listening for quite a while as our group of spectators got larger when more sailors would return to board Indy. After beating one prisoner after another, tossing them out and bringing another in for "interrogation," finally someone must have 'squealed.' We couldn't understand the Turkish shouting and talking but the body language and actions were easily interpreted. The military police waded into the crowd of prisoners and identified the culprit. They handcuffed him and put him in the back of a "paddy wagon" which roared off down the road. Heaven only knows what happened to him.

The Turkish police shouted some things to the prisoners, probably warnings and threats of consequences for bad behavior. Then they removed the rope corral and "shoo-ed" the prisoners out to the road and their freedom. The show was over so we went aboard Indy. You don't want any part of Turkish "justice" and I think their prisons are very brutal as well.

SIDE NOTE: You don't want Turkish "Measurement" either. The previous year on a visit to Istanbul a Turkish tailor was measuring my wife for a custom-tailored suede leather coat. His hands were taking liberties on intimate parts of the female figure. She was very embarrassed and I became angry. A "Turkish Measurement" has been a family joke ever since.

BEIRUT BACKFIRES

THE FLEET CANTEEN TO PROTECT
SAILORS HEALTH GOES AWRY

THE INDY AND other ships in the battle group sailed into Beirut, Lebanon. This was before the Middle East fighting destroyed the city. In 1966 Beirut was known as the "Paris of the Middle East." It was a beautiful city architecturally. It had a rich cultural tradition. There was a prominent American ex-pat community. The American University of Beirut (AUB) was founded in 1866, officially chartered in New York and offered excellent college and postgraduate education including MD and PhD degrees. Beirut even had a branch of the Lido, that famous high-end night club in Paris. Everyone was in great anticipation of our port call in Beirut.

During the Med Cruise we had diagnosed and treated a fair number of cases of infectious hepatitis. The virus was obviously contracted by eating ashore and the supposed culprit was salads, unwashed fruit or other foods prepared by people with questionable hygiene. Our Medical Department had expressed concern over the visit to Beirut where the prevalence of hepatitis was known. There were always advance personnel and planning before a port call so it was decided to set up a Fleet Canteen ashore where sailors could eat at no cost. The food would be prepared on Indy and thus eliminate the risk of eating hepatitis-causing foods ashore.

The advance team established contacts with the American ex-pat community and the AUB. Arrangements were made with the Phoenix Hotel to set up a canteen to provide food, beverages and entertainment for sailors on shore leave. The ship would supply the food and ex-pat volunteers would set up and serve the food and beverages. Everyone was happy with the plan, the arrangements and the benefit of avoiding infectious hepatitis.

In we sailed to Beirut and moored to the pier. The Phoenix Hotel was an easy walk from the ship. Our mess deck crew prepared an array of food for transport to the hotel. All was well.

UNTIL …. THERE I WUZ … one evening on the Indy as the MOD expecting our usual collection of drunks and minor injuries. Gradually we began receiving sailors with diarrhea and vomiting. First just a few came into sickbay and we paid little attention. Then more arrived, then more.

Something was going on. Most of the sailors felt terrible but after throwing up and having a few bouts of diarrhea, they felt better. On examination none had signs of an "acute abdomen" which would require surgery. The diagnosis was acute food poisoning. All the sick sailors had eaten at the Fleet Canteen and none said they had eaten any other local food.

After their bowels calmed a little and we were sure they were stable, the sailors were released to their berths. The criteria were that the vomiting had stopped and they could tolerate clear liquids by mouth. Four sailors were significantly dehydrated with abnormal vital signs so were given intravenous fluids and admitted to a hospital bed.

Finally, after three or four hours the inflow of patients slowed, then stopped and we received no more after about an hour interval. We counted ninety-three cases. Only those four needed IVs and admission. The rest were released to their bunks with some antacids and anti-nausea, antidiarrheal medications. Crisis over.

As the crew of corpsmen and I sat around enjoying sandwiches and coffee we had obtained from MidRats, we discussed the events of the evening. It was like nothing any of us had ever encountered before. The discussion led to speculation as to what had caused the outbreak.

Eureka again. We needed to do an epidemiological study to isolate the culprit food. Since our medical library was loaded with texts on most every aspect of medicine, I retrieved a volume on Public Health and Epidemiology. There was complete coverage including example questionnaires for doing a study. It also occurred to us that if we did not do a complete study, our Senior Medical Officer, who was ashore until the morrow, would initiate one that would plague us for a week or more. We remembered that master's degree in public health he touted and how he pestered and harangued the corpsman assigned to sanitation.

That corpsman and I got to work on a comprehensive questionnaire for an epidemiological study. We contacted the mess decks and obtained a list of all the foods they had prepared and sent ashore to the Fleet Canteen. We printed a hundred copies, then dispatched a team to the berths of all the sick sailors to have them completed. It included a section on demographics of the sailors, a list of all the foods, etc. It included everything we needed for a good study.

Earlier during the evening amid receiving and treating so many cases, I had "read up" on acute food poisoning. It is caused mostly by staphylococcal enterotoxin and is commonly called "staph food poisoning." Here is a synopsis and pertinent details ….

What is staph food poisoning?

Staph food poisoning is a type of food poisoning caused by infection with the Staphylococcus aureus (S. aureus) bacterium. The bacteria multiply in foods and produce toxins especially if food is kept at room temperature. The toxins may be present in dangerous amounts in foods that have no signs of spoilage, such as a bad smell.

What causes staph food poisoning?

Most people get staph poisoning by eating contaminated food. The most common reason for contamination is that the food has not been kept hot enough [140°F (60°C) or above] or cold enough [40°F (4°C) or below].

Foods that are associated with staph food poisoning include:

- *Meats.*
- *Poultry and egg products.*
- *Salads such as egg, tuna, chicken, potato, and macaroni.*
- *Bakery products such as cream-filled pastries, cream pies, and chocolate eclairs.*
- *Sandwich fillings.*
- *Milk and dairy products.*

What are the symptoms?

Symptoms of staph food poisoning include nausea, vomiting, retching, stomach cramping, and diarrhea. In more severe cases, dehydration, headache, muscle cramping, and changes in blood pressure and pulse rate may occur. Symptoms typically come on quickly. How severe they are depends on your susceptibility to the toxin, how much contaminated food you ate, how much of the toxin you ingested, and your general health.

After the questionnaires had been completed and returned to sickbay, we analyzed them. Every sick sailor had eaten some or a lot of the macaroni salad …. made with macaroni, pickle relish and mayonnaise. No other food was common to all the sick sailors although a few others had some overlap. We contacted the Chief on the mess decks and did some further investigation. It turned out that after the food had been offloaded from the ship and loaded into the ship's van for delivery to the Phoenix Hotel, the van had broken down. Before it could be repaired and the food delivered to the hotel, the van and its macaroni salad had sat in the hot sun on the dock for four hours. Voila! We had our etiology.

So, we put together a comprehensive Epidemiological Study Report which was ten or twelve pages long including the questionnaire and various background information. We put a copy on the SMO's desk. It was an "all-niter" for us working on the study and report, but we had prevented the harassment of doing one with the SMO directing and nit-picking it.

Next day SMO saw and read the report. He asked a bunch of questions and we could tell he was "p----- off" that we had headed off and undercut his "thing." That was it. All the sailors completely recovered as expected. No further studies nor reports ensued. The sanitation corpsman and I "high-fived" in private and for the rest of the cruise were big buddies sharing wide smiles every time we saw each other.

In retrospect this is a perfect example of the Law of Unintended Consequences.

JERUSALEM AND DAMASCUS

SIDE TRIP TO THE HOLY LAND

JERUSALEM ... WE flew from Beirut to Amman, Jordan, then drove by bus across the Jordan River into Israel. (See elsewhere for details of the flight.) This article will make no pretense to list, describe or comment much on the usual Holy Land sites that are "must-see" for tourists.... and that's a good thing because it was a "can't see anything" on crossing into Israel. The delay of that flight was so long it was pitch-black on our bus ride to the hotel. We pulled up to the Hotel of the Good Shepherd and dinner was ready. We were hungry. The meal was meat, vegetables and bread ... not sure what exactly ... we just ate and went to sleep. In retrospect we lost a whole afternoon of our limited sightseeing time because of that late arrival.

Next day we were up early and made a circuit to the usual tourist sites. They are fuzzy in recall but I remember the streets of Jerusalem and walking the "Way of the Cross." I think we saw the Wailing Wall but it must have not been impressive. Gethsemane had some ancient olive trees. I don't remember exactly the crucifixion site but am sure we saw it.

We drove through the countryside out to the Sea of Galilee then back to the Dead Sea. The density of the water was utterly amazing. We didn't go swimming, no time, but it was worth seeing it and feeling that water. We had a nondescript lunch and stopped on the Jordan River for souvenirs. The river was disappointingly small, about Louisiana creek or bayou size. There were some camels whose size was impressive as were their feet. Camels are notorious for bad breath and that reputation is truth.

It was a quick trip really, but worth the experience. We flew back to Beirut and the ship.

Damascus, Syria ... While we were going to the Holy Land Al Cohen was driving to Damascus in a hired car with driver. We though he was crazy since he was Jewish. There he was driving alone into Syria but he was hell-bent to see Damascus. I wondered if perhaps his family was from Syria originally, maybe even Damascus?

Al was a great guy, but sometimes eccentric. Several examples might illustrate. In Italy he decided to buy a used Ferrari and have it sent back to Richmond, his home. He went ashore, looked up some dealers, bought the car and arranged shipment.

Later in Virginia Beach he developed that "spin-around butt check" technique. Al was single and a younger brother had died. He may have been living on the edge a little. I think he went into an anesthesia residency after he left the navy. He didn't say much about Damascus except that it was a pretty city.

IDENTIFY YOURSELF

ISRAELI MIRAGE JETS WITH THE STAR OF DAVID

AFTER A SUCCESSFUL visit to Beirut, except for that food poisoning episode, Indy sailed back into the eastern Mediterranean. The second day out we resumed flight operations as part of our ongoing training and skill-honing exercises.

Two F-4s were flying around when suddenly they saw six, count'em six, Mirage jets with the Star of David painted on the tail. It was one of those "THERE I WUZ" stories. The Israeli fighters tuned to the radio frequency and keyed, "Identify Yourself" in English. The F-4s explained they were U.S. Navy from the *Independence* flying a routine training mission.

The Mirage flight leader said, "We knew that but you have just overflown Israeli air space and we scrambled to check you out. Please watch your coordinates and keep over international water." With that the Mirage and Phantom fighters all headed for home.

The next day Israel launched a massive air attack against Egypt. They had speculated that Egypt had heard what was planned and that our two F-4s were a preemptive strike from Egypt. The massive airstrike from Israel destroyed much of the Egyptian air force capability and essentially there were no more hostilities at that time.

However, the potential for an international crisis was there. Indy received orders to stand ready for any contingencies. We found a clear spot in the eastern Med and sailed in two-hundred-mile circles for two or three weeks. There was speculation that the Russians might support Egypt and strike Israel. We were prepared to come to the aid of Israel if necessary.

Nothing happened except we just sailed around for an extended period, longer than our usual underway at-sea cycles. I recall that we had been scheduled for a port call in Athens but had to cancel it. That was disappointing because Athens is filled with antiquities and interesting historic architecture, plus the lifestyle and cuisine are fun.

As a substitute for Athens, the ship sailed into Argostoli Bay for a giant beach party.... beer, barbecue and bathing in crystal clear waters.

ARGOSTOLI BAY

A GIANT BEACH PARTY ... R & R IN GREECE

AFTER THAT FIST-BUMP confrontation with the Israeli Mirage fighters and the Israeli-Egypt hostilities we spent the next thirty days or so circling in a giant two-hundred-mile circle "holding pattern" in the eastern Med. We were poised and available for any action that might be required of us. Waiting with no end in sight is tough on everybody. The Navy knows from long experience that sailors perform best when there are occasional interludes to get off the ship for some rest and relaxation, a.k.a. R & R. Without really recalling the details or true facts I think we had been scheduled for port call in Athens but had to skip it. Having previously been to Athens I was looking forward to it. So it goes.

Anyway, the powers that be in our military hierarchy decided we would drop anchor in Argostoli Bay on the west side of Greece. Argostoli Bay is a large gulf of the Ionian Sea on the island of Kefalonia, Greece. Regardless of the exact geography it was beautiful. It was calm like a huge cove protected from waves. Crystal clear blue water and bright white sand beaches would be a good description. We were there for about four days so everyone on the ship would have opportunity to go ashore.

Beach party time! The ship pulled out all the stops to make it special. Getting off the ship was the main reason for being there, but the sand, water and sunshine were highly attractive. The crew boats and officers' launches made regular back and forth trips from the ship to the shore. You could go for a short visit or stay all day. We saw a few cases of sunburn in sickbay later.

The ship offloaded probably a thousand cases of beer. Undoubtedly, we had a huge stash in the hold somewhere that wasn't discussed but was ready for just such needs as our lengthy beach party. It was American beer in twelve-ounce cans. I don't remember the brand and maybe there were several.... but it did have the characteristics that are favorites of navy men everywhere.... "cold and free."

Barbecue stations were set up and fully equipped for high-end ribs, brisket, burgers, dogs, steaks.... with all the trimmings. (This time caution was taken to not let any foods "cook off" in the sun.) The beer flowed like water. Soft drinks, bottled water et al were also plentiful.

Volleyball nets and courts, horseshoes, tetherball poles, basketball goals and more were set up for an array of sports activities. By far the favorite sport was swimming. A fabulous aspect of the swimming was how clear the water was and how the fine grains of white sand swirled up at the slightest disturbance. The specific gravity of the sand appeared remarkably close to the water as it wafted up freely and settled back slowly. For the next month or so in sickbay every sailor we examined had some of those fine white grains of sand in their ears. The sand did no harm and it eventually worked out with the cerumen in the normal migration pattern.

Argostoli Bay was a huge success.... then we hoisted anchor and returned to the open Med.

THE DAY TRIP TO FLORENCE

I WAS EXCITED AND NO ONE ELSE GAVE A HAPPY.

INDY WAS GOING to dock in Livorno (Leghorn) on the west coast of Italy about midway up the boot. Livorno is directly opposite Florence (Firenze) about 90 kilometers drive in an hour or a little more. I was excited because of having been there in the fall of 1965 when touring Europe. The few days taste of the culture and historical importance of Florence as the cradle of the Renaissance only whetted my appetite. Museums, architecture, Tuscan cuisine including great wines beckoned and begged for another visit.

The plan was to get a small group together, rent a car or van, drive over early one morning and arrive about when the museums opened. After a few hours we would have a fine lunch somewhere, then do a few more museums before the drive back to Indy in Livorno.

I went all over the ship with the plan.... to ready rooms, ward rooms, everywhere.... no one seemed to give a happy damn about it.

NOTE: The standard modus operandus for the squadron flight officers in port was to go ashore and set up a squadron lounge somewhere. They would rent a large hotel room somewhere, stock up a plentiful bar and sit around to get loaded until time for a meal. Most of the time their idea of fun and sightseeing was walking from the hotel room to the restaurant. Of course, there were some exceptions, but no one was interested in a day trip to Florence.

Finally …. I recruited three other people. The protestant chaplain, the Catholic chaplain and a gay A-6 Bombardier/Navigator who wanted to see the David, Michelangelo's huge sculpture of a nude man. (We all knew the B/N was gay, nobody cared. He didn't make a big deal out of it, didn't bother anyone, he was a good officer and a competent aviator.) The two chaplains had studied at seminary enough to understand and appreciate all that was in Florence.

Eureka, the trip was going to be fun. We rented a car and took off early. First stop was the Uffizi Gallery, then the Pitti Palace, a stop at the Ponte Vecchio to buy souvenirs, then we walked around town to admire the Duomo et al. Next, we found a delightful place for lunch…. Sabatini. We of course had good Tuscan red wine, antipasto, a primo piatto of pasta, a secondo of meat, a salad, some cheese, fruit* and a taste of dessert…. and left with huge smiles and great satisfaction. Sabatini is still there and highly rated. (I ate there again on a subsequent visit.) After lunch we went to the Accademia Gallery to see The David, maybe visited the Medici Chapel … some of the trip fades after that vinous lunch. It was a long day but we had an experience of a lifetime really. The drive back to Indy was a "piece of cake," or should I say, "pezzo di torta?"

*It may have been here that I discovered that magnificent combination of gorgonzola cheese with a fresh pear. It was certainly somewhere in Italy and has been a favorite of mine for half a century.

BARCELONA SECOND VISIT

A SEASONED SAILOR MAKES THE BEST
OF HIS LAST CRUISE PORT CALL

THERE WAS AN interesting contrast between the first and the second visit to Barcelona. On the first visit I was a green newbie mostly just looking for some decent bath towels. There was a lot of discovery, some exciting, some embarrassing, all interesting. On this second visit I mostly knew exactly what I wanted to do and had become an experienced port call visitor.

Formal Dining In … First the Airwing had scheduled an "all-officers" Formal Dining In. This is a banquet where everyone is required to attend (except those required to stay on duty aboard Indy.) A large hall had been reserved at the Avenida Palace Hotel where several hundred officers in dress uniforms could be seated and served in elegant style. I think we all had the cost automatically deducted from our paycheck. The seating was arranged "by the numbers." That means strictly according to rank seniority. If there were thirty Commanders in our group, each one's Date of Rank determined who was senior. The SOPA (Senior Officer Present) was at the center of the head table. It went down the line from there. The lowest ranking Ensign was at the bottom of the seating arrangement and was known as "The Boot."

Of course, there was plenty to drink.... cocktail hour, then seated at table. A round of toasts ensued. Whenever someone proposed a toast, ex. "To the President of the United States" standing with glass raised, everyone would stand and also raise their glasses ... then the Boot would respond, on behalf of the whole group, 'To the President of the United States." Then another toast... and the response from the Boot.... throughout the evening. It was an exercise of us all being "Officers and Gentlemen." It was impressive and fun. It was my first and only "Dining In."

The food and wines were good, not great but good. It was hearty cuisine in Spanish style and very appropriate for the occasion and the young men present.

Los Caracoles Again ... The snails were so good the first time, I had to go back again. It was winter now so lunch was indoors. I knew what to order and selected a much better wine as well. The restaurant had a charcoal fire grill on the street for advertising and to allow passersby to warm themselves. Delicious ... A+ for Los Caracoles.

Guria !!! ... A++++ One A+ for the steaks, three for the gorgeous young ladies serving the tables. See separate article on Guria. I ate there once on the first visit, but twice on this second port call. My eyes feasted more than my stomach. Did I say gorgeous?

Buying Wine in a Restaurant to Take Home ... From time to time, one orders a wine in a restaurant which is outstanding. The likelihood of finding it in a retail shop is slim. The restaurant price is usually escalated. So, one doesn't often buy wine to take home from the restaurant wine list. My first experience in doing this was in Barcelona that second visit. think I was in a hotel restaurant, but don't remember exactly. I ordered a half bottle of a Rioja which was about twenty years old. I think it was the "Imperiale" Rioja C.V.N.E. (Compania Vinicola del Norte de Espana = Wine company of north Spain.) It was delicious. My palate and my knowledge were much better now than on that first visit. The price was reasonable although I don't recall what. I bought four half-bottles and took them with me.

La Rambla ... was fun as usual. It appears as if the whole city has turned out for a stroll. It is a people-watching paradise. The leaves were gone from the trees this time and the people bundled in heavy coats. Sunset was sooner but Spanish hours don't seem to slow down the locals. We sailors really strained to wait until 2100 for the restaurants to open.... but it was okay if we were planning to feast at Guria. Didn't I say gorgeous? It was time to get back stateside.

So, after about a week in Barcelona we cast off our lines and sailed for home.... waving goodbye to the statue of Cristoforo Colombo standing guard over the harbor. Out south into the Med, around west to Gibraltar where we were met by the "Bear." (See separate article.) Then we sailed into the open Atlantic to make a beeline for Pier Twelve in Norfolk.

The Sneaky Navy ... The carrier steams about five hundred miles a day at normal cruising speed. That is about the span of a time zone. It took five or six days for a leisurely pace back and forth across the Atlantic from Norfolk to Gibraltar or return. So, the time changes each day and all the clocks are reset. Going east you lose an hour each day so the time change is made in the wee hours of the night. Going west you gain an hour each day so the change is made during the daytime working day. Sneaky Navy.... steals an hour of sleep from the sailors on the way over and adds an hour to the workday on the way back.

Nobody really seemed to care and ten percent never got the word.

XI

MEMORABLE MOMENTS

THE ARAB INCIDENT
AT THE IOIC DOOR

RATTLE, RATTLE, BANG, BANG …. GENERAL QUARTERS, GENERAL QUARTERS

IT WAS BACK in Naples after Beirut, Jerusalem and Argostoli Bay. We were moored to the pier and having visitors onboard for public relations and good will purposes. It was "Foreign Nationals Day." Some of the crew were ashore for R & R with others remaining aboard. Both officers and enlisted were stationed all around the ship to serve as tour guides and for security.

The Information and Operational Intelligence Center (IOIC) was the locked and guarded spaces where all the "secrets" were kept. (Now named CVIC on Nimitz class carriers.) There were maps, protocols for launching nuclear weapons, targets for them … lots of classified documents. There was a strong steel door, always locked. Next to it was a one-way window with an armed Marine posted behind it. You couldn't see him, but he could see everything going on in the passageway by the entrance door. Access to the IOIC required top secret clearance AND a need to know. (I had top secret clearance but was often not admitted due to lack of need to know.)

Foreign nationals coming aboard were logged in by name and address on an ID card or some form of identification. We knew how many were aboard and who they were if the IDs were valid. That day in Naples we had about a thousand foreign national aboard when …. an Arab in a flowing white robe, "fan-belt" head covering with face covered, dashed up to the IOIC door, started rattling the handle and banging on the door, shouting in unintelligible language, then ran off. The Marine guard hit the "Ooo-gah Button" to raise the alarm.

Immediately came the 1MC …. 'GENERAL QUARTERS, GENERAL QUARTERS, All hands man your battle stations … This is NOT a drill; this is NOT a drill." The usual mad dash ensued and we waited for about two hours as the foreign nationals were cleared from the ship. I couldn't see from my Forward Auxiliary Battle Dressing Station but heard that the visitors were all escorted to the hangar deck and logged off the ship one-by-one to match the log-in information. All were matched so none were left aboard. Meanwhile others of the security detail were doing a clean sweep search of the entire ship. They were looking for anybody who shouldn't have been there and looking for that Arab costume. Neither were found and the Arab zuit-suit never showed up later. The whole process took about two hours and we were both tired and disgusted when it was over.

Afterthoughts and Opinion … Flight surgeons have lots of eyes and ears within the airwing. It is part of our job. We listen for conversations and look to see things as trained observers. It is for the sake of health and safety of flight crew personnel mostly, but we hear and see lots of scuttlebutt. I think I know who perpetrated the Arab Incident. I think it was one of the helicopter pilots whose stateroom was close to the IOIC and where he could slip out with no one in the passageway, bang on the door, then dash back into his room to strip off the Arab suit, stash it (maybe in the same void under the drawers where I stashed wine), then proceed to general quarters battle stations with the rest of us.

THE BOSUN'S INCIDENT

[NOTE: This was written on 6-9-15 as a stand-alone piece so it contains some repetitive explanatory sections.]

"BOSUN" IS THE pronunciation of a Boatswain's Mate aboard a Navy ship. The term Boatswain traces its origin and history back over a thousand years. Essentially a "bosun" is the chief sailor on a ship. He is the chief deck hand and supervisor of all other deck hands onboard. The modern Navy has many specialists among the enlisted crew who have expertise and training in various things like electronics, aviation mechanics, quartermasters, etc. It is a long list. The ratings as they are called indicate what the specialties are and insignia patches on uniforms show the duties.

Boatswains Mates insignia are two crossed anchors. Entering enlisted crew who are "striking" for higher rank begin as seaman apprentice, then seaman, then seaman third class, then second class, then first class, then Chief Boatswain's Mate of various grades. Boatswains Mates (BM) are the sailors who oversee the physical plant and are the physical human muscle of the ship. They do all the painting, anchor hauling, maintenance, repairs, firefighting and a host of other duties. On a Navy ship there is always an Officer of the Deck and a Bosun of the Deck on duty. They serve 4-hour shifts in rotation. The Bosun of the Deck is always a senior experienced sailor and he carries a Bosun's Pipe on a chain around his neck. (Sometimes a Boatswain or bosun is also called "boats.")

The "Pipe" is a thin metal tube about five to six inches long with a ball on the end which contains a small hole. The pipe can make four basic sounds: steady low (fingers close over the ball), steady high (fingers raised), flutter (opening and closing the fingers and it sounds something like a canary) and trill (by trilling the tongue). Just like there are various bugle calls in the army, there are similar "pipe calls" in the navy which are used to announce various activities during the day such as attention, all hands on deck, sweepers man your brooms, chow time, etc. In the modern navy an advanced loudspeaker system is used and the pipe calls are broadcast over the "1MC" (number one master communications system) then the announcement is made verbally. This occurs all day and night on the ship. The most serious notice is "General Quarters" in which the bosun pipes "attention" then announces, "General Quarters, General Quarters, all hands man your battle stations." followed by repetitive alarm gongs. Most people have heard this in the movies and other announcements such as "Now hear this. Now hear this. This is the Captain speaking.... etc." [I'm not sure why it's common practice to repeat commands twice but suspect it's because with lots of noise on a ship it increases understanding and retention. There is literally nowhere on an aircraft carrier where the loud sound of the 1MC cannot be heard, even with machinery and the noise of the flight deck. Yet with four or five thousand people on the carrier there always seemed to be ten percent who "didn't get the word."]

Anyway, one of my favorite pipe calls with announcement onboard the carrier was the "Sweepers' Call." Cleanliness onboard a navy ship is traditional and great energy is used to keep everything "shipshape." Periodically during the day, the Bosun pipes attention (long low sound, followed by high sound) then the following verbal announcement, "Sweepers, sweepers, man your brooms. Make a clean sweep fore and aft. Take all trash and garbage to sponson eight." A sponson is a small projection from the hull or deck and on the aircraft carrier, "Sponson eight" was portside aft and was where all the various garbage and trash was thrown overboard periodically. [The other most interesting pipe call/ announcement was for smokers since with all the aviation fuel aboard the carrier smoking was a significant fire hazard if caution were not used. The call was "attention" on the pipe, then the verbal announcement of "The smoking lamp is lit throughout the ship in all authorized spaces." I never did see an actual lamp but figured this was just a traditional historic reference.]

As you probably know the Navy is famed for slang and special terms for just about everything. Front and rear are called fore and aft. Right and left are starboard and port. There are no floors or doors since they are known as decks and hatches. The toilet was a head. It goes on and on. Learning the lingo is an important part of being an effective crewmember.

So, when at sea a trash can is often called a "shit can." [I don't know if this is still the practice since women are part of crews, but in the days of all male sailors it was in common use.] Thus the "sweepers call" was announced with, "Sweepers, sweepers, man your brooms. Make a clean sweep fore and aft. Take all trash and <u>shit cans</u> to sponson eight."

Another little bit of lingo that is important for the understanding of this "Bosun's Incident" is the word "belay." If some command or announcement were made in error, it was common practice to say, "belay that" or "belay my last" or some such. This meant to ignore the previous command or announcement, to resume previous status, to cease doing something, etc. Belay was/is a term used to make a correction of an error.

So...... there we were on the carrier in port, tied up to a pier in Italy. It was visitor's day and there were over a thousand visitors on board touring the ship. We called them "foreign nationals." During the 1960s in the Mediterranean, it was common practice to have open house days for foreign nationals from time to time to promote good will. We always had crew, both officers and enlisted, stationed throughout the ship to serve as hosts, to answer questions and of course to ensure safety and security. Life and activity on a ship is "24/7/365" so regular activities go right along no matter if visitors are aboard.

When in port the Officer of the Deck and his assistant who was a senior experienced bosun's mate were always stationed at the top of the gangway by which people walked on or off the ship. The quarterdeck had a podium with various logs for recording routine activities and any unusual incidents. There was a mounted bell for signaling the passage of time as is traditional on a ship. The 1MC was used to broadcast all over the ship as usual. The bosun had a sidearm for any emergencies.

When coming aboard, even though you could not see the flag flying astern, a crewman saluted aft toward the flag, then said, "Request permission to come aboard, sir." When leaving it was the protocol to salute aft and then, "Request permission to leave the ship, sir." The officer of the deck would respond with a salute to you, then, "Permission granted." There was a lot of formality and historical ritual as the life and activities aboard ship just rolled along. The OD (Officer of the Deck) had the option to grant or refuse permission, to search you or your belongings, even to arrest someone if need be…. and even to announce, "General Quarters" and lock down the ship if necessary. Usually everything was just routine formality, but it was an important element in the safety and security of a Navy ship of war. When lots of people were coming and going it must have been grueling for the OD to be constantly returning salutes and granting permission.

One day while about a thousand foreign nationals were visiting aboard, I was the Medical Officer of the Day and was stationed in "Sick Bay" (term for the medical department and area.) Then the "Bosun's Incident" occurred.

The 1MC blared out the low-high "attention pipe call" then the announcement, "Sweepers, sweepers, man your brooms. Make a clean sweep fore and aft. Take all trash and <u>shit cans</u> to sponson eight." There was immediate silence all over the ship. In those days, the word "shit" was not used in polite conversation, especially with ladies present and certainly not in a public announcement with a thousand visitors aboard.

You could hear the crackling open mike from the quarterdeck and hear the OD in the background excitedly telling the bosun he had just "messed up" by saying "shit can" over the 1MC. After another moment of crackling silence there was a tap-tap on the mike and the bosun came up and announced very loudly....... **"Belay that shit can."**

You could hear the shocked silence aboard ship turn to peals of laughter as the OD again admonished the bosun and the 1MC went silent.

PLEASE KEEP ME FROM KILLING HIM

THE CLASSIC PSYCHIATRIC PLEA FOR HELP

THERE I WUZ … my first night on the Indy and one of the squadron commanders came by our stateroom. I first met my flight surgeon roommate, Al Cohen, MD, earlier that day and I had not even unpacked my gear. Al introduced me to Commander "X" (as he will hereafter be called.) Al then proceeded to pour whiskey and we sat around sipping and talking …. i.e. they talked, I listened. Al and I didn't sip much but CDR X was not bashful on refills. The conversation was casual, not "business" and not just social either. It was obvious that Al and X were good friends and that this sort of conversation and drinking had been going on for some time.

By and by X was sufficiently lit that he thanked us, said his goodnights and departed to his stateroom. After he left Al explained the situation and here is the story.

X was a Naval Academy graduate, high in his class and a very accomplished pilot, one of the best. Sometimes he "got his kicks" by making a supersonic pass to the side of a destroyer at fifty feet off the

354

deck (ocean) ... at night .... just to bang them with the sudden sonic boom. X was married and had multiple children. As his career advanced X had been stationed in an overseas country. He and his wife hired a local governess to help with the young children. The governess was a young woman in her early twenties who spoke good English and who was attractive. The governess became a mistress as X started an affair and began "screwing her on the side." Likely Mrs. X knew all about it but I never heard that.

By and by the overseas tour ended and the X family moved back stateside. They brought the governess/mistress back with them. The affair continued. At some point the governess/mistress decided that there was no future for her with X, so she began a relationship with a military-connected civilian who was single and stable. X came unglued. His phallic prowess and macho manliness had been challenged. About that time X deployed to sea and was not a happy camper.

For some time, Al had been telling the CAG (Commander Air Wing and X's direct commanding officer) that there was a problem with X. CAG would not listen or even respect Al's input because of the cult macho of naval aviators, especially Naval Academy graduates, that they could "do anything, anytime, anywhere." CAG just blew it off and Al was stuck to deal with it however he could. The pattern developed with X coming every evening to get drunk politely and sleep it off.

X had a plan. He was going to check out in a jet, refuel in the Canary Islands, then fly stateside and kill that S.O.B. who had stolen his macho manhood. He was serious about it.... and could have done it easily as no one would have challenged him on the trip. X was making a classic psychiatric "plea for help" by coming to our room to dull the night.

[**SIDE NOTE**: There was a wonderful book published in 1998 that describes a person like the situation of X. The book is "The Professor and the Madman." The madman was a U.S. Civil War surgeon who had demons afterward, went to England and killed a man. He was committed to a mental hospital and later became the largest contributor to the Oxford English Dictionary. During the daylight hours he was sane and brilliant, but at night the demons made him insane. He was a paranoid schizophrenic. During the day he was compensated, at night he became decompensated. Paranoid schizophrenics are frequently very accomplished people and go all through life so… if they stay compensated.]

Back on the Indy in 1966. It was thirty years before that book was published but Al and I had enough training in medical school and later at NAMI to diagnose X. Without anything ever in writing, we discussed X and both agreed he was likely a paranoid schizophrenic who was highly compensated but was at risk of decompensation. I think Al had been trying to tell CAG and explain it to him, but CAG just "wasn't buying it."

The nightly alcohol was keeping X compensated. He was functioning at high level during the day and completely normal in all respects. Nightly he would come by for relief and release from the demons. This went on for a while, maybe a month at the most. By now I was fully into the situation, it's treatment and its risks. X became increasingly on edge, sometimes even fidgety which was very unusual for a cool pilot.

X started stopping by to see me in sickbay every few days, complaining that the exhaust fumes from the ship's stacks were making him cough. Lungs were clear as was a chest film, but X kept stopping by. He seemed more and more stressed. One day I auscultated some expiratory wheezes in his lung periphery. It was easy to make a diagnosis of asthmatic bronchitis … an acceptable diagnosis for an aviator. I issued a "down chit" to take him off flying status. X was quite happy about it. His plea for help was being answered. X was an intelligent man and basically a good guy. He understood exactly what was going on and exhibited signs of relief. In effect, from a medical standpoint, X had become so stressed and "uptight" that he had induced bronchospasm, hence the wheezes.… but "it was that damned stack smoke that was kicking his butt."

Al and I conferred and were in complete agreement, X needed to go the Naval Hospital in Naples to be admitted to the psychiatric ward. We were due into Naples within the week. We were going to arrange a "good guy, bad guy" situation. Al would be the "good guy," friend, confidant, support person …. as he had been doing from the beginning. I was to be the "bad guy" who was busting X for a medical (non-psychiatric) problem.

I arranged with communications to have a ship-to-shore radio/ telephone call with the psychiatrist at the hospital in Naples. He agreed to receive X and take care of his needs. After we docked in Naples, CDR X packed his gear for transfer to the hospital. All the paperwork showed asthmatic bronchitis, but X knew exactly what was happening and which unit at the hospital where he was going. He was onboard with it all … seemed happy with it. By now Al had again advised CAG as to the situation and explained what was happening. At last CAG understood and accepted. So, X and I departed Indy. I took him to the Hotel Excelsior and bought him lunch. The hotel was close to the Castell dell 'Ovo and quite near the dock…. easy walking distance even with X's gear. Hotel Excelsior was also one of the top hotels in Italy at the time, part of the CIGA chain, and noted for its restaurant food. It was really a superb lunch and a proper sendoff for X. After lunch we took a taxi to the hospital where X was received with all the courtesy and respect that a Navy Commander should have.

Several weeks later I received a post card from X which said, "Thank you. You don't know how much I appreciate your help. By the way, you guys could mess up a steel ball bearing." I still have that postcard. We later heard that X had been transferred back stateside to the Portsmouth Naval Hospital. We surmised that with proper medication and counseling X probably finished a twenty-year career at a desk job…. but we never heard any more. Here's hoping that he stayed compensated and resumed a good life.

UP THE NOSE BY A HAWSEHOLE

THE INDEPENDENCE WAS a warship and a powerful one. Americans were in combat in Viet Nam when in 1965 the Indy and its Airwing Seven had distinguished themselves supporting those operations from the South China Sea and they won the Navy Unit Citation "for exceptionally meritorious service." The Cold War was still in progress. We had a ready plane on the carrier loaded with a nuke and capable of launching with thirty minutes notice.

However, the Indy was also performing a diplomacy mission all around the Mediterranean during our 1966 cruise. At every port of call we and the other ships in our task force would display a string of bright white profile lights from stem to stern, peaked at the highest mast in the center. The ships were impressively outlined and our presence could be seen for miles.

During the daylight hours on some days, we would host visitors with over a thousand foreign nationals (men, women and children) onboard at one time. Also, sometimes we held formal dinners in the main wardroom to entertain local dignitaries and officers from ships of the countries we were visiting.

We were in port in Naples. We had invited about three dozen officers from the Italian Navy to join us for a formal dinner aboard the Indy. They were of most rank levels and were selected both because of outstanding performance records and because they spoke excellent English. The guest of honor and our speaker was Angier Biddle Duke who was at that time the U.S. Ambassador to Spain. Ambassador Duke had a distinguished career in the U.S. Army Air Corps during WWII and in the diplomatic corps off and on thereafter.

At age 25 Mr. Duke had enlisted as a private in 1940 and rose to Major in 1945. The navy has a term for officers who start as enlisted men and advance into the officer ranks. The U.S. Navy term for such people is "Mustang." In the Royal Navy, officers who advanced from enlisted are said to have "come in through the hawsehole." For background, ships are tied to piers with huge ropes and/or cables called hawsers. They pass from the ship to the dock through a hole with rounded edges which is called a "hawsehole."

THERE I WUZ ... gathered in the wardroom with several hundred fellow officers including the three dozen Italian Navy officers. We were all in full dress white uniforms. The Italian officers were almost indistinguishable from the host Americans except for the rank and other insignia differences. The Italian officer guests were deliberately interspersed among us to promote conversations and interactions and to make them feel at home with us. Because of the large number of us crowded into the space we were seated almost shoulder to shoulder.

Now Mr. Duke was a distinguished man who served his country during wartime and who had a distinguished career in public service. He was also very wealthy, educated and a gentleman. However, what he said at the Indy dinner in Naples was certainly not diplomatic and was closer to a--hole than hawsehole.

After gathering and everyone being seated, we had time to become friendly and chat with our Italian guests. As in all formal military dinners the seating was arranged by rank so we were with our same rank Italian peers. Dinner proceeded with the usual formalities. At the appropriate time our Captain, the senior officer presiding over the occasion, called for attention and introduced Ambassador Duke.

As is often customary for speakers, a joke or two is told to "loosen up" and relax the audience.

I have no idea how many jokes Mr. Duke told, what they were …. nor even anything he said in his talk. The only thing I remember is the one joke he told that froze the group.

Said Ambassador Duke, "Do you know how to break an Italian's finger? Hit him in the nose."

The silence was deafening. It was the proverbial 'could have heard a pin drop.' All the Italian officer guests understood the English perfectly and the implication of the "joke."

THERE I WUZ …. embarrassed for our ambassador to Spain, Mr. Duke; embarrassed for our country, embarrassed for our navy, ship and officers…. embarrassed with the young Italian officer seated next to me and who for the rest of the evening was polite but rather stiff and unfriendly in contrast to the previous cordiality and camaraderie we had shared.

I don't know if Mr. Duke realized that so many Italian officers were in our midst, that they all understood English perfectly or even how undiplomatic his comment was. Even without any Italian officers being present the comment would have been inappropriate.

It has been a memory for half a century and led to the title of this chapter.

Hawsehole indeed.

TEN DAYS MIDCRUISE LEAVE IN NOVEMBER

GENOA TO MADRID TO PALMA .... VIRGINIA AND T Y G

BY NOW I was a seasoned sailor with over four months of carrier life. The learning curve had reached a high plateau and most everything seemed comfortable and to some extent routine. By then I had explored most all the ship, knew lots of people and was an accepted part of my squadron families. The cruise was about halfway through its eight months so it was a most appropriate time to take ten days leave. (Navy personnel accrue 2.5 days of leave per month which is 30 days a year. I had accumulated 25 days by then.)

It worked perfectly. Virginia would fly to Genoa as the Indy arrived there for a week of port call. Then we would fly to Madrid for the ten days that Indy was at sea again. I would rejoin the ship in Palma de Mallorca as Indy sailed into port there. The ten days leave was during the ship's sea time.

Virginia's parents kept Elizabeth who was now about six months old. They were probably glad when she returned. All went well. I swapped some days of MOD call, Palma for Genoa. The other guys were delighted because Palma had more to offer them than Genoa. That allowed me to be ashore in Genoa more days after Virginia arrived. As the ship sailed, we flew to Madrid to visit my cousin Tracy Eubank and her fiancé Gonzalo Rodriguez de Castro (a.k.a. T y G.) They were married back stateside soon thereafter in 1967.

Tracy was from Alexandria, started college at Randolph-Macon for one year, then transferred to Smith for three more years. After graduation she went to Madrid to become more fluent in Spanish. She met Gonzalo in Madrid that year. Tracy spoke impeccable Spanish. She was our tour guide in Madrid. We did it all. Museo Nacional del Prado (The Prado) was a biggie. There were several other impressive museums close at hand. The Spanish cuisine was another biggie. Tracy was excellent at introducing us to the traditional foods, the delicacies and some exotic foods. Fresh fish and shellfish of every description are everywhere in Madrid. That is amazing because Madrid is landlocked and hundreds of miles from the coast. It seems a fleet of trucks loads up every evening on the north coast with the days fresh catch and then drives through the night to deliver the fish at daybreak. The seafood is everywhere, very fresh, superbly prepared and reasonable in cost.

We had a wonderful culinary exploration in Madrid. Percebes (barnacles), Centolla (big round crabs), mussels, huge shrimp of several kinds, many varieties of flat fish…. we tried it all. The chefs all seemed to have a real touch for perfectly cooking seafood. The percebes are served with their hard foot and tough skin. Tracy showed us how to extract the tender and delicious interior edible part. The centolla has a large round and deep shell about the size and shape of half a softball. The shell is cleaned of innards and used as a serving dish. The crabmeat is picked from the claws and body parts, mixed with the edible eggs, liver et al of the crab and served hot.

I was especially enamored with angulas which are baby eels that are born in the Sargasso Sea and then drift for three years to the estuaries of Spain. They are cooked in olive oil in little brown flat earthenware dishes with a few thin slices of garlic and a small slice of a guindilla chili pepper that is of medium heat. They are so slippery they must be eaten with a wooden spoon. They are expensive but both delicious and exciting for an adventurous developing epicure.

Some of the meat dishes were new and exciting as well. Two deserve special mention. *Cochinillo asado* is a roasted baby suckling pig. The cooked piglet is so tender the chefs cut it with the edge of a plate to demonstrate their perfection. The meat literally falls off the tiny cartilaginous bones. The skin is crispy brown. A quarter of the piglet is a standard serving size as a main dish. My favorite was the similar *Cordero asado* which is a roasted suckling lamb. It is cooked and served similarly. Maybe it was my favorite because I prefer lamb over both pork and beef.

When Tracy couldn't be with us for daytime excursions, she would explain what to do and how to do it. In the evenings Gonzalo would join us for dinner most nights. He brought some delicious wines from his parents' cellar that were twenty years from the vintage or more. We ate one night at Horcher which is a famous restaurant of German origin. Horcher was founded in Berlin in 1904 and served prominent Nazi leaders during the 1930s. Then Goebbels closed restaurants to help the German war effort so Horcher moved to Madrid in 1943 and began to serve Franco's fascists and German people planning escapes from Europe. In any case in 1966 the food and service at Horcher were excellent and exceptional respectively... and the company was the best of all.

That ten days of leave time in Madrid was special for multiple reasons. It was a welcome vacation from shipboard life and it was great to have Virginia fly over to share the experience. Seeing Tracy and meeting her soon-to-be husband Gonzalo was a highlight. We forged a lifetime friendship. The exposure to Spanish culture with insider guidance was exceptional.

That wonderful interlude was not just what the doctor ordered, but also what the doctor needed. So back to the Indy refreshed, reinvigorated, relaxed and ready to resume duty.

THE GLEAMING BASTARD

[Author's Note: This chapter was written about twenty years ago in 2000 or 2001 with the intent to proceed in writing the book. If the "road to hell is paved with good intentions," this is one of the paving stones. Because of the twenty-year lapse a good bit of repetition is evident in this chapter. Rather than edit it out I have left it as written for several reasons: 1) It is a shortened synopsis of my navy story, 2) It illustrates the vividness of my memory of the event in Cannes, 3) The repetitive first part is a good introduction to why and just how significant that ray of sunshine was to me on 25 December 1966.]

IT WAS CHRISTMAS Day 1966. I was alone with over 4,0000 men aboard the *U.S.S. Independence* (CVA-62) deployed in the Mediterranean for an eight-month cruise during the thick of the Vietnam War. I had worked extremely hard at the Naval Aerospace Medical Institute in Pensacola to be on the attack carrier in the Mediterranean rather than with the new Marine Air Wing in the Vietnamese jungles where 29 of the 35 physicians in Flight Surgeon Class 112 spent their tours of active duty. Elizabeth was about a month old when we left Pensacola and drove to New Jersey and then to Virginia Beach to find an apartment. There was an airline strike during July which caused about a week of delay before I could fly out of McGuire Air Force Base to join the carrier where I was assigned as one of two staff flight surgeons for Carrier Air Wing

Seven (CVW-7.) The ship had sailed in early June and was on station in the Mediterranean doing the initial at sea flight operations to hone the skills of all onboard.

My transatlantic flight landed at Torrejon airfield in Madrid, then I flew on to the Naval Air Station at Rota, Spain where the ship support activities were based. The aircraft carrier was a few days from arriving in Barcelona for port call of about a week. After spending the night in the BOQ at Rota I flew onto the carrier in the "COD" which was the nickname for the propeller driven light plane that carried the incoming and outgoing mail, personnel like myself, machine parts or whatever was needed onboard... hence the origin of the nickname for "Carrier Onboard Delivery." It was an exciting time in history, an exciting assignment for me and an exciting arrival to my duty station.

Yet I was homesick already because it was tough to leave a wife and a six-weeks old baby. So, I just dived into the melee of activity on the carrier doing both medical duties and aviation activities. The squadrons were highly professional in their mission and performance of duty. Mostly all the personnel were open and welcoming so I made many friends and many more acquaintances, particularly among the airwing as opposed to the ship's company.

The flight operations were dramatically exciting and I thoroughly enjoyed flying off and on the carrier in F-4 Phantoms, A-6 Intruders, A-3s, helicopters and "Fudds" which had a huge radar dome mounted on top. We also had A-4s but these were single seat planes. It didn't take long to settle into the daily routines of sick call, squadron ready room rounds, hops on the various aircraft and learning the intricacies of the convoluted spaces in the bowels of the carrier.

Except for letters back and forth and an infrequent ham radio telephone patch call there was mostly isolation from family back stateside for all the four thousand plus men on the ship. We broke up the flight operations at sea with port calls. The usual pattern was to be at sea for about ten to fourteen days then in port for a week to ten days. Seeing new places was just as exciting as life on the carrier. In late November Ginny flew to Genoa just as Indy arrived in port then I took ten days' leave while the ship was next at sea. We flew to Madrid, visited Tracy Eubank and her fiancé Gonzalo Rodriguez de Castro, then rejoined the ship in Palma.

By the time Christmas arrived I was ready to get back home. I still enjoyed life on the carrier, but winter had arrived and the sea and sky were mostly grey, windy and cold so "outdoor" strolls on the catwalks were more problematic. Six months were enough in one stretch. Since I didn't have the duty on Christmas Day and we were anchored off Cannes, I decided to have a good Christmas dinner in town somewhere, hopefully to find excellent French cuisine. Officers could wear civilian clothes ashore so I put on a suit and took the Captain's gig shuttle to the docks and walked into town. After some inquiry and from previous reading it was apparent that the best meal in town would be in the dining room at the Carlton Hotel on the beach. The beach was devoid of people on the blustery overcast day as I walked toward the hotel. The wind was brisk and chilly as I hurried along. The small boats anchored in the marina were bouncing on the choppy waves and I could see the huge carrier at anchor in the distance. The hotel itself was a square block high-rise structure of rather undistinguished architecture from a distance…. but as I neared, the trappings of elegance that adorned the outside became obvious, particularly around the front entrance. The interior of the hotel was understated posh and I immediately felt luxuriously comfortable. The dining room was nearly deserted with only one couple seated near the windows. No doubt only idiots and deployed lonesome sailors would be there on Christmas Day for noon dinner rather than home with family.

The waiter spoke perfect English and made me feel both welcome and relaxed. He suggested a Loupe au Fennel which he said was their Christmas special. The medium-sized sea bass was stuffed with fennel and baked. It was presented whole on a silver platter, then masterfully dissected and served by the waiter. It was delicious. I don't recall the accompaniments. After having recommended the fish and noting my order the waiter had brought the wine list and suggested I might try the 1959 Batard-Montrachet. I had read about wine of this caliber but had never before tasted a top level French white Burgundy. These wines are vinified entirely from chardonnay grapes and matured in small Limousin oak casks. Of course, I had learned about the elegance of chardonnays in California where I began a lifelong avid pursuit of fine wines. I was open to the waiter's pronouncement that not only was 1959 a superb year and this a top-level vineyard bottling, but also, he had tasted the wine on several occasions and found it to be consistently among his best selections. Further he thought it would be particularly excellent with the loupe. I had noted that it was priced at a very reasonable thirty francs which was about six dollars. I had read enough to remember that "Batard" meant "bastard" in English but that this designation did not denigrate the wine. The name only connoted a bit of history and the origin of the vineyard's name. Batard-Montrachet was generally recognized as equal to the famous Le Montrachet, Bienvenue-Batard-Montrachet, Chevalier-Montrachet and other Tete de Cuvee white Burgundies from the area. This was the bottle for my Christmas Dinner!

The waiter seemed pleased that I had taken his recommendation. As he went off to retrieve the bottle from the cellar, I gazed out the large windows at the beach, the sea and the sky. It was the totally familiar totally grey scene. The overcast heavy grey sky and the choppy grey sea with whitecaps and foam framed the deserted grey beach. It seemed an apt vista for the greyness of my spirits in dining alone on Christmas Day in a foreign country.

As the waiter silently came up behind me, he remarked, "Sir, you are in luck. This is the very last bottle we have of the '59 Batard-Montrachet." I began to feel that perhaps today was going to be okay after all. He presented the bottle for my perusal of the label which was like the hotel in its understated simple elegance. The vintage date was prominent on the neck label and the main label simply stated Batard-Montrachet in large letters with Appellation Controlee in smaller print beneath. The estate bottler was inscribed at the bottom but at this date I don't recall the exact provenance of the wine. No matter. I was pleased with the choice and the luck of getting the last bottle.

After my nod of approval, the waiter expertly cut around the capsule with the little blade on his waiters' style pocket corkscrew and efficiently slipped the lead disk into his jacket pocket. He carefully cleaned the top and deftly inserted the point of the corkscrew worm into the cork. As I observed every motion, I heard the faintest of squeaks as the cork released its seal and eased out of the mouth of the bottle. Immediately the most incredible and delicious aroma reached my nostrils. It was the smell of very ripe chardonnay grapes and the vanilla overtones of Limousin oak. The waiter then presented the cork, took a quick sniff at the top of the bottle, then leaned over and began to pour my glass. My spirits soared as the bouquet of bottled sunshine overwhelmed my olfactory senses and reached into my heart. Then at the very instant my glass was filled.... suddenly there was a tiny break in the overcast cloudy skies outside and a single beam of bright golden sunshine shone directly through the windows into the glass of wine. The green gold of the viscous liquid leapt into glorious brilliance capturing my soul into the glass and then up the golden sunray into high spirits after all.

The enjoyment of the wine was almost anticlimactic although I must say the waiter was correct in his pronouncement of a perfect wine and food match. Could there have been a better wine for the fish or a better dish for the wine? I don't think it possible. Was life good? Indeed, yes! That ray of sunshine bursting into the Batard-Montrachet somehow elevated everything to a higher meaning and erased all the initial greyness of spirit, weather and situation. I savored every sniff, every sip and every swallow. It was not only intrinsically one of the finest wines I have ever tasted, but also the circumstances enhanced the wine just as much as it enhanced the fish and me. After drinking the whole bottle and finishing the meal with probably some great dessert which it is not necessary to recall, my attitude was remarkably adjusted. I was satisfied and happy. Ahhh.... is there any substitute for the tranquil transition that wine brings? On Christmas Day 1966 the balm of that Gleaming Bastard made me at peace with myself and with the world.

MUSIC

Three Important Songs of the Navy and the Bosun's Calls

1. **The Star-Spangled Banner ...**
   O say can you see by the dawn's early light
   What so proudly we hailed at the twilight's last gleaming
   Whose broad stripes and bright stars through the perilous fight
   O'er the ramparts we watched, were so gallantly streaming?
   And the rocket's red glare, the bombs bursting in air
   Gave proof through the night that our flag was still there
   O say does that star-spangled banner yet wave
   O'er the land of the free and the home of the brave.

2. **The Navy Hymn** ... (a.k.a. "Eternal Father, Strong to Save")
   Both words and music are moving. Here are the lyrics of the original song and then a stanza added for Naval Aviation. There are multiple other verses added for Army, Air Force, Marines and even more for Seabees, Submarine sailors and a host of others. Please search the internet and find it sung by an all-male choir... as well as some interesting history... and the additional verses.

Eternal Father, strong to save,
Whose arm hath bound the restless wave,
Who bid'st the mighty ocean deep
Its own appointed limits keep;
O hear us when we cry to thee,
For those in peril on the sea.

O Christ! Whose voice the waters heard
And hushed their raging at Thy word,
Who walked'st on the foaming deep,
And calm amidst its rage didst sleep;
Oh, hear us when we cry to Thee
For those in peril on the sea!

Most Holy Spirit! Who didst brood
Upon the chaos dark and rude,
And bid its angry tumult cease,
And give, for wild confusion, peace;
Oh, hear us when we cry to Thee
For those in peril on the sea!

O Trinity of love and power!
Our brethren shield in danger's hour;
From rock and tempest, fire and foe,
Protect them wheresoe'er they go;
Thus evermore shall rise to Thee,
Glad hymns of praise from land and sea.

The Stanza Added for Naval Aviation

Lord, guard and guide the men who fly
Through the great spaces in the sky,
Be with them always in the air,
In dark'ning storms or sunlight fair.

O, hear us when we lift our prayer,
For those in peril in the air.

3. **Anchors Aweigh** ... This was originally a football fight song but the words have been changed to fit the whole Navy more appropriately. The music is played by Navy bands at ceremonies: changing of command, sailing and arrival of ships. It is uplifting and spirited usually and is played at optimistic times.

Anchors Aweigh **(1906 version)**, still used today at the Naval Academy and Enlisted Boot Camp.

Stand Navy down the field, sails set to the sky;
We'll never change our course, So Army you steer shy-y-y-y.
Roll up the score, Navy, anchors aweigh!
Sail Navy down the field and sink the Army, sink the Army grey!

Get under way Navy, decks cleared for the fray;
We'll hoist true Navy Blue, So Army down your grey-y-y-y;
Full speed ahead, Navy; Army heave to;
Furl Black and Grey and Gold, and hoist the Navy, hoist the Navy Blue!

Blue of the Seven Seas; Gold of God's Great Sun
Let these our colors be till all of time be done, done, done,
By Severn's shore we learn Navy's stern call:
Faith, Courage, Service true, with Honor, Over Honor, Over All.

Revised Lyrics of 1926 by George D. Lottman:

Stand, Navy, out to sea, Fight our battle cry;
We'll never change our course, So vicious foe steer shy-y-y-y.
Roll out the TNT, Anchors Aweigh. Sail on to victory
And sink their bones to Davy Jones, hooray!

Anchors Aweigh, my boys, Anchors Aweigh.
Farewell to college joys, we sail at break of day-ay-ay-ay.
Through our last night on shore, drink to the foam,
Until we meet once more. Here's wishing you a happy voyage
home.

Revised Lyrics of 1997 by <u>MCPON John Hagan, USN (Ret)</u> which is used today by the Navy:

[FIRST TWO STANZAS ARE THE SAME WITH THIS LAST NEW STANZA ADDED......]
Blue of the mighty deep, Gold of God's great sun;
Let these our colors be, Till All of time be done-n-n-ne;
On seven seas we learn, Navy's stern call:
Faith, courage, service true, With honor over, honor over all.

4. **The Collection of Bosun's Calls ...** These are fascinating. There are four basic sounds which in combination have different meanings. It is worth your while to go on the internet and listen to an explanation and some demonstrations.

Search for "Sounds of the Bosuns Call ... 2010 Sea Scout Manual, 11th edition."
YouTube ... Dan Maker ... 20 Feb 2013

THE LARGE BORE SHOTGUN
ON AN AIRCRAFT CARRIER

FOR MID-OCEAN UNDERWAY REPLENISHMENT

CAN YOU GUESS why we had a large bore shotgun aboard? Probably we had several as backup in case of malfunction. It must have been about a six gauge, maybe four gauge. It shot a single steel ball. It was used for mid-ocean resupply of fuel, food, munitions, etc.

Before *Nimitz* and *Ford* class carriers with nuclear propulsion, conventional supercarriers needed LOTS of fuel. It was heavy fuel oil and I saw a plaque on the *Lexington* that listed the consumption of fuel at flank speed at sixteen gallons to the foot. You read that correctly: **sixteen gallons to the foot**. The supercarriers are larger. Of course, flank speed against the considerable water resistance was rarely necessary but still LOTS of fuel is used. Re-supply while at sea must be done maybe weekly to keep the tanks topped. Jet aircraft mostly use JP-5 which is a hybrid kerosene. Combat readiness required regular replenishment. Even nuclear carriers need millions of gallons of jet fuel. Empty or low tanks for either fuel is a no go.

That's why we had the large-bore shotgun. An oiler ship would come alongside the carrier, always on the starboard side, and the two ships would match speed and direction for relative stability. Our flight deck was so high we looked down at the other ship. Someone would shoot the steel ball over the supply ship. Attached to the steel ball was a strong cord that would uncoil and follow it across. The oiler crew would remove the steel ball and attach a larger and stronger line to the fly-line. The carrier crew would pull the fly line and its stronger line back to the carrier. Whereupon successively larger and stronger cables would be passed from ship to ship back and forth until a strong enough cable was secured to send the fueling hose over. The hose had rings above it which rode along the cable.... much like shower curtain rings hold the curtain on the rod. Once the fuel hose was attached to the carrier tanks, pumping began.

A second hose was used for pumping JP-5. Another line could be used for passing munitions, crates of food and other equipment. Often the oiler sent over only fuel while a separate supply ship would arrive with the food and other supplies. The crew of four to five thousand young men consumed lots of chow. Like ship and jets, crew doesn't function well with empty tanks.

We didn't have to re-fuel and re-supply at sea too often because everything could be topped up while we were in port. On our Med cruise we mostly alternated ten to fourteen days at sea with a week in port.

Occasionally a person would need transfer and we had a special chair with an extra line to pull it between ships. If it were a stretcher case, we had a clamshell wire basket of body size so we could transfer even an unconscious patient.

That's an extreme simplification of the logistics of our supply chain, but it explains the large-bore shotgun .... and was interesting to watch.... another of those THERE I WUZ deals.

SENDING THE INDY'S VW VAN TO DAVY JONES' LOCKER

IT WAS DURING the Med Cruise of 1966. We had just anchored for a port call and were preparing for a few days of R & R ashore in balmy autumn weather. Since the pier facilities could not accommodate a ship our size, it was necessary to "anchor out" and take boats from the Indy to the pier. The *Independence* had a Volkswagen van that was put ashore for port calls and used to pick up supplies including fresh vegetables, to deliver personnel and messages and generally to run errands as needed. The van had to be transferred to a boat, taken ashore and unloaded on the pier.

The word went out that there was a scene topside that was good entertainment. Upon arrival on the flight deck there were several hundred sailors gathered just aft of the island watching the scene unfold in the water below. It seems that after the VW van had been lifted away from the ship with a boom to be transferred to a barge, it had slipped out of its harness and was floating free in the sea. The van was watertight as it had good seals on all the doors and windows, so it was bobbing up and down in the water. There were three or four sailors swimming around the van in their clothes. They were trying to get a line around the van to secure it and to lift it into the barge with the boom. Of course, there were shouted comments and kibitzing from the growing crowd on the flight deck watching the whole procedure.

A line would be put around the van and tension applied by the boom operator. The line would begin to raise the van, then slip off. As this happened the van would begin wild gyrations and the crowd of observers would roar with laughter and catcalls. A myriad of suggestions was shouted to the frustrated and increasingly frantic sailors in the water. Several different approaches were tried but the line kept slipping off. A horizontal tie was attempted. A round and round vertical tie was tried. No good. Every time the line would just slip off and the van bobbed more and more. The crowd kept growing as the cheers and shouting drew the attention of more people.

All this was indeed good entertainment. By now there may have been four or five hundred of us watching the whole scene. One of the sailors in the water decided to try to secure the line by looping it through the driver's side door handle to keep it from slipping over the top of the van. As the boom operator increased tension on the line this suddenly popped open the door.

The water rushed inside and the van proceeded to sink rapidly beneath the surface down to the bottom of the harbor. The roar of the crowded observer gallery no doubt could be heard ashore. It took quite a while for the laughter to stop and the assembled sailors to dissipate and return to their assigned duties.

We had sent the Indy's Volkswagen van to Davy Jones' locker.

[This story was written 11-2-18]

THE DOUBLE WHAMMY

"FLIGHT SURGEON", M.D. (Dr. FS) and I met and became friends at the NAMI Flight Surgeon School in Pensacola. He and his wife had three children. FS was a tall friendly guy from the Midwest. He worked hard and when the final class rankings were published FS was the one who bested me by .002 of a percentage, so he had a billet choice just before mine. There were two carrier billets available. FS selected one and I selected the other. Both airwings and carriers were slated for Mediterranean deployments in the Atlantic Fleet and both were based at Norfolk (carriers) and NAS Oceana (airwings.) So off we went for our two years active duty as carrier flight surgeons.

The First Whammy ... FS was deployed at sea on a short proficiency training cruise to GITMO when his accident occurred. After an F-4 Phantom flight and trap he was caught in a gust of wind as he dismounted to the flight deck where he landed off balance and tore a hole in the knee of his flight suit. He went into the squadron ready room where they had a tradition that if someone didn't keep their flight suit repaired, i.e., holes sewed or patched, the others in the squadron would rip the suit off them. FS was new in the squadron and didn't know that. In the friendly attack and scuffle to rip off his flight suit FS banged against a bulkhead. Several weeks later back in Virginia

Beach he became aware of a retinal detachment. Whammy. THERE HE WUZ…. incapacitated and unable to perform his duties. He went to Portsmouth Naval Hospital for surgery on his eye. Hospitalization was for two weeks then he returned to NAS Oceana and the airwing billet. One day "out of the blue I got a call from BUMED (Bureau of Medicine and Surgery) telling me my new billet was NAS Norfolk as the Naval Aviation Reserve Training Unit (NARTU) flight surgeon." [quoted from Dr. FS.] His carrier and airwing were soon departing for a six-months Med Cruise and BUMED decided he was at risk of a re-detachment if on a carrier participating in flight ops. Dr. FS's arguments and pleadings were denied, a replacement flight surgeon went with the carrier and Dr. FS was sent over to NARTU for shore duty.

The Second Whammy … THERE HE WUZ one morning at NAS Norfolk (1 November 1967) when he received another call from BUMED and the caller said, "Dr. FS, we have an immediate need for a flight surgeon with a Patrol Squadron [Flying P-3 Orion patrol aircraft for anti-submarine warfare (ASW) missions.] deploying to NAS Sangley Field in the Philippines for six months. Would you like to volunteer to go with them?" Dr. FS only had seven months left on active duty. He was to start a residency in Internal Medicine in July. He was married with three young children. It didn't' take him long to say, "Actually, no, I would not like to volunteer to do that. You said recently that my retinal detachment kept me from a fleet deployment." The BUMED caller responded, "Well there are ophthalmologists at Clark AFB an hour from Sangley and a retinal specialist in Yokuska, Japan, so it's too bad you won't volunteer because we cut your orders this morning. Get packed, you leave the day after tomorrow."

THERE HE WUZ … Whammy again and off to the Philippines for six months. I haven't seen him since but recently found him and exchanged correspondence. He is doing well.

THE CENTURION AND THE
FLAMING HOOKER

BEFORE STUDENT NAVAL aviators graduate from flight school and receive their "Wings of Gold" as Naval Aviators they must successfully complete "Car Quals" (a.k.a. CQ) which is navy lingo for Carrier Qualifications. They of course have practiced carrier landing techniques on solid land airstrips with the Fresnel lens ("meatball") approach system to make precise touchdown where the arresting cables are on a carrier.... but there is nothing like the real thing. Carrier decks are NOT solid stationary landing strips. They bounce in varying and differing ways. Each student pilot must qualify by performing twelve day landings and eight night landings on a real carrier. (In 1966 it was 20 and 10.) So off they go for Car Quals.

Later when deployed with a squadron on a carrier they fly regular hops (sorties) both day and night. Records of each trap are carefully kept .... not only how many, but also the quality of technique. Each landing receives a numerical score from Zero (bolter) to ten points (perfect approach and trapping on #3 or #4 wire. A perfect ten-point landing is called an OK-3 or OK-4.

Eventually an aviator has become experienced and executes his ONE HUNDREDTH trap on that carrier. (Previous traps elsewhere don't count.) He has earned the title of CENTURION. In celebration and recognition, the ship's cooks prepare a special cake with decorations (planes, ships, his name, etc. in keeping with the theme) and wording for "Congratulations Centurion." The squadron has a brief congratulations ceremony in the ready room to cut and eat the cake and celebrate the milestone achievement. Various invited guests assist with the celebration. [Two hundred traps and you are a Double Centurion, three hundred a Triple Centurion…. after that everyone wonders why in heck you are still on the same carrier.]

Then …. next time you are ashore as a Centurion you must be initiated into the Flaming Hooker society. A "flaming hooker" is perhaps not the image some people might conjure when reading this. In naval aviation a "flaming hooker" is the term used for a night carrier landing because when a steel tailhook at 130 knots hits the steel deck, sparks and flames shoot out in all directions. It's a little mesmerizing to watch these. They are a little like fireworks and especially sparklers.

So, Joe Centurion is ashore in a bar somewhere with his squadron aviator mates. They order a shot glass with one ounce of brandy and light it afire. This drink is known as a "Flaming Hooker" and the new Centurion initiate must down it in one gulp. The secret is to do it immediately while the brandy is still room temperature. The flame is immediately extinguished in the mouth and not much different from a regular shot of brandy. Of course, the trusty? buddies try to toast and delay the initiate's performance, hoping to let the brandy heat up …. which it does. The hot brandy becomes a serious problem as it can burn the mouth and throat and if spit out… which is the usual reflex action … burns of the face are common. I had to treat several such cases in sickbay because the initiate didn't know the "secret" of rapid quaffing. The new Centurion must wear his "burn beard" for a week or so until it heals……… and that takes us to the CIRCUMCENTURION……

THE CIRCUMCENTURION

OUR SHIP'S COMPANY general surgeon (A.T.) didn't have much to do in the way of surgery. He helped with sick call medical care, took his MOD rotation every fourth day and had some occasional surgical cases. There were a few appendectomies, some abscesses to be drained, some broken bones to set and cast, lacerations to suture, etc. but not that much surgery because our sailors were basically healthy or they would not have been there.

So, Al got bored. He decided to offer circumcisions to any sailors who wanted one. Among that large population of sailors there were a significant number who wanted to have their foreskins removed. In addition to the benefits of the surgery the postop recovery period allowed the sailor to have a few days or a week off work for recuperation.

The word went out over the ship and sailors started signing up for a circumcision. Al started doing a few cases every day or so when we were at sea. (No one wanted to forfeit shore leave time to do it when in port.)

By and by the number of cases began to add up and someone had the idea that the 100th case should be celebrated like a pilot's hundredth trap. So, we had the cooks bake a large cake and decorate it appropriately. Use your imagination about the creative artwork decorating the cake in colorful icing.... things like a scalpel and .... Of course, the patient/

sailor's name was on the cake and emblazoned across the middle was "CIRCUMCENTURION" in prominent position.

We had a little celebration party with the medical department and others in attendance. A brief ceremony was done including photographs of everyone involved. After congratulations all around the cake was CUT (pun intended) and enjoyed. Dr. Al was congratulated on his milestones (pun intended) achievement…. and our sailor patient was certainly the proudest among us and delighted with the attention even though he had given up a lot to get it.

JESUS MAKES A VISIT
TO SICKBAY

THERE I WUZ in sickbay one morning when a call came in from the radar decks. There was a Radarman Third Class (hereafter called RM3) who was "acting funny" and they were sending him down to sickbay for evaluation. Down he came and arrived escorted by two shore patrol. We gave him a thorough physical exam and found nothing amiss. However, his affect was strange and it was obvious he either had some mental disturbance or perhaps a stress reaction.

I was the newest flight surgeon, junior in seniority and most recently graduated from NAMI and its psychiatry courses, so I got the duty as the Indy's psychiatrist. Even though Marine flight surgeon Gene Purvis was planning a psych residency after his tour, dealing with all the emotional problems on the Indy was tedious and frustrating…. so, I was stuck with the emotion-disordered sailors. It took time away from more desirable duties…. but THERE I WUZ.

During the cruise it was not uncommon for a sailor to go "stir-crazy" and have various emotional/mental problems. Usually, some psychological counseling and a lot of listening would resolve the difficulties and the sailor would return to functional capacity. Sometimes the etiology of the aberrant behavior was just immaturity. There was an urge to give the sailor a good spanking and tell him to grow up. We did some of that with the counseling.

So RM3 was admitted to a hospital bed in sickbay where he could be monitored and observed by the duty corpsmen and so I could interview him regularly. Most important was to make an accurate diagnosis and disposition. We had that padded cell room which we used as a private consultation room. It had a desk and several chairs and was the appropriate venue for interview of psych cases. Over the next several days I used that padded cell room for multiple hour-long discussions with RM3.

Remembering all I could from medical school and NAMI psychiatry training, mostly I just listened and let RM3 talk and lead the conversation. Some of his verbiage was rambling and almost incoherent. Sometimes he was more lucid but still strange. RM3 thought he was Jesus Christ. He was aloof to reality and his surroundings. He talked with religious cliché sometimes, was all-understanding and all-forgiving of other people's transgressions. I just listened.

After multiple hour-long sessions over three or four days I was about to decide RM3 was schizophrenic. He was talking and I was listening, but not giving him much feedback .... including not indicating whether I did or did not believe he thought he was Jesus. RM3 kept talking and gradually it dawned on me that he was more and more trying to convince me that he thought he was Jesus. Eureka! If he really thought he was Jesus Christ, he wouldn't have to convince me. He was malingering and faking the whole thing. I confronted him with my diagnosis and his reaction essentially confirmed my interpretation. He continued the façade but the wind was out of his sails because I wasn't buying it. He stopped trying to convince me that he thought he was Jesus, but the cat was out of the bag.

So how did it all work out? The resolution was simple and effective. If he really were schizophrenic and mentally unstable, he was at risk for suicide by jumping off the fantail. I discussed that with him and told him how easy it would be. If jumping off at night when the flight deck was deserted, no one would even miss him until too bad, too late. RM3 wasn't happy that I even suggested that.

For his personal safety I confined RM3 to the brig… for his own protection and self-preservation. Off he went under Marine guard for a stint behind bars. (Refer to the section about the brig for the routines there.)

I saw RM3 several times on MOD rounds and inspection of the brig. He was behaving less and less disordered but was a most unhappy sailor. After about a week in the brig he confessed that it was all a big scam, that he was normal and please "let me out of the brig."

There was no way RM3 could be trusted in the radar center doing his previous work helping with air traffic control and monitoring aircraft. So, he was assigned to the mess decks where he helped with clearing, cleaning, washing, hauling garbage and the like. I saw him from time to time when making rounds of the mess decks. We never spoke or even acknowledged recognition. He didn't show any signs of resentment.

RM3 finished the cruise on the mess decks and I have no idea what happened after that. My guess is that he left the navy.

That is the story of when Jesus made a visit to sickbay.

THE CONGRESSIONAL
INVESTIGATION

THE FAMOUS SIGN ON HARRY TRUMAN'S
DESK, "THE BUCK STOPS HERE"

THERE I WUZ ... Minding my own business, trying to finish routine sick call. We were in port; I don't recall where. I was MOD (Medical Officer of the Day) so finishing early would allow making some of the "inspection rounds" and having a little free time before the usual evening arrival of drunks and minor injuries. Standing there was a nervous corpsman and a sailor. They had come aboard from a destroyer in our Battle Group.

The Medical Department on the carrier had the only physicians and the best medical facilities in the Battle Group so we provided backup care for the whole group. Each of the smaller ships had one or two Independent Duty Corpsmen (IDC) who had to be E-4 to E-7 and enroll in a twelve-month intensive medical training program. It wasn't as lengthy or as comprehensive as medical school but in one year it covered the basics including some clinical experience. The IDCs were widely respected in the navy medical brotherhood. They took care of a wide range of injuries and medical problems and knew when to refer a sailor up the line for more care.

So here was an openly nervous IDC from a tin can with a smug sailor in tow…. and a health record about three inches thick, maybe more. It appeared that the sailor had contracted a rash on his skin, the IDC had diagnosed it correctly as tinea versicolor which is caused by a harmless skin fungus by the name of *Malassezia furfur*. The fungus is quite common on the skin, especially in warm humid conditions … like a Med cruise. The fungus causes completely harmless pigmentation variations in the skin, often called pseudoachromatic spots. These are spots and patches where the skin doesn't make normal pigment so the spots are lighter color than the normal skin. The effect is magnified when the person gets a suntan…. like working without a shirt, topside, on a Med cruise.

There are no symptoms, it is not contagious and easily treated. Lotions and creams like Lotrimin, Tinatin, Selsun and others are effective at eliminating the fungus, but the light spots on the skin persist for months, even a year.

Repeat: the IDC had correctly diagnosed the spots on the sailor's shoulders, back and arms. He had prescribed the correct treatment to cure the problem by eliminating the fungus.

Problem: those spots persisted and the sailor wasn't' happy that his skin had not returned to normal … even though the IDC had explained it would take months or longer. The unhappy sailor was from Maine and wrote a letter to his then U.S. Senator, Margaret Chase Smith…. complaining that he was not getting good medical care, that his health was in danger, etc.

Senator Smith bucked it over to SECNAV, who bucked it to CNO, who bucked it to CINCLANT, who bucked it to ComSixthFleet, who bucked it to ComBattleGroup, who bucked it to the Captain of the destroyer who bucked it to the Independent Duty Corpsman and asked him, "What in the H--- is going on?

You can see why the IDC from the destroyer was nervous and

perhaps why the sailor was smug at all the attention he was getting and the results from his letter.

That's where the Harry Truman quote comes in … that letter went buck, buck, buck, buck, buck right down the chain of command until that day on the Indy in sick bay with me as MOD …

"The buck stops here."

The way to diagnose a case of Tinea versicolor is to shine a Wood's light on the skin and to do a skin scraping with KOH prep and look for fungal elements under the microscope.

Wood's light is an ultraviolet light in a handheld lamp. We had one on the Indy. If *Malassezia furfur* is present on the skin it will fluoresce. Subject sailor did not fluoresce so there was no active fungus on his skin.

Skin scrapings were mounted on a slide with KOH and examined under the microscope. There were no fungal elements. There was no active fungus on the skin.

Sailor cured, still had pseudoachromatic spots. Long discussion, long explanation, long note in his health record … and then I explained to him that he might have a problem with future presentations to sick call. Every time a corpsman or doctor reviewed his chart, there would likely be a speculation that the sailor was a smart-ass. I gave soothing reassurance to the now less-nervous IDC ……. and then came the hard part.

Goodbye extra freedom that day, goodbye the rest of the day or more. I had to write a Congressional Investigation Report for Margaret Chase Smith. You should have seen the packet of papers and the forms that had to be done. I don't think it went directly to her. I think it bucked back up the chain of command whence it came. I wasn't a particularly happy MOD that day, but thereafter it has been fun to tell the story. Even as I write this it is still amusing and smile-inducing.

Yep, THERE I WUZ…. an Official Investigator for the U.S. Congress. Should it be on my resume'?

IN MEMORIAM

CDR Harold F. Hicks
VA-75 ... A-6 Intruder
16 August 1966

LT Harold L. Quint
VA-75 ... A-6 Intruder
16 August 1966

THE A-6 INTRUDER launched from the angle deck catapult and retracted the flaps instead of the gear. Flying speed was immediately lost, the plane flipped upside down and flew into the water. All we found was 100 grams of tissue floating on some buoyant padding.

LCDR Monard L. Lilleboe
VQ-2 ... A-3 Skywarrior
3 November 1966

AT1 Lawrence Gallagher
VQ-2 ... A-3 Skywarrior
3 November 1966

LTJG James H. Stilz, Jr
VQ-2 ... A-3 Skywarrior
3 November 1966

ADJ2 Keith A. Kleis
VQ-2 ... A-3 Skywarrior
3 November 1966

LTJG Victor C. Vogel
VQ-2 ... A-3 Skywarrior
3 November 1966

ATR3 David W. McCusker
VQ-2 ... A-3 Skywarrior
3 November 1966

The A-3 was developed as a carrier-based nuclear bomber but later converted for use as an airborne electronic warfare platform and as a tanker for inflight refueling. It was the largest and heaviest carrier aircraft and consequently nicknamed "The Whale." The A-3 carried pilot and copilot plus one officer and three enlisted men to operate the electronic equipment.

The A-3 was completing a routine flight and descending for its trap recovery when it flew into the water. According to radio and radar records the pilot had misread the altimeter by ten thousand feet. The Three-Pointer Altimeter in the A-3 had one pointer indicating 10,000 feet per number on the dial, one indicating thousands of feet, the third indicating hundreds of feet. The pilot called "descending through ten thousand feet" just before he hit the water.

One body was recovered because a survival vest toggle had caught on something in the crash and inflated the flotation bags. Our surgeon insisted on doing an autopsy although the rest of the physicians didn't think it was appropriate and that we should just send the remains stateside. The final diagnosis was "Multiple Injuries Extreme." The other details are best left in the distant past.

Rest in Peace these eight…. "There but for the grace of God, go I."

THE MOST DIFFICULT TASK
OF THE ENTIRE CRUISE

I HAD GONE ashore in Barcelona, then we went back to sea. It was my first time with at-sea flight operations. I had several flights including a flight in an A-6 Intruder with the XO of VA-75, Commander Hicks. That was on the fourteenth or fifteenth of August. The A-6 has a side-by-side cockpit with pilot on the left and Bombardier/Navigator on the right so the visuals are unobstructed and it was a fine flight. The *Independence* was due to "make port" in Naples a few days after that.

A day or two after my flight CDR Hicks and his regular B/N, LT Harold Quint, took a cat shot and flew into the water killing both. Apparently, the flaps were retracted before the gear and the loss of lift resulted in insufficient lift for the drag, so the plane stalled, flipped inverted and flew into the water.

There were thirty or forty wives who followed the ship from port to port. Mostly they were officers' wives. Some had children. When Indy sailed out for a sea period, the wives would go to the next port, find an apartment to rent and be there for that next port call. The wives were required to notify the squadron of complete contact information, where they were and how to contact them. The group of wives and their assorted children became close friends, sharing their ashore activities, bonding with the common interest of why they were there … undoubtedly sharing their fears and emotions. They were a support group for one another.

Harold Quint's wife was in an apartment in Naples with their two or three children. After the accident, the squadron commander put together a team to notify Mrs. Quint in person. No advance information was sent ashore. The team would be the squadron skipper, the chaplain and me as a physician. I'm not sure why I was selected because Al Cohen (the senior flight surgeon) knew Harold much better. Al probably just didn't want the unpleasant task.

The day of arrival in Naples the skipper, the chaplain and I took the Captain's Gig ashore about 0600 before Indy docked and any message could get to Mrs. Quint. We had the address and location of the apartment. Naples navy authorities provided a car and driver to meet our launch and take us directly to the apartment building. We took the elevator up and knocked on the apartment door. There was a brief delay, probably as Mrs. Quint threw on a housecoat.

When she opened the door, she knew exactly why we were there. Not a word was spoken, but she knew. She of course recognized the squadron skipper, but the chaplain and I were strangers. She may have seen the chaplain's cross insignia and my medical corps insignia.

The wives and families all know full well the risks and dangers of carrier aviation. When Mrs. Quint saw the skipper, she knew immediately there was only one reason he would be knocking on her door with two other officers that early in the morning. She absorbed the initial shock surprisingly well, did not break down emotionally, but her distress and grief were immediately obvious.

The skipper told her what happened. He minimized the details. That could come later if she wanted them. The CO introduced the chaplain and me. We each offered condolences and any spiritual or medical assistance she might want or need. I had brought along a small supply of sedatives and tranquilizers and gave them to her with instructions for use if she needed them. She said probably not because she had the children to care for…. and she would have to explain to them what had happened.

Mrs. Quint was amazing. She maintained calm despite the obvious shock, grief and distress on her face. I think the children were stirring in the background but the tension was so great those details are now vague.

The CO offered to provide any assistance Mrs. Quint needed.... help with packing, help arranging return to the United States, help notifying others stateside and/or the other wives. The chaplain and I offered similar assistance in any way we could at any time. After probably thirty minutes, maybe it was an hour ... but it felt like forever ... we offered our condolences again and our offers of help and departed for the ship.

That was the most difficult task of the entire cruise. Definitely .... and among the most distressing of my medical career.

NOTE: Physicians are trained for and must deal with death regularly. It is never easy and always stressful to tell someone of the death of a loved one. In many cases the death is expected or forewarned and that helps both the physician and the family of the deceased. In many cases the deceased is elderly and not in the prime of life with young children. Even in sudden accidents the family usually knows their loved one is dead before a conversation with the physician. That day in Naples provided no forewarning for Mrs. Quint except perhaps the unspoken gut-fear that it might happen. The grief of all four of us when she opened that apartment door is just not describable.

XII

FLIGHT SURGEON ASHORE

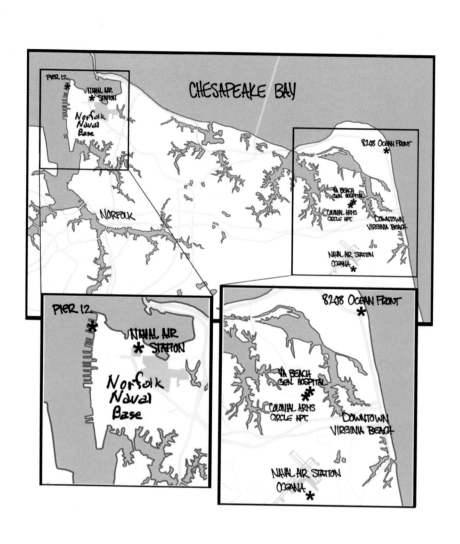

SHORE DUTY IN VIRGINIA BEACH

FLIGHT SURGEON LIFE AND MEDICAL ANECDOTES FROM NAS OCEANA

IN FEBRUARY, THE Airwing Seven aircraft "fly-off" was the day before the Indy tied up to Pier 12 at the Norfolk Naval Station. Sailing into Norfolk was impressive on its own. Naval Station Norfolk is the largest naval station in the world. It is known as Sewell's Point and is on the Hampton Roads peninsula. It is the home of the U.S. Fleet Forces Command. There are four miles of waterfront space and eleven miles of pier and wharf space with seventy-five ships along the fourteen piers. Impressive would be an understatement. There are usually two or three, sometimes more aircraft carriers at the piers.

They knew we were coming. There was a huge crowd of family waiting to be reunited with their loved ones who had been at sea for so long. Mooring at the pier with flags flying, bands playing and the throngs of people was just as impressive as sailing in and seeing all the ships. It took most of the day for those going ashore to offload and depart the dock. Of course, a functional contingent crew remained aboard.

My how Elizabeth had grown. From a month-old newborn in June, she was a cognitive baby now. Babies double their birth weight in six months and triple it in a year. It was good to be home. Bubbling with stories from the cruise and hearing all about the goings-on stateside consumed untold hours of conversation. Fresh seafood was a treat at lots of meals. I never had any complaints about the food on the Indy, but home cooking is always the best.

So, family life was reestablished and orientation at NAS Oceana began. Getting an ID sticker for my TR-4A made gate passage quicker. There was always a stream of cars. The military guard would see your sticker and salute you through. Although my primary assignment and responsibility was to the Airwing, mostly the workday was in the Infirmary a.k.a. Dispensary a.k.a. "Sickbay" even though it was on land.

The airwing command and staff was based at NAS Oceana. VF-84 and VF-41 (F-4 Phantom fighter squadrons) and VA-75 (A-6 Intruder squadron) home-based at Oceana while the A-4s were at NAS Jacksonville, Florida. The other squadrons and detachments returned to their respective home bases. So now I had just three squadrons. Even so, visits to the ready rooms became less frequent because of the distance from the Infirmary to the hangars.

The routine at the Infirmary was little different from on the carrier except we now provided medical care for the large number of wives and children in the families of the active-duty personnel. Because other airwings and squadrons were also based there, we usually had fifteen or so flight surgeons to help with the load. That gave us all time to visit our respective squadron ready rooms, to fly with our squadrons, give training programs, et al. We shared the annual flight physical responsibilities. It also meant that we were only on call about twice a month. As Medical Officer of the Day (MOD) we stayed overnight in the infirmary. There was a small but comfortable room with private bathroom facilities for the on-call doctor.

The senior medical officer oversaw overall care and scheduling of physicians for call duty, times for clinic, times for squadrons and flying, etc. Like on the ship he was more an administrator than a practicing physician. The infirmary was a long low building. At one end was the main entrance with registration desk, records department, administrative offices and a comfortable lounge where patients could await their turn. The commanding medical officer's office was there to the right of the main hall. Patients, both sailors and families checked in at the front desk, their records were pulled and they were escorted to the middle section where there was a bank of examining rooms, treatment rooms with lots of equipment, physician offices/consultation rooms, rest room facilities et al.

On the left at the end of the long hall was a hospital ward with nurse's station and various support side rooms, heads, etc. We had five or six beds available for inpatient observation. Only occasional patients were admitted. They were sick but non-critical patients. We referred major problems to the Portsmouth Naval Hospital by ambulance, as necessary.

Also, at the back to the right of the end of the hall was a large Aviation Medicine section. It had all the Vision Lanes, slit lamps and refraction equipment we needed for flight physicals. Our sound-proof booth for audiometric testing was soundproof!!! The corpsmen would begin with history and vital signs including weight. They would do vision and audiometric testing and various other testing batteries. After all was ready, the physician physical examination would follow. We had a large central room which was the site of doing the flight physicals quite often in groups of thirty or forty.

We usually had three or four flight surgeons working simultaneously and we practiced division of labor. Since I was going into an ENT residency, I would check ears, nose and throat. Another flight surgeon would examine eyes, another would listen to chest and heart, another check abdomens, hernia and hemorrhoids.

It was all men in those days so the examinees would stand in a row, stripped naked except for skivvies. [The occasional exams for women officers and of course for female patients would be done in private rooms with female nurse attendants.] The corpsmen would have the men in the line do range of motion exercises for arms and legs, squats, etc.

Then the flight surgeons would go down the line checking our respective areas. It was efficient and allowed us to do a significant volume without undue waiting for the examinees.

Spin-Around Butt Check ...A great anecdote evolved from these examinations. My Indy flight surgeon roommate, Al Cohen, developed a unique and unorthodox way to check for hemorrhoids. He would sit on a revolving stool in the middle of the room, have the examinees form a circle around him, then turn around with their backs to the center. On command they would lower their skivvies, bend over, spread their cheeks and Al would rotate around on his stool to visualize each rear end for hemorrhoids or other abnormalities. If any pathology were present that individual would be sent to a private room for further evaluation. (a.k.a. "up-the-kazoo" rectal exam et al.)

Here is a collection of THERE I WUZ stories from the infirmary at NAS Oceana:

The Bleeding Pervert ... THERE I WUZ at the infirmary when one night about 0100 the Shore Patrol (SP) brought in a young sailor in handcuffs with blood all over his white sailor trousers. The SP said, "Doc, look at this pervert before we take him to the brig. We arrested him on the boardwalk exposing himself." [Virginia Beach had a boardwalk downtown (like the more famous one in Atlantic City.) It was all along the oceanfront between the ocean and beach on the front side and various stores, hotels and apartment buildings behind on the land side.]

The story was that the Shore Patrol had spotted the sailor bending over on the boardwalk with his pants down so they arrested him for indecent exposure. They were on the way to the brig but thought medical ought to check out all the blood.

The sailor was not drunk in the infirmary. (Believe me I had sufficient experience with drunk sailors in sickbay on the ship and some of them were brought in handcuffed by the SP.) The sailor's story explained everything. He had been at a party in a friend's apartment overlooking the boardwalk. He had a pint of whiskey in his back pocket and was sitting on a low privacy wall in front of the first-floor apartment.

Suddenly he fell backward onto the boardwalk and landed on his butt. It didn't hurt much but when he stood up, he noticed blood running down into his shoes. He pulled down his trousers to see where he was bleeding…. and that's when the SP saw him and arrested him.

Examination showed multiple lacerations on the sailor's gluteus maximus cheek … exactly where his hip pocket held the whisky bottle. He had landed on the whiskey bottle which smashed and cut his behind… hence the blood running down into his shoes. I sterilized the wounds, administered a local anesthetic and sutured the lacerations. Multiple Band-Aids were sufficient dressings. I wished the sailor good luck as the SP hauled him off back in handcuffs…. and offered to certify his medical need to drop his drawers if that would help him.

The lacerations were not serious and would all heal with no long-term effects. It was all kind of funny in a way if not for the serious charges against him. I had fixed his end, but never heard how his case ended.

The Six-months Sprained Back … On another MOD occasion a sailor and his wife brought in their twelve-year-old son with a laceration that required suturing. The usual procedure is for family to wait outside the treatment room while surgical procedures proceed, even minor surgery. But the mother was insistent that her little boy needed her support while the suturing was done. I relented and let mother and father come along into the treatment room. The mother was an exceptionally large woman. The young boy was quite brave and dealing with it all very well, when suddenly the mother fainted. As she fell her husband jumped over to catch her and break her fall. She came around rapidly, but the husband sailor was in agony from his back hurting. I finished the suturing and turned my attention to the sailor's back. It was Musculo-skeletal sprain. I ordered pain medication, muscle relaxants, heat and gave him an appointment for sick call in a few days. X-rays were negative and further examination ruled out any pathology except the muscle strain. It took six months and multiple trips to sickbay to get his back well and get him off light duty status. THERE I WUZ …. with another interesting story. The little boy was fine, the mother was fine .... the sailor suffered for the laceration.

Fridays Off ... One of the squadron enlisted men had a serious motorcycle accident and sustained multiple fractures of arms and legs. He was lucky not to have been killed. He was in traction at Portsmouth Naval Hospital and required several operations. Finally, after several months he was discharged and sent back to Oceana. Voluminous reports and records were sent with him including specific orders for him to return to the Orthopedic Clinic every Friday for follow-up. He dutifully followed orders and reported to Portsmouth every Friday. His squadron chief and personnel officer got used to him being gone every Friday for Orthopedic Clinic. After a few months, the sailor was discharged from the ortho clinic...... but by then he was feeling well and was getting accustomed to having Fridays off.

So.... he just kept taking off on Fridays but without going to Portsmouth to the clinic. That went on for about six months or longer before anyone wondered when he was going to be discharged from ortho clinic and returned to full duty. Someone called Portsmouth and found out that our sailor had been discharged six or seven months previously. I don't know what happened to the sailor.

Very Few Sailors for Friday Sick Call ... Friday sick call was always lighter than the Monday through Thursday load.... and there was a good reason. When sailors came down with the usual common colds, throat infections, strained muscles, gastro-intestinal disorders and the like, they reported to the infirmary to sick call. We prescribed the appropriate treatment and frequently that included light duty or no duty for a day or two. From time to time, we would have a sailor at sick call who didn't really seem to be sick. Maybe it was worry ... or maybe it was malingering. Sometimes it was obviously malingering. Somehow the malingerers seemed to always show up at the Friday sick call. Hmmmmm? .... early off for the weekend?

So, when we had a suspicious case of malingering on a Friday, we would admit the sailor to one of our infirmary beds "for observation."

We would keep him until late Sunday or early Monday morning in time to return to duty. The word got out, as the saying goes, and that is why we didn't have many sailors report for sick call on Fridays. The ones that did were sick.

Free-loader Attitudes ... Most of the sailors and their families appreciated the healthcare they received, respected the physicians and corpsmen, only requested help when necessary. However, there were a few with "free-loader attitudes" for lack of a better word for it. One such was an officer who wanted "medical" to give him free 100-count packs of cotton-tipped swabs to clean the recording/playing heads on his tape deck. A few people wanted free aspirin and common over-the-counter medications. Another was a man who showed up one Saturday morning at 0500 wanting all four of his children examined. They were on the way to go fishing that day and he wanted to be sure they were not getting colds. There were other examples, but not in the scope of this discussion.

Those Lousy Navy Doctors ... The local Virginia Beach General Hospital (VBGH) was small in 1967. It had a staff of physicians with good qualifications and who practiced a good brand of medicine. It was before the days when hospitals were mandated to have physicians in their emergency rooms, but the staff physicians preferred paying one to be there rather than each of them having to make multiple visits to the ER on their call nights. The pay was $55.00 for a 12-hour shift (1800 hours to 0600 the next day), Sundays through Thursday nights and $65.00 for a Friday or Saturday night shift.

Since we had fifteen or more flight surgeons at NAS Oceana most all the time, we were on call only about twice a month. About a dozen of us signed up to moonlight at VBGH because in 1967 before all that inflation hit a decade later, the money was a fine supplement to our income. We each took the call at VBGH maybe three nights a month.

The Oceana Infirmary received patients 24/7/365 and the MOD was there to evaluate and treat anyone who came. It was not uncommon to have a significant number in the evenings for various reasons. Maybe daddy got home from work and wifey or kiddie-pie was sick. Sometimes the wait would be an hour or two if the evening clinic were busy. Invariably one or two navy family members would go to the infirmary for medical care and for a variety of reasons they would not be happy about it. They would go to VBGH for care.... the proverbial "second opinion" before the term was popularized.

The patients didn't know that the same doctors staffed both places. Often, they would be critical and say negative things about the lousy care they received "at the base." At VBGH we would evaluate the problem, confirm or change the treatment as appropriate in our opinion, listen to the patient a lot and counsel them if needed. After they left if we weren't too busy, it was fun to call whichever of our fellow flight surgeons was the MOD at Oceana and tease him a little about being a "lousy Navy doctor." A few nights later we would be MOD at Oceana and some of our patients would be unhappy about our treatment, go to VBGH, then we would get the call and take a turn at being the "lousy Navy doctor."

Psychiatrists don't do professional courtesy for physicians or their families because they insist that patients who don't pay for care don't respect it. That may be true for some other services and goods besides medical care. Some of that psychology was behind the daily trek of patients from the NAS infirmary to the VBGH Emergency Room. The same physicians provided the care at both places. Most likely the problem was that at the NAS Oceana infirmary patients received good medical care, but no satisfaction.

You Dirty Rotten S.O.B. ... One of my pilot's wives came to me one day at the infirmary requesting assistance in stopping smoking. A great many people smoked cigarettes in those days and the wives especially seemed to have a problem with it. At squadron parties, picnics and other activities everyone got to know most everyone else. We were mostly on a first-name friendship basis as by then I was part of the squadron family. "Susie" (fictitious name) described her habit and some of her lifestyle reasons for smoking and not being able to quit after several previous attempts. Could I help and would I help her. Of course.

So, we began a regimen of the various lifestyle modifications, medications and behavioral recommendations. I saw "Susie" a few times over the next month or so ... both in the infirmary for tweaking and reinforcement as well as at social events. She was doing great and was almost over the nicotine addictive phase ... really doing well.

Then one night at a squadron party, as was usual, we were all standing around having a few alcoholic drinks and I casually mentioned to husband "Joe" (also fictious name) how proud I was that "Susie" was doing so well stopping smoking. The party went on as usual with drinks flowing and smoke in the air.

About fifteen minutes later THERE I WUZ .... backed against a wall by an irate Susie cursing me in very direct terms. "Dirty Rotten S.O.B" is polite compared to some of the things she said. The problem was that I had violated a patient confidence and had betrayed her by telling her husband that she was trying to stop smoking. My assumption that "Joe" knew all about it was wrong. She didn't tell him because she didn't want him to know in case she failed again.

Boy, did I learn a huge lesson. I had my ass royally chewed by a fluent professional. Ever since that occasion I have been Dr. Tight-Lips. I have seen patients and even operated on some who were best friends of my spouse ... or spouses of some of my best friends ... or relatives ... or anybody ... and like in the famous story, "He don't say nuthin'."

The Italian Tetracycline ... Tetracycline is a good broad-spectrum antibiotic that was commonly used for infections in the sixties.... particularly if a patient were allergic to penicillin and/or couldn't tolerate erythromycin. The Navy (maybe the entire military?) had apparently put out bids for a large supply of 250mg tetracycline tablets. An Italian company got the contract and the Navy bought a gazillion tablets. Problem: their effective strength was about half potency. I'm not sure how we knew that, but someone apparently noticed they were not working right and tested the potency. Solution: Use twice as many. So, if we wanted a patient to take 250mg every six hours, we ordered 500mg every six hours. The Italian low-bidder didn't save the Navy any money.

FUBIT ... As previously discussed, there were always personnel coming and going, changing duty stations, deploying to sea, getting out of the Navy entirely. They were known as "short timers." In some cases, their dedication, motivation and attitude deteriorated the closer they got to leaving, particularly those being discharged and leaving the Navy permanently. They developed what was known as a 'short-timer attitude." Some were rather cynical and some very blunt and outspoken about it. "What are they going to do about it? …. throw me out of the Navy?" When receiving an unpleasant or unwanted instruction and/or criticism, etc., it was not uncommon to hear a short-timer mumble under his breath "FUBIT." [F… You Buddy, I'm Through.]

30,000 NAILS AND 12 FEET
OF SAND BUILDUP

[Author's Note: This lengthy chapter is not strictly about naval service but is included because it was an integral part of my time in Virginia Beach while in the Navy. On the carrier one is 24/7 with little personal time and no family time. On shore duty those become essential. So, this is the story of how I used my BAH ... basic allowance for housing.]

AFTER RETURNING FROM the Med Cruise, we were staying in the small apartment in the Colonial Arms Apartments in the Hilltop area of Virginia Beach. The apartment was modern, reasonably priced, and close to NAS Oceana. However, it was small, upstairs and only one-bedroom. Elizabeth was approaching one year old and "had her legs" but there was nowhere outside for her to play. We had found and rented the apartment the previous June in a big hurry as related elsewhere. We had little furniture. Our one-year lease was almost completed. For multiple reasons it seemed right that we should look for a bigger place, one with two or three bedrooms, one with a yard.

A local realtor was recommended by a more experienced navy friend as someone to be trusted. Surveying the market there just were not that many apartments available, probably because navy personnel kept the area saturated with renters. The realtor suggested buying a house because there would be lots more space. The mortgage payments would be about the same as apartment rent. Resale would not be too much of a problem because of the same navy demand for housing.

So, house hunting began in earnest. The realtor, Scott Taylor, showed us a few houses for sale. One was up the beach closer to Fort Story right where Highway 60 came in from Norfolk and turned south at the Atlantic Ocean. The house for sale was right on the ocean with nothing between it and water except the beach and a low sand dune. Suddenly it occurred to me that "they aren't making any more ocean shoreline" and the likelihood of investment value growing would be best right on the ocean.

The lady who had owned and lived in the house for decades had recently died. She had run a gift shop downtown for many years. Several children had moved away and had no interest in living in the house or keeping it. Partly that was because maintenance had been deferred for some years. The cedar shake siding was dried, curling and in disrepair. Gutters leaked. It was a "fixer-upper." Being built on sand the middle of the house had settled some and there was a visible sag in the middle of the roofline. Because of all that the asking price was reasonable.

Through the realtor we contacted a building contractor who came out to evaluate everything. His report was that the house was basically sound and in good shape except for the sag from settling foundation and the deferred maintenance items. He said the sagging/settling foundation was not uncommon on the sand and he thought it could be corrected inexpensively.

8208 Oceanfront, Virginia Beach became the new address. There was a great fenced back yard with a lawn and there was that expanse of beach and ocean in front. There was a huge picture window in the living room looking right out at the ocean and a fireplace for cold weather. Two bedrooms with bath were downstairs on the right and upstairs were two more with dormer windows, one being quite large, with full bath… and there was a second full kitchen upstairs. A small enclosed porch at the back entrance led into the ample main kitchen downstairs. Left of the kitchen was the dining room. From the dining room there was an open view through the living room and picture window to the ocean.

The contractor said he had fixed settling/sagging foundations before and the technique was interesting. He and his crew went under the house and poured a 3 X 3 feet square concrete pad with a concave dome underneath. The engineering concept was that as weight was applied to the pad the concavity underneath would force sand into the center, essentially packing it into a column to support the weight and prevent settling. Once the reinforced concrete had set, they went back under and put a house jack between it and a major weight-bearing floor beam right where the settling and sagging had occurred. Then every week the contractor would come by and turn the jack about an eighth to a quarter of a turn. Slowly this applied uplift to the sagging beam and remainder of the house. Over about six months the house slowly went back to its original configuration and there was no longer a sag in the roofline.... and nothing cracked or split as the house was raised back to original configuration.

Furniture was needed and that is when we found a retired navy man who was buying used furniture and selling it from a medium-sized warehouse. Some wonderful pieces were available at reasonable prices. We furnished our new home in short order. It was not much further to Oceana for the daily commute than the apartment had been.

Our realtor said that after we left the Navy, he could rent it by the week in the summer for amazing rent, if it were furnished. Typically, a grandparent couple would rent for a week and gather their two or three adult children with spouses and all the grandchildren for a week at the beach. Our furniture man had those great old beds from the Atlantic City hotel that had been demolished so we outfitted the upstairs. We could sleep twelve adults and a few additional children. Realtor Scott was right. Except for the weeks we were there for the next several summers doing Navy reserve stints, the house was rented every week from Memorial Day to Labor Day. The rent we received was hard to believe. During the rest of the year, about nine months from September to May, the monthly rent was normal going rates but at least covered monthly costs. It was never empty because of that location on the beach and ocean.

I set about doing the deferred maintenance required. First was repairing the leaky gutters. Some sections were sound and just needed scraping and painting. Other areas had rusted holes which were scraped and sanded to fresh metal, then painted with anti-rust undercoat paint. Then an appropriate length of sheet aluminum was cut and bent into a U-shape (flat wide bottom and an inch lip on each side) to fit up under the defective gutter suctions. With the aluminum patch in place holes were drilled through both it and the existing gutter at regular intervals. The aluminum patch was removed and layered inside with exterior caulk, then pushed back into place and secured with short metal screws in all the holes. Finally, a coat or two of white paint finished the job. Standing back from the house you didn't notice the patches. It might have been easier to just replace all the gutters but it was fun figuring out how and then putting on all the section patches. Except for the time and energy of my labor it was a lot cheaper to patch than to replace.... and it worked! The gutters stayed sound and functional with normal maintenance for the next eight years we owned the house.

Next was revitalizing the cedar shake siding. With lots of consultation with the local hardware supplier, he recommended nailing all the curled shakes with mostly 4-penny galvanized common head nails (with occasional 6d or 8d where longer bite was needed), followed by caulking, followed by one or two coats of oil stain to restore the oil in the shakes rather than just paint over dry shakes. It took some time, some on a ladder, to nail all around the house. It took one hundred pounds of nails!! That is about 30,000 nails!! There were no air-pressure nail-drivers in 1967. Each nail was hand-held with the left hand and hammered in with the right hand. Caulking was much faster even with ladder time. I selected ... what else? ... Navy grey oil stain. The cedar shakes sucked in the first coat of stain like a sponge so a second coat was required. Some places in direct sunlight even required a third coat. At last, when finished, the house looked great. Except for my labor it was much cheaper than replacing all the shakes with new ones. The roof was sound. Some of the hinges on windows and doors were rusted from the salt-water air/spray exposure that is common on oceanfront property. I replaced them with brass fittings. Next was caulk and putty all around and painting the window trim.

The interior was all cedar woodwork and cedar walls. The floors were peg-pine boards. All of this was in excellent condition, so nothing was needed. One of the most distinctive and wonderful characteristics about that house was the distinct aroma of cedar when you entered. It was like walking into a cedar closet except it was the whole house.

I still have the sturdy Great Neck screwdriver I used. Also in that drawer at my office is the putty knife that I used so much the corners are rounded. They mean nothing to anyone else, but the hours they were in my hand make them meaningful to me. They are very personal souvenirs from 8208 Oceanfront.

Wood Box … The kitchen had a thinish vertical cabinet door on one wall and inside was a pull-down ironing board like a Murphy bed…. very convenient. Like other various discoveries here and there the house had a brilliant fireplace accessory. There was a large box for firewood on the outside attached to the wall right next to the chimney of the fireplace. There was a door on the outside for loading firewood into the box and a door on the inside to retrieve the wood to put into the fireplace. This eliminated the need to carry wood through doors and over carpets. It was such a neat idea I have installed such wood boxes in every house where I have lived since…. and built one at my mother's house. It's so easy to fill the box from the outside, then just open the inner door for wood to put on the fire. For security there is a lock on the outer door.

Lawn … There was a fine grass lawn in the large back yard. It was sheltered from the ocean wind and salt air. Little did I know there was a real technique for watering it in dry weather. Of course, the base was sand. If you just watered with a hose, the water went straight down into the sand and one foot away stayed dry. There was no spread. It required a sprinkler and careful moving around to cover the entire extent of the grass that needed watering. There was a chain link fence with high hedges and a sturdy gate. Just outside was a one-car garage at the gate and at the end of the packed gravel and stone driveway.

The Dune ... All along the oceanfront in Virginia Beach is a high sand dune which protects the homes from wind and water to some extent. Several years before I bought the house a severe storm or hurricane had washed away lots of the dune in front of the house and several neighboring lots. That was another reason the price of the house was reasonable. Again, I consulted the hardware man. He suggested putting up a snow fence, a.k.a. sand fence, and let the wind build up the dune. So, I bought rolls of six feet high wooden slat fencing.... the kind that has the slats connected with twisted heavy-duty wire and gaps between. Also needed were a stack of metal fence posts.... those ones with the flat plate on the bottom for an anchor and the half-I-beam shaft with little hooks cut and sticking out all along the length. I drove the posts into the dune at the point where more height was wanted, one about every five or six feet. Instead of a solid fence across or leaving a gap for walking down to the beach, I offset the fence coming from each side in the middle so there would be a continuous wind/sand barrier, but you could zig-zag through the offset gap to walk through. It was a sturdy fence when the rolls of slats were wired in position.

A year later when we returned the dune had built itself up a full six feet and completely covered the fence. As sand from the beach blew from the ocean wind it would hit the slats and fall to the ground, slowly building up and spreading out to give width as well as height. I installed another six-foot sand fence right on top of the now-covered first one. A year later <u>another</u> six feet had built up on the dune.... and the width had grown accordingly. Amazingly I had helped nature restore twelve feet to the dune. By then a lot of beach grass had grown so the roots could stabilize and strengthen the new dune. I was both amazed and satisfied at the whole evolution.

The Beach ... Of course, the ocean views every day were wonderful. In good weather we often went down to the beach, sometimes with a picnic basket. Elizabeth played in the sand. It was just a huge sandbox for her. Gazing at the ever-changing ocean ... sky, waves, wind and weather was just as satisfying as those interludes on the catwalk of the carrier every evening after dinner. There is something fascinating about the vista. I think some of the same satisfaction is derived in mountains looking down and across wide areas.

Snow in the Picture Window ... There was a spotlight shining out toward the dune and ocean for lighting the front entrance. At night it didn't really carry all the way out to the ocean, but when it snowed every snowflake caught the light and reflected to your eyes. So, at night when the snow was falling and the wind was swirling, it was fascinating to just sit in the living room with a warm fire, a glass or two of fine wine and watch that dancing, flickering show.

The Breeze and the Sound of the Waves ... When I bought the house, it had aluminum screens that were in poor condition because of the salt air corrosion. So, I replaced them all with copper screens. In the bedrooms and elsewhere the house had windows that opened inward with those little handle-cranks and rods. The inshore breeze was almost constant and it carried the sound of the waves. What a pleasant regular experience to enjoy that breeze and ocean wave sound when weather permitted open windows.

That ocean breeze and the sound of the waves is enough to make you want to join the Navy... and it was enough to entice grandparents to pay big bucks in the summer to share it with their grandchildren.

Don't Leave Me and Wuh-Wuh Banki ... In late June 1968 as we packed to move to New Orleans for the ENT residency there were stacks of cardboard boxes awaiting the movers. The day arrived and the moving van and crew rolled up. Most of the furniture would stay in the house for "furnished" rentals, but some was going to NOLA. The movers began hauling things out of the house. Elizabeth was two years old and had not learned to pronounce "L's" yet. She had a yellow blanket that was her constant companion, the proverbial security blanket. She called it "Wuh-Wuh Banki." Time for Elizabeth's nap and she went to sleep in her crib. While she was asleep the moving crew took virtually everything that was going to NOLA out to the van. The crib was the last to go, so when Elizabeth woke up, a worker folded up the crib.... clack, clack, slam... and hauled it outside. Elizabeth was wide-eyed and walked around clutching and sucking on her wuh-wuh-banki. We were busy with last minute things, checking around to be sure all was in the van or going with us in the cars.... including that last case of twelve bottles of the best special wines from the cruise smuggling/bootlegging.

Then we realized that Elizabeth had disappeared. Searching the house didn't find her. I worried that she had wandered off to the beach and ocean, so made a mad dash out. No Elizabeth anywhere to be found. Finally, I went out to the car and there was Elizabeth sitting in her car seat clutching wuh-wuh-banki. We had moved around so much during her first two years of life that she knew about that car seat and was making danged sure we were not going to leave her behind. There was great relief from worry at the time.... and then it was a little funny .... but it was also sad in a way.

Two Weeks Active-Duty Reserve Training Every Year ... I stayed in the Navy Reserve for four years during residency (1968-1972) and was able to arrange the two-week summer TAD (Temporary Additional Duty) training billets in the Virginia Beach and the Norfolk tidewater area. (See separate section for more details.) Lydia was born in December 1968 so in the summers of 1969, 1970, 1971 and 1972 we were able to live in our house for two weeks and enjoy the beach, ocean, et al. With small children it was a lot of fun and we could see why grandparents brought their families for vacations. Virginia's parents joined us several summers so we were the same three-generation vacationers. After daytime active-duty work at the Navy TAD job, I spent some time those summers doing upkeep and repairs on the house as needed. After starting private practice in July 1972, we kept going back in May every year to spiffy-up the house for the high rent season.... finally selling the house in the fall of 1975.

It was an evolution taking two small children, a dog and a cat on the airplane from New Orleans to Virginia Beach. (See "Cat Eyes.") One summer our Shetland Sheepdog, Cabernet, ran off down the beach and it was a dramatic scene finding him. When I finally sold the house in 1975 it was for four times the purchase price. Besides the tidy profit there were some wonderful times shared in that house at 8208 Oceanfront.

NAS OCEANA INCIDENTS AND OBSERVATIONS

EXCEPT FOR TWO shakedown cruises I lived in Virginia Beach from mid-February 1967 to end-June 1968, just over a year subtracting nine weeks of shakedown cruise time in the spring of 1968. Here is a potpourri of incidents and observations, (some more interesting than others), presented in random order, a collection of THERE I WUZ stories:

F-4 Phantom II ... some facts:

1. 5,195 built, most ever for U.S. supersonic jets.
2. Exceeded Mach 2 on its first Air Force flight in 1963. Top speed: 1,473 mph.
3. 98,557 feet altitude record set in 1959.
4. In 1962 set a time-to-climb record of 29,500 feet in 61 seconds.
5. Only jet aircraft to be flown by both the Navy Blue Angels and Air Force Thunderbirds.
6. 528 F-4s were lost in the Viet Nam war.
7. At 63 feet long with 35,000 pounds of thrust the F-4 was nicknamed the "triumph of thrust over aerodynamics."

F-4 Pilot Height Limits ... To qualify to be an F-4 pilot there were some height limits. If you were too short, you could not see over the console. If too tall, an ejection would probably kill you. So, the lower limit was about 5 feet six inches and the upper limit, 6 feet six inches. We had one pilot who was on the lower end of the scale. He was an excellent pilot but it was always a little amusing to see him in full flight gear climbing up into the cockpit carrying a large very firm seat cushion about six inches thick. I enjoyed flying with him because he was not only an excellent aviator, but also a fun guy.

Flying in the Rain ... It didn't matter much. You got a little damp mounting to the cockpit, but once strapped in and canopy closed it wasn't a problem. Taxiing out to the runway sometimes the rain was so hard you had difficulty seeing. There are no windshield wipers on a jet. Takeoff solved the problem. Headed down the runway as speed picked up suddenly the windshield was crystal clear as the airflow blew all the water away.

Preflight the Aircraft and Preflight Briefings ... It is important to do a safety walk-around of your aircraft before climbing into the cockpit and taking off. Even though the maintenance people, the plane captain and others are meticulous with their safety precautions it is standard procedure for pilots to "eyeball" their aircraft. Inflation of tires, strength of struts, stability of ailerons and flaps, pitot tube cover removed. ... anything and everything.... the preflight inspection "walk-around" was standard. In the ready room before going out to the plane there is a preflight briefing if there are two or more planes to be flying together. Someone is designated the flight leader; the planned mission and details of the flight are discussed .... everything important for everyone to know. Some briefings take a while and some are shorter, even hurried when necessary. The pilots had a joke about preflight briefings and preflight inspection of the aircraft: "Kick the tires, Light the Fires... First one out leads."

The Huffer ... In the old days of early propeller planes the pilot would turn on the magneto and call "contact" over the cowl, whereupon someone would crank the propeller for an engine start. (Early automobiles had an external crank for the same purpose.) Starters for propeller aircraft have become standard now. Jet engines are similar and different. They are started by having the blades of the engine turning but starters are too heavy to be within the jet. An external forced air generator is used. Hence the name "Huffer." That was the common term for the external air blower that was attached to the jet for a start. "I will huff and I will puff until I blow your house down" … er, ah, start your engine.

The "Huffer" was a low, squared-off, rectangular machine on small wheels used to start jet engines on the ship and on an airstrip tarmac. Restarts in the air after a flameout are done (hopefully) using the air forced through the engine intake by the speed of the plane. It's sort of like old stick shift cars when you could push it in neutral then release the clutch in first gear hoping to start the engine. Both techniques are great …. when they work.

Pilot Lost at Oceana … After return from the Med Cruise one of our F-4 pilots left active duty but stayed in the Navy Reserves based at NAS Norfolk. He had been in the airwing and on Indy for the 1965 Viet Nam deployment where he had flown many combat missions without mishap. Likewise, his regular flying on Indy in the Med was without mishap. One weekend as a reservist he took off from NAS Norfolk in an older F-4B and experienced hydraulic problems. He called Mayday and approached the Oceana airstrip for an emergency landing. Whatever happened his aircraft rolled sideways from straight and level, struggled to say airborne, then crashed, killing him. We all knew him and were greatly stressed. He had survived extensive combat in Viet Nam, then was killed on a weekend reserve flight.

Infirmary Senior Medical Officer … Previously mentioned was that he was more an administrator than a physician even though he was an M.D. Like the SMO on Indy, he was picky about military protocols, etc. I don't remember the details but for some reason he called me into his office and admonished me for some decision that wasn't "like in the military" or "according to Navy protocol" or whatever. It had been a medical treatment decision of some kind. In my defense I replied, "Sir, I am a doctor first and a naval officer second." It was obvious he didn't like that and its implications. Undoubtedly my next Fitness Report reflected his irritation.

Flight Surgeon's Health and Safety Programs ... Our function in this area was a prime responsibility as previously discussed. Ashore at Oceana we continued regular lectures and information programs for the squadrons in their ready rooms. The pilots and flight officers were interested in learning things about health and safety, BUT the macho in them mostly made them <u>seem</u> nonchalant, unconcerned and reluctant to hear the material. It was necessary to keep them interested and the hardest part was making important but perhaps basic and mundane topics perky. One day in talking about decompression and altitude sickness, the bends, the dangers of SCUBA diving, then flying, etc.... I got their attention by saying I was going to talk about "formication." That is a sensation of itching or that feels like ants crawling on the skin. The pilots perked up at the title of my program. A cold-water survival lecture was entitled, "How to shrivel your genitals" or "How to freeze your ass off." You get the idea.

One lecture was about proteins, vitamins and aspects of nutrition in survival situations. The title was "Rolling Your Worms in a Leaf." It was fun thinking up catchy titles and gimmicks to keep attention during educational programs.

One serious program I initiated was for pilots who were to deploy to combat in Viet Nam. In an extended time surviving if not captured, nutrition would be a major consideration. Pilots were known to stuff whole salamis, high-energy/protein bars and all kinds of food items in their flight suits. If overdoing it, the excess weight could compromise their survival of an ejection. Few ever considered vitamins. Fat soluble vitamins would be okay for a long time, but water-soluble Vitamins B & C only last 2-3 months without replenishment. A supply of Thera-Combex-HP vitamin capsules was donated by Parke-Davis pharmaceutical company and I made up little packets of six. They were very lightweight and taking one a month would likely keep you out of deficiency,

Lobsters from Maine ... The peak season for lobsters is July. In the summer it was not uncommon for a pilot to fly to NAS Brunswick, Maine to bring back a load of lobsters for a party. Usually, it was a propeller aircraft with some storage space, but the distance and time were not too great in the air. Now that sounds like the taxpayers were subsidizing a luxury lifestyle for the aviators, but not true. The pilots must log flight hours to maintain proficiency. There were always some staff or ground-based pilots who needed some flight time and they would be flying around doing nothing anyway just to log the hours. It was not a problem to find a volunteer, especially if rewarded with a few lobsters. The lobsters were always purchased with private personal funds.

A Wedding in Florida ...One of my cousins was getting married in St. Petersburg, Florida in the spring of 1967; I arranged for one of my staff pilots to check out an F-4 and fly me to the wedding. I drove my wife to the airport in Norfolk to take a commercial flight, then drove back to the hangar at Oceana. My friend and I jumped into a Phantom and zipped it to MacDill Air Force Base in Tampa. I rented a car and was waiting for the commercial plane to land at the civilian airport. He flew back to Oceana and logged an hour or two of flight time.

After the wedding weekend it worked the same in reverse. Another pilot in one of the F-4 squadrons was happy to visit his parents in Florida, so he flew down a day before my return to Oceana. I dropped off my wife at the airport for the commercial flight home, drove to MacDill, returned the rent-a-car, strapped in and zipped back to Oceana in the Phantom. That could be called a "perk" in the military, but it did give purpose to the required flight time we had to log.

Terre Haute, Indiana ... That was exactly why I flew to Terre Haute, Indiana in May of 1968. Since my replacement had already arrived, I didn't sail with the airwing and Indy off to the Med for another cruise. With my squadrons all deployed I needed flight time elsewhere. A pilot's mother was in the ICU back home so he booked a flight to Terre Haute. I was on the log room list to pick up some flights, so they called me. Off we went. The boring part was sitting in the staff room at the Air National Guard hangar waiting for the pilot to return from the ICU and fly us back.

Fun in the Air ... By now you should appreciate how exciting it was to fly in military jet aircraft. There were the usual flights that became routine, but there were also some unusual and particularly exciting flights from time to time. My favorites were the

1. High Performance Takeoff ... As I understood it this technique was developed at NAS Key West to the purpose of having fighters at altitude in just minutes in case some threat from Cuba was inbound. Pilots would be in full flight gear in the hangar ready room. The F-4s were on the tarmac with engines already turning. On signal the pilots could mount up and be at thirty thousand feet in a couple of minutes. The technique was exhilarating. From the far end of the runway the pilot would accelerate out with military power (full throttle with afterburners) but instead of a slow climb, he would "keep it at the deck" at about fifty feet above the runway and accelerate as much as possible before the opposite end of the runway. Then pulling back the stick the F-4 would trade airspeed for altitude and pop up to the top. You felt weightless as actually you were slowing down, but the ground would rapidly disappear below you. It was sort of like riding a fast elevator without the feel of gravity. Wow and whoooeee.

2. Low-level Flights ... These were carefully planned and mapped flights through the hills and mountains of western Virginia. The idea was to fly below the screen of radar detection. We flew in the valleys and gaps lower than the tops of the hills and mountains. Planning and study of very up-to-date topography maps showed a safe route, especially one without any highwire power lines in the path. It was like movie photography you see now with drone technology. We would. take off and do a circuitous route out and back.

3. <u>Air Combat Maneuvers (ACM) a.k.a. "Dog Fighting'</u> .... This was a blast for several reasons. First it was not your straight and level flight like that trip to Terre Haute. Second it was competitive. Two or-more pilots would be trying to best each other as if in real combat with enemy planes. Third the pilots would often delight in trying to "make the doc sick." So, all high jinks were permissible. Most of the time I kept my lunch, but sometimes ... with negative G's especially ... I would lose it. Just in case I always had a barf bag in my flight suit leg pocket.

As the ACM engaged there would be lots of G-forces and lots of aeronautic maneuvers. My favorite was the **Split-S Maneuver**. Flying along straight and level you suddenly roll inverted and pull back hard on the stick. The aircraft does a vertical 180 degree turn and you are flying in the opposite direction from whence you came. The G-forces are huge. Pilots are always watching the gauges so as not to exceed the airplane's safety tolerances. When they did get over the safe limits that was known as "bending the airplane" and it required extensive maintenance .... and usually earned the pilot a butt chewing from the CO.

Loops, rolls, spins, Immelmann's, Cuban Eights, etc., etc. The list goes on and there are dozens of configurations. Complex combinations are many more. It would take an extensive study in aerobatics to cover it all. The pilots were accomplished and practiced most of them. They often explained what they were doing but some of it was not in my understanding. l was a back-seater, observing, enjoying and sometimes clutching my barf bag.

4. <u>Bombing Practice</u> ... There was a little island in the middle of Chesapeake Bay that we practically bombed to smithereens. Rather than full-sized bombs that would have caused a lot of damage and been expensive, not to mention local percussions and repercussions, we used eight-pound practice bombs. They were dense little things with a smoke charge in the nose. When

it hit the ground a big puff of smoke would erupt. We could spot the smoke from the air to see how accurate the bombing run had been. We practiced a lot of bombing runs and it was satisfying to watch how accurate the pilots were.

Insurance Physical Examinations ... Besides moonlighting at the local hospital ER, I picked up some extra money by doing insurance company physical examinations. Several companies hired me to go around to the homes of people applying for an insurance policy. The pay was good and it didn't take a lot of time. A salesman would call me with the name and address of a customer. I would go out, locate the person to be insured and then do a history and physical. That included a urine specimen to be sent in with my report. Over the year I became familiar with most of the Virginia Beach/Norfolk area. The extra income was welcome.

Weekends ... Most of the Navy duties with the squadrons and at the infirmary were weekday work. When I was not MOD at the infirmary or moonlighting in the ER ... and if there were no squadron parties over the weekend.... we took some trips around the area on weekends.

Williamsburg ... The colonial restoration was magnificent and close at hand. We went there a few times. Elizabeth was now a year old and a good traveler. My mother flew in for Thanksgiving and we had dinner at the King's Arms Tavern. On the way up were Hampton Roads, Newport News and Yorktown ... all interesting for different reasons.

Carters Grove ... was part of the Williamsburg restoration and a particular favorite. It was a huge old mansion overlooking the James River.... beautiful vistas, beautiful interior, interesting history and more. Jamestown was nearby.

Charlottesville ... Western Virginia hill country, Monticello, other historic places. The Boar's Head Inn had just opened and was a fun place to stay. Coming back down the west side of the James River were Surry, Smithfield and Suffolk. We picked up some of those salty dry hams in Smithfield and peanuts in Suffolk. There was a great old-fashioned, home-cooking, family-style restaurant in Surry that we enjoyed. They welcomed our one-year-old.

<u>Delmarva ... a.k.a. Eastern Shore</u> ...The peninsula across Chesapeake Bay from Norfolk. There was a bridge and tunnel making access easy. There wasn't a lot of development but there were some rustic seafood restaurants of note.

Seafood ... Seafood was fresh and wonderful everywhere. Stormont's was a local fish store who caught their own fish and would deliver it fresh every day right to your house if you called before their delivery run to see what was fresh. (Gene Berry's father was in VB and married a Stormont daughter some years prior.) There were several excellent restaurants at the Lynnhaven Inlet.... and many more actually. She Crab Soup was a biggie, fresh Chesapeake oysters were special, Shad and Shad Roe in the spring .... it goes on and on.

The Lynnhaven Bridge Disaster.... The four-lane Highway 60 had two separated two-lane bridges over Lynnhaven Inlet ... one bridge with two lanes going east and the other bridge with two lanes going west. THERE I WUZ working in the VBGH Emergency Room one night when the ambulance brought in a young sailor who had been coming home after midnight from his duty station at the Little Creek Amphibious Base. Those Lynnhaven restaurants also had bars that were popular. Some drunk had pulled out of one of the bars and turned up the wrong highway bridge and crashed head-on into the sailor as he crested the top. The drunk was unhurt, the sailor was killed. Damn.

The Ambulances That Never Arrived ... Sometimes the ER nurse at VBGH would get a call from one of the ambulances saying, "Get ready, we just picked up a bad casualty from a wreck at so-and-so location. We'll be there in fifteen minutes." If I were asleep in the wee hours, the nurse would awaken me with the message so I could be alert and ready. In more cases than were logical the ambulance would never arrive .... and they never called. We didn't know if they went to another hospital in Norfolk which might have been closer, or if the patient died, or what ... they just "no-showed" after we waited an hour or two.

Officers Clubs ... We had a wide choice in the area. There were Officers Clubs at Navy facilities in Oceana, Little Creek and Norfolk. All had good food and it wasn't all the same. The Army Officers Club at Fort Story was available to us as well. We tried them all from time to time. After regular participation at Happy Hour at the O-club of Oak Knoll Hospital in California during the summer of 1963, I didn't frequent the Happy Hours much in Virginia Beach. I was single in '63 and there were some young Nurse Corps ladies at Oak Knoll plus that Medical Service Corps Ensign that seemed to have a fondness for hanging out with me.

In Virginia Beach I mostly enjoyed just going home to wife and baby most days. On some occasions one or another squadron would plan some carousing at the Oceana O-club and I would join them...... ALWAYS careful to remove my cover before entering lest the bartender clanged the bell and I had to buy a round for the house.

Navy Exchange ... These were the retail stores for military people. The prices were excellent and the selection good in a wide variety of categories. By now I was seriously interested in wine. The Oceana exchange had a fine liquor and wine shop. The Navy Exchange in Norfolk was bigger and had a better selection. We went there sometimes. I browsed the others around the area when opportunity presented. The commissary was for groceries and the prices there were very favorable also.

Antique Furniture ... There was a retired navy man who developed a business buying and selling antique furniture. He operated out of a medium-sized warehouse building. For example, he bought about 100 beds from a hotel being demolished in Atlantic City. He bought three beautiful mahogany writing desks that had been in the lobby of the Astor Hotel in New York City. Each had a large multi-paneled, beveled glass, ornate mirror across the back. I still have one in my bedroom and enjoy it every day.

SURVIVAL SCHOOL

CAN YOU HACK IT IN RANGELEY, MAINE?

ALL NAVAL AVIATORS are scheduled for the survival training program in Rangeley, Maine. I think it has been modified from how it was in 1967 so this description is only about the time we were there. Since its founding in 1962 over 50,000 Naval Aviators have been trained at the 12,000-acre facility just east of Rangeley Lake in northwest Maine.

The purpose of the training is to prepare aviators for basic survival in the wilderness if ever downed, to teach them how to evade the enemy if in hostile territory, to prepare them psychologically for a potential enemy POW camp imprisonment and torture, and to enhance the likelihood of escaping from it. The training is abbreviated as SERE which means Survival, Evasion, Resistance, Escape. Few aviators would volunteer for the training. They are just scheduled. During the Viet Nam war it was especially important because a significant number of them were shot down. If not killed, they sometimes endured extended years in the "Hanoi Hilton" POW prison.

[NOTE: In Viet Nam 539 Navy personnel were POWs or MIA. (153 Accounted For/ 386 unaccounted For. Total military: 1,565 (1,053 Accounted / 512 Unaccounted)]

So, THERE I WUZ at the Naval Air Station, Brunswick, Maine in the spring of 1967. Virtually all the flight officers in CVW-7 (from Oceana, VF-84, VF-41, VA-75) were there including the CAG. There were also some enlisted flight crewmen. It was a large group of maybe sixty or seventy. The program was four days. We flew into Brunswick the afternoon before the program was to begin at 0800 next day. Some of us went out for a fine lobster dinner.

The first day was classroom instruction in Brunswick. Topics covered were (1) Survival: basic fire, food, shelter as learned by Boy Scouts as teens and preteens; (2) Evasion: wilderness map navigation, hiding in natural surroundings, et al; (3) Resistance: the POW camp/stockade experience … what to expect, how to deal with it psychologically including from physical torture; (4) Escape: Some ideas about how to do it. This program is called SERE training following the Navy tradition of abbreviations…. SERE being derived from the first letters of the four phases.

I was there as an observer and not as a direct trainee. Physicians are non-combatants and were not allowed to fly combat missions at that time. I participated in all phases of the program including the stockade POW part which was my major responsibility. My role there was to observe the group and the individuals for physical illness, injury, harm, psychological/mental problems, etc. (see below.)

The lectures on Day One were good. The survival topics were new to some, but old hat to those who had been scouts. Only a brief overview was given as most of the skills would be taught "in the field" the next day. Interpretation of topographical maps was quite informative. Many tips were given on how to use terrain to navigate from point to point, how to do it without being seen, when to crawl, when to run and much more.

There were lengthy discussions about the physical and psychological pressures exerted on prisoners of war to break them. "Hard" torture was physical abuse of many kinds. "Soft" torture was stressing the emotions and mind with various techniques. In a real situation both would be used. Probably half the time was spent on this phase, just a little on the escape orientation.

After class we loaded up in buses and drove out to Rangeley. There were still several hours of daylight, enough to establish camp, build fires, cook dinner …. the little there was of it… and bed down for the night. Day two was spent in on-the-job training in basic survival skills with lectures, demonstrations and practice …. again a "piece of cake" for former scouts. Wilderness survival was the training including foraging for food.

The staff of instructors was professional and quite good at their instruction. They were all active-duty Navy personnel, including some hospital corpsmen. They were mostly enlisted with several chiefs and an officer leading the unit. Probably there were several dozen but they were not all together at one time. There was a deliberate mystery about their identity and organization to promote and simulate the unknowns and fears of a real situation. The instructors who ran the "escape/capture" day and the POW/stockade phase were not in the field during the survival training. This was because they would wear black uniforms and be the enemy. It was necessary for them to be unknown and not recognizable by the trainees.

Mostly the instructors were guys who were accomplished outdoorsmen, had volunteered for this duty and had been given extensive training themselves. The survival phase instructors wore outdoors clothing without rank insignia. The trainees wore flight suits like would be the case if shot down, in wilderness survival and imprisoned if captured.

So … Day One was classroom instruction in Brunswick, Day Two was survival in the field with instructions and practice doing it. Day Three was the Escape and Evasion phase. Day Four was 24-hours in the POW stockade.

At the end of Day Two everyone had a campsite established, ate what they had foraged and tried to get a little sleep before sunrise the next morning to begin the Escape and Evasion phase of Day Three.

Sunrise came too early. Another scanty meal and it was the last the trainees would have until the whole four-day program was finished. Maps were marked with checkpoints and each individual trainee would have to find each one then keep tracking to the end destination. (See below.) Everyone wore a nametag because the instructors were evaluating and grading performance for each person. You didn't want to score poorly on any phase of the program and have it go in your service record. It was known that Promotion Boards paid particular attention to Survival School performance. Everyone was off separately into the wilderness with canteen of water and their map. The goal was to evade capture while getting to each checkpoint and the destination. The "enemy" was lurking in the woods to capture you if they could…. and they knew the terrain.

I didn't have much to do that day as I was not in the woods either trying to evade capture or to try to catch anyone. One of the instructors drove me to the large comfortable cabin/barracks where staff lived. The cabin was only fifty yards or so from the POW stockade training compound that was surrounded with a high fence and barbed wire on top.

The cabin had a small entrance door/lock for cold weather and it opened into a large lounge/den with television, et al. A spacious kitchen and dining area was adjacent. Several hallways provided access to the bunkrooms and heads. The instructor took my gear and showed me to my private bunkroom.

A few of the instructor group were there lounging around in their black "enemy" uniforms that had red-star patches above the shirt pocket. Their black military covers also had red stars. They retrieved a few beers from the reefer and explained the protocols a little.

All the trainees were in the woods tracking the checkpoints to the last rendezvous spot. If they were captured at any time, they would go straight to the POW compound … with no food and no rest time. That would be additional time in the POW compound added to the twenty-four hours mandatory duration of the stockade sequence. If a trainee successfully evaded capture, tagged all the checkpoints, and reached the rendezvous destination, he would be given a small meal of bread and a bit of cheese and permitted to sleep a little before the start time of the 24-hour compound phase. The instructors kept a log on each trainee noting grades and scores for each part of the whole three-day program after the first classroom day.

The 24-hours in the compound was from about noon of the third day to noon the fourth and last day…. or maybe it was 4PM to 4PM? Once all the trainees were in the stockade, the program began. Instructors in the black uniforms functioned as enemy guards and they had well-planned protocols for harassing the group collectively and everyone separately. I was fitted out in a black "enemy" uniform and a black hood with eyeholes and a mouth hole for breathing. It completely covered my face to hide my identity as all the flight crew knew me. They were to see no friendly face for the 24 hours. My role was to be around and observe for health and safety.

The trainees were given no rest and no sleep for the entire time. Instructors rotated in shifts so they could enjoy normal life with meals and sleep. When supper time came, a new set of "enemy guards" relieved us. We went back to the cabin and cooked big steaks for dinner. There were a few pangs of guilt … but not too many … at enjoying that steak while the trainees were being put through the paces with nothing to eat at all. I made sure to not tell them about it later either.

Some of the stress exercises were interesting, both the physical torture elements and the psychological ones. The yard of the compound looked like one might see in a movie of a prison…. high walls with barbed wire, guard towers, etc. These were all rustic wooden structures. There was still some snow and ice on the ground when we were there. One of the stresses was to have everyone strip naked and stand in the open compound. They were at least given arctic boots (thick air foam insulation) to prevent frostbite of toes and feet. It was maybe in the high forties or low fifties with a slight breeze. There was some shivering and shaking but forced calisthenics helped maintain a healthy core body temp. There was a large icy puddle of water in the yard and from time to time someone would be forced to lie down in it for a few minutes. The others would be threatened with it if they didn't "cooperate." The instructors were inventive and lots of it was preplanned.

All the while loudspeakers were blaring with "Tokyo Rose" type of enticements, "Agree to tell us about your military unit and you may come inside and have hot soup." It was well orchestrated.

Inside there were always a few trainees being grilled, belittled, humiliated and stressed emotionally. Some physical pain was inflicted both inside and out in the yard as part of the torture indoctrination and attempt to "break" the trainee. I walked around with my black hood, peering out the eyeholes and watching everything for health and safety. The instructors had even given me suggestions on what to look for and things to guard against. As mentioned, they were very professional and well-trained.

Some of the trainees were selected to wear dresses and called all sorts of terrible names .... in front of the yard group. Some were made to kneel for long periods. Some were put in "the box" to cramp muscles and induce claustrophobia. The ongoing physical and psychological stresses were lengthy, varied and non-stop.

Some of the officer "victims" (if I may use that term) held up very well, some broke down and some were in the middle. Their reactions and responses to the stresses went across the gamut like a classic bell-shaped curve ... some excellent on one end, some terrible on the other end, most in the middle. One of the best performers was an enlisted air-crewman. One of the worst was a very senior officer. The survival school score of each probably affected promotion later .... positively for the enlisted top-performer and negatively for the senior officer who totally "broke."

It was an enlightening experience for the trainees and for me as observer. After the twenty-four hours were over everyone could dress and a small meal was offered. It was NOT a fun experience for the trainees but likely was valuable to them later if ever in a POW situation. After it was completed, we returned to NAS Oceana, perhaps a little wiser.

NOTE: As I write this fifty years later a thought occurs ... with the growing number of female aviators in the Navy, I wonder how they handle SERE training? Do they do all female groups with female instructor teams? Or is it like that scene with Demi Moore in the movie "G.I. Jane" ... or do they do mixed gender training to add to the stress and make it more like the real thing in an enemy POW camp?

GITMO AND THE SHAKEDOWN

PREPPING FOR ANOTHER MED CRUISE

ON RETURN FROM the Med Cruise in February 1967 Independence went into dry dock at the Norfolk Naval Shipyards for overhaul, repairs and updates. Over the life of a carrier various items of maintenance are required and updates keep the carrier "state-of-the-art" for frontline service. While in drydock only a skeleton crew remained aboard.

The CVW-7 Command and Staff of the air wing departed for shore duty at NAS Oceana in Virginia Beach along with the F-4 Phantom squadrons (VF-84 Jolly Rogers and VR-41 Black Aces) and the A-6 Intruder squadron (VA-75 Sunday Punchers) … all to maintain proficiency. The other squadrons returned to their respective home base air stations. Remember the regular turnover of personnel in all units of the navy. After a year at Oceana there was probably a fifty percent rotation in and out of the squadrons. Activity and life at Oceana are described elsewhere.

On 19 September 1967, the Indy had to leave drydock early to make way for fire-damaged *Forrestal*. Refurbishing of Indy was completed out of drydock and crew was built back up. By early 1968 *Independence* was again ready for sea duty but as with all ships following overhaul a test of the repairs and upgrades is necessary. Call it sea trials, call it a test cruise ... whatever ... the Navy term was "shakedown cruise." We had two .... one of three weeks and one for six weeks. The three-week shakedown was in the Atlantic off the coast of Virginia and no port calls were included.

All non-flight crew personnel of the airwing boarded Indy at the pier in Norfolk and the carrier sailed into the open ocean. Next day was the "Fly-On" where each aircraft completed a trap onboard and our shakedown/training exercises began. Of course, all the new equipment had to be used and tested but that wasn't the main purpose of the shakedown cruise.

Remember that a large proportion of the crew, both ship's company and airwing were new with varying levels of experience on a carrier ... from none ... to old hands with previous cruises under their belts. Coming out of drydock, maybe three quarters of Indy's ships company were newbies. They had been trained for their jobs, maybe had previous sea duty on smaller ships, but carrier ops were new. The senior officers and especially the Chiefs and First-Class Petty Officers had the knowledge and experience to train them. By now I was the senior flight surgeon in the airwing and an "old salt." By moving up in seniority, I moved down to the lower bunk in our room. Rank has its privileges.

The previous ships company general surgeon, Al Taquino, had been replaced by Bob Corcoran, M.D. We became good friends and after Navy days Bob moved to New Orleans for private general surgery practice. We enjoyed visiting and reminiscing at various Louisiana State Medical Society meetings and other events until he died in 2014.

So off we went early in 1968 to test, train, try out and prepare for frontline service again. The three weeks went by rapidly with lots of flight ops.... then back to Norfolk and NAS Oceana.

Maybe a month later we departed again, this time for a six-week shakedown cruise with planned port calls in Montego Bay, Jamaica and GITMO ...which was the fond term for Guantanamo Bay, Cuba. This six-week cruise was to prepare for a planned long, regular Mediterranean Cruise scheduled for departure on 30 April.

Routines were quickly established after Indy sailed from Norfolk and Fly-On the next day. Flight ops rapidly escalated as everyone refreshed their proficiency and newcomers learned their jobs.

Montego Bay, Jamaica ... We were there just long enough for everyone in the crew to rotate and enjoy one daylong visit ashore. That was the purpose ... to break up the six weeks with a couple of port calls. We were in Montego maybe three days. I went ashore one day. Montego Bay was and is a resort community but the posh clubs, hotels, golf courses, et al were too far out from the downtown and port area for a sailor on foot to visit.

So, I walked around town as I had habitually done in port calls on the Med Cruise. The commercial area seemed rather dilapidated, but interesting to see. There were no steel drum performers around to liven my pace. I visited a few shops which displayed local crafts, then found a comfortable outdoor café for lunch. It was hot in Jamaica, even at that time of year, but the prevailing winds kept it reasonably comfortable.

Voila! Remember that discovery of flank steak in Pensacola? There was another discovery in Montego. On the table was a little bottle of Pickapeppa Sauce, made in Jamaica. It was thick like ketchup, dark brown, aromatic, spicy but not too hot .... and just delicious with my lunch, the remainder of which I don't recall. I made a point of stopping in a grocery and buying three or four bottles to bring back stateside.... alas, big downer back in Virginia Beach.... Pickapeppa Sauce was on the shelf at the NAS Oceana Commissary right beside the Tabasco, Lea &Perrins, A-1 steak sauce and other condiments. My "discovery" mostly just displayed my naivete in the world of condiments.... but the "discovery" was fun while it lasted.

Back to sea ... where else for sailors? More flight ops and training exercises. I got tired of General Quarters drills to hone firefighting and other skills. At least as the senior flight surgeon my battle station was at the "Midships Auxiliary Battle Dressing Station" ... located at flight deck level in the island. There wasn't the tedium and boredom of the "Forward Auxiliary Battle Dressing Station" where I was during the Med Cruise GQ drills.

GITMO, Cuba ... By and by we tied up at the pier in GITMO for about five or six days. I was able to go ashore two or three times. Again, it was hot but the continual winds that are common in the Caribbean kept it tolerable. We had some rain showers. The Officers Club was top-notch so we enjoyed the libations and meals. The Navy Exchange held an interesting new discovery .... monkeypod wood plates and bowls from the Philippines.... and this "discovery" held up after returning stateside. I bought two dozen large ten- or twelve-inch wooden plates for entertaining occasions in the future and an assortment of wooden bowls. The plates served well for some years but are gone now ... to wherever things like that go. I still have a darling bowl carved like a pineapple and use it regularly for nuts, chips, crackers, etc.

One of my NAMI, Pensacola student flight surgeon classmates was stationed at NAS Leeward Point so I visited him and he came across to visit me at the O-club. The main base at GITMO is on the east side of the bay and Leeward Point is on the west side, is smaller and rather isolated. All the facilities are on the main base side and my classmate said it was a royal pain to have to take a launch across the bay for shopping, dinner at the O-club, to get a haircut or whatever. He was not happy about his duty station on the offside at GITMO.

At least he was close to being what is known in the navy as a "short-timer" ... which means it's only a short time to discharge from active duty or transfer to another duty station. He was looking forward to FUBIT.

After another week or ten days of sea trials and flight ops we again tied up at the pier in Norfolk in the early part of April 1968. That was my last time on the carrier at sea deployed with the airwing. Flying on and off the carrier had become routine enough (except for the night hops) that I don't specifically recall the last trap, nor even realizing at the time that it was.

Good News … Departure for the Med Cruise was scheduled for 30 April. I had been accepted for the ENT residency at Tulane and was to start 1 July. My active duty in the Navy would be finished a few weeks before that. I was planning to deploy with the airwing and carrier to the Med, then fly off and return stateside at the appropriate time. It would have been something of a logistics problem moving to New Orleans with household goods, two cars, a two-year-old child and a newly pregnant wife…. all in a short, compressed time frame.

The good news was that my replacement, a newly graduated flight surgeon, came onboard the airwing staff in April. I did not have to sail with CVW-7 and the Indy! I received orders to detach from the airwing staff and be TAD at NAS Oceana until discharge.

There was one minor "downer." My replacement flight surgeon was already a Lieutenant Commander even though he was "fresh out" of NAMI Pensacola. As a newbie he outranked me and I was a seasoned veteran of sea, steel and sky. The Navy was attempting to retain more physicians, particularly flight surgeons, on active duty, so they had escalated the promotion timetables to automatically promote the NAMI graduates to LCDR before their assignment to the fleet. I was "a day late and a dollar short." At least I had done my tour in carrier ops and not in Viet Nam.

The last two months in Virginia Beach were routine but I had lost my squadrons, the friends there, the familiarity and excitement of carrier life and the thrills (with attendant adrenalin rushes) of carrier aviation flight operations.

THERE I WAS … a classic case of "leaving the fleet with great nostalgia, but no regrets."

THOUGHTS AND OBSERVATIONS
ABOUT VIRGINIA BEACH

VIRGINIA BEACH (VB) is a remarkably interesting community for a lot of reasons.

History ... Cape Henry was the site of the first landing of English colonists who settled at Jamestown in 1607, thirteen years before the Plymouth Colony of the Pilgrims in Massachusetts.

Size ... The incorporated city includes about 500 square miles, half being land and half water. The current population is nearly half a million people. (The Greater Metropolitan Statistical Area of Hampton Roads includes 1.7 million people). Average elevation is twelve feet above sea level.

Relative Size ... VB is the largest city in Virginia by both land area and by population. It also has the longest pleasure beach in the world (Guinness Book of Records.)

Flavor ... With all that size VB has the flavor of a suburb and a beach resort tourist town. There is a large military presence, mostly Navy, and many military retirees.

Growth ... When I was there in 1966 there were huge open fields across from our apartment in the Hilltop area. Now it is all shopping malls, a huge new hospital and a labyrinth of residential housing. The area between downtown VB on the ocean and the city of Norfolk was mostly open spaces and undeveloped land in 1966. No longer. It is now one continuous megalopolis and they have run out of land to develop. Government agencies and developers are having legal battles.

Naval Air Station Oceana ... NAS Oceana is a major naval aviation center but there is talk of closing it in ten years or so. Oceana (with other Navy installations) has been a major draw for a significant portion of the population. The developers would love to get their hands on the acreage, but without the active fighter base would there be as much demand for development?

The Cavalier ... Originally a hotel from the Big Band era it was converted to a high-rise apartment building. I looked at several apartments but the rent was too expensive. Now it has been returned to a luxury resort hotel by the Marriott company. That same summer/ winter swing in rates has July rooms at about $400. per night and up ... with winter rates half that.

Seafood ... Still an important part of the local scene and there are now a multitude of restaurants. She-crabs are illegal, but crab soup is still good; oysters, shad and shad roe, fish of all kinds are abundant ... just fond memories of the wonderful seafood that remains available.

The Boardwalk ... and the surrounding areas = "Tourist City" of hotels, gift shops, restaurants, bars, apartment buildings ... everything you would expect at a beach resort. Significant economic center.

Up Beach ... Expensive homes and high-end residential apartments.

Return ... About forty years later I went back to visit: dramatic changes but similar "feel." The house at 8208 has been expanded and upscaled. All the empty lots are developed. Lots more high-rise buildings. NAS Oceana still has testosterone shooting all over the landscape and macho swagger still rules. The people change and the people stay the same. Anchors Aweigh .... Go Navy .... THERE I WUZ.

XIII

NAVY RESERVES

THREE YEARS IN THE READY RESERVE

WEEKEND WARRIOR AT ALVIN CALLENDER FIELD, BELLE CHASSE, LOUISIANA

AFTER RETURNING TO New Orleans for a four-year residency in Otolaryngology at Tulane University it occurred to me that if there were a national emergency and a sudden need for Navy flight surgeons, the only ones already trained and current were those just discharged and recently out of the Navy. It would be like in the movie "Bridges at Toko-Ri" when the Navy pilot played by William Holden was called back.

It made sense that if I were to be available, I might as well get paid for it. The Navy had been educational, rewarding and exciting. Why not continue. Even though I was a LCDR now the income wasn't much .... but it was a welcome supplement to the very meager salary of a resident in those days. The responsibilities were not onerous either. It would require one weekend a month for a Saturday and Sunday plus two weeks active duty in the summer. With the house in Virginia Beach, it would be a vacation if I could get billets in the Tidewater/Norfolk area. I already had all the uniforms required so it really was an easy decision. I "re-upped."

My duty assignment as a "Weekend Warrior" was at NAS Alvin Callender Field in Belle Chasse, Louisiana … just across the Mississippi River south of New Orleans. The normal duty was muster at 0800 on a Saturday with an eight-hour workday and another workday the next day on Sunday. From the beginning there was a small problem. Hospital rounds lasted until about mid-morning on Saturday even when not on call. I could get to Belle Chasse by about noon. However, there was a solution. There was only one physician at Alvin Callender Field. He was on call every day, 365 days a year. I arranged to stay overnight at the dispensary on the Saturday nights of my duty weekends so he could be completely off one day a month. Instead of two eight-hour days I would be on station for about 28 hours.

I was not on flight status so could be there all that time. The medical duties were light with only an occasional emergency so I could bring books and journals to study and read.

Water-skiing in a Float Plane in the Mississippi River … On August 17, 1969 Hurricane Camille veered off Louisiana at the mouth of the Mississippi River and slammed into the Mississippi Gulf Coast. it was a Category 5 hurricane and second only to a 1935 storm in intensity. Wind velocities were 175 mph or more but nobody knows how much higher and stronger it really was because Camille destroyed all the wind velocity measuring equipment. The tidal wave that hit Mississippi was 24.6 feet high. About 500 people were killed.

The Louisiana Department of Health decided that all offshore oilrig workers should be immunized against typhoid and tetanus. The oil companies decided it would be easier and cheaper to fly the injections to the oil rigs than to bring 500-600 workers in for the shots. Our group of Tulane ENT residents had a collective/joint moonlight job and were covering Saturday office hours for the Industrial Medicine practice of Morgan Lyons, M.D. and Manny Paine, M.D. One of us not on call would work the clinic. Since there were seven or eight of us on the rotation that meant one Saturday morning every few months. Drs. Lyons and Paine had contracts with several of the oil companies and wanted one of the residents to fly down to the rigs with their nurse to give the shots on two successive weekends. Since I was the flight-experienced one in our group, I got the nod.

The first weekend the nurse and I drove out to the airport with a large bag of medicine and supplies. A pilot was waiting for us with a two-engine float plane and off we went. We would land near a rig then taxi up to the rig. The workers would line up and we would give two shots each to fifty or sixty or more men. Then we would load up and fly to the next rig. That first weekend we probably visited 5 or 6 rigs and inoculated maybe 300 workers. It was like the "piece of cake" expression from the Navy days.

The second weekend the nurse and I arrived at the airport to find the pilot and a single engine smaller float plane. Off we went again. We stopped at three or four rigs as before to finish the job by injecting maybe another 200 or so workers. The last rig we visited was right on the bank of the Mississippi River…. it wasn't much bank as the edge of the river is mostly water that far down with some low vegetation delineating the edge. We landed directly in the river and taxied to the rig, gave the shots and were loading up to depart when a large worker came out to the airplane with a large hard-shell suitcase. He said he was supposed to fly back to New Orleans with us. Our single engine plane had four seats…. pilot left front, me right front and nurse in one of back seats. The worker weighed at least 250 pounds, probably more. The suitcase was heavy. He crawled in the other back seat with the suitcase on end in his lap.

The pilot taxied into the river. There was an amazingly strong current. He pointed us down river going with the current and added full power for takeoff. The plane would not lift off. We were overloaded and the extra weight of the worker with suitcase had added too much weight to overcome the drag and resistance of the pontoons which were now lower in the water. THERE I WUZ … water skiing down the Mississippi River in a small float plane. The pilot was irritated, frustrated and perturbed by the worker and the problem he presented. With us skiing down the river with full power the airspeed would not accelerate and the plane would not lift out of the water. The pilot mumbled, "Maybe I can rock it off." He started pulling back on the stick to lift the nose, then forward to let it rock back. Pull the nose up, rock it back.... ever greater rocking and the airspeed was indeed beginning to increase a little.... at about the same time as the propeller blades started flicking the water on the down rock. Damn ... Dilbert Dunker in Ole Man River here we come.

With all that flying in the Navy I had never been so apprehensive. In the jets we had ejection seats and parachutes if we needed to get out in a hurry. Had this little plane flipped over in the river upside down as simulated by the Dilbert Dunker, we would have been goners. Had we been able to get out of the plane I doubt we would have survived because of the current.

Since I lived to write this story half a century later, obviously the little plane picked up enough speed and lift to take off. Nobody said much on the way back to NOLA. We were all glad to get out of that water-skiing coffin.

Summer Active-Duty Training ... I was able to get three billets in Norfolk for each of the next three summers. The rule was that you couldn't do the same one twice, but there were enough Navy installations in the area that billets for reservists' two-week TAD were available. It wasn't easy getting there and back but otherwise all worked well. (See "Cat Eyes.") (Also see the section "30,000 Nails.")

Trouble in River City ... After about three years and nearing the end of my residency there was a change of command at NAS Alvin Callender Field in Belle Chasse. It may have just been the officer in charge of the Reserve Training Unit. Anyway, he took exception that I could not "make muster" at 0800 on the Saturdays of drill weekends. The explanation of me covering the dispensary duty for the only physician there (see first section above) made no difference to him. The new officer in charge was rigid about the rules and insisted I would have to "make muster" at 0800 on Saturdays .... so, I resigned. Except for this I would probably have stayed in the navy reserves for twenty-plus years.

Letter to BUMED ... I wrote a letter to the Navy Bureau of Medicine and Surgery explaining the situation. In effect the Navy needed me more than I needed them. They didn't need to respond because I was out with that proverbial FUBIT.

Later ... So, with "great nostalgia and no regrets" I left the Navy and started practice in Alexandria in July 1972. About two or three years later I received a letter from BUMED literally begging me (and any other physicians) to participate in the Navy Reserves.... NO weekend duty, NO summer two weeks TAD, absolutely NO requirements except to just be available for any national emergencies. They offered a generous monthly stipend and of course accrual of time for retirement pay after a few decades or maybe it was a certain age. "Sorry, Charlie," too late for me. You had your chance. FUBIT. By then I was far too busy with private practice medical responsibilities.... so much so that we could no longer take the time for vacations in Virginia Beach. That is about when I decided to sell the house there.

The Navy saw this coming at least six years before in 1968 when the graduating NAMI flight surgeons were accelerated to LCDR promotions. It was just another example of entrenched bureaucracy being behind the curve, a day late and a dollar short.

There was a crisis in the Navy (and probably other military branches.) They could not retain physicians, on active duty or in the reserves. Professional pay of $250.00 per month after four years of medical school just couldn't compare to private practice.

As of 2020 an internet search indicates the Navy will repay up to $120,000 of student loans (subsidizing medical school), provide a medical officer generous and going rate competitive base pay, housing, liability insurance, retirement etc. which all combined makes it competitive with private practice.... AND the Navy offers both competitive Incentive Pay (IP) and a Retention Bonus (RB) annually on top of that ... of varying amounts according to specialty. The black shoe brass finally figured it out.

CAT EYES

[Author's Note: This piece was written on 20 August 2000 so there is some repetition in the first paragraph which is a preamble to the body of the article. Also please note that the title refers to real feline animal eyes and not the thousand eyes watching aircraft being launched from a carrier catapult.]

UPON DISCHARGE FROM active duty in the Navy in June 1968 it occurred to me that if there were an emergency or crisis requiring military action or buildup anywhere in the world and if additional Navy Flight Surgeons were required, there was only one immediate source which would be those of us already trained and recently discharged. An act of Congress could call us back into active duty just as happened for the Korean Conflict and which was the subject of the movie "The Bridges of Toko-Ri" starring William Holden. So, I figured if I were logically available already, I might as well get paid for it. I decided to do a three-year stint in the Navy Reserve at Alvin Callender Field in Belle Chasse just south of New Orleans where I began my four-year residency in Otolaryngology at Tulane. The extra income would be a fine supplement to the meager resident's salary of $350.00 per month. Additionally, I had always found the Naval Air experience exciting. The requirements were minimal: one Saturday and Sunday weekend drill per month and two weeks on active duty each summer. Since we had kept the oceanfront house in Virginia Beach it would be a great way to have a paid working "vacation" at the beach every summer so long as I could arrange the two weeks active duty in the tidewater Virginia area …. which ultimately was the case.

So, in June 1969 the time arrived for the two weeks active duty and I had arranged to do it at the Naval Aviation Safety Center in Norfolk. Elizabeth had just turned three and Lydia was nearly six months old. We still had Gigi, the Siamese cat from San Francisco internship days and had recently acquired a fine Shetland Sheep Dog named Cabernet. We booked roundtrip airplane tickets to Virginia Beach and bought two airline kennels for the animals. In those days air travel was still formal in that most men still wore coat and tie and ladies travelled in high heels and dresses. In fact, we even dressed Elizabeth in a red and green plaid taffeta pinafore party dress with fancy white blouse, lace-topped white socks and black patent shoes. She was a fancy little blonde doll and during the layover in Atlanta drew the attention of several Delta Airlines employees. Ultimately, she was photographed and became the cover girl on the Delta Digest magazine.

However, the most dramatic moment of the trip occurred before we left. On the morning of departure, we prepared the menagerie and dressed in our finest clothes. When the taxi arrived at 1710 Valmont Street it was fortunately one of the large old sedans. The four of us had multiple Samsonite hard-shell suitcases with enough "stuff" for a six-month trip including the paraphernalia for a six-month-old baby …. plus, the two bulky wooden kennels with metal mesh windows. It was a major evolution to get all the suitcases out to the taxi and packed into the trunk while keeping Elizabeth tidy and Lydia in a clean diaper. I put Cabernet in his kennel on the front passenger seat and we would take Gigi in her kennel on our laps in the back. The dog was not a problem, but when I went to put the cat in her kennel, she freaked. She jumped out of my hands, ran out the front door and went under the house.

What a dilemma! We had just barely time to get to the airport for our flight and now the cat was under the house with an already frustrated and anxious wife and kids in the taxi. There was no way the cat would come out on its own. We couldn't leave it alone for two weeks without food. Eureka! It occurred to me that the cat wore a collar and if I could hook it with a coat hanger, I might be able to pull her out. But how to crawl under the house in a suit and tie without becoming a filthy, dirty, dusty mess? There wasn't time to change clothes, shower and change back. Aha! I would just shuck the coat and put on my old orange Navy flight suit over my clothes. This done and with a coat hanger in hand, suitably straightened with a hook on the end, under the house I crawled.

Fortunately, our old New Orleans raised house allowed enough crawl space for hands and knees technique as opposed to belly crawl only. The previous owners (named Stufflebean) had built an addition in the rear which provided an entrance hall and closet by the staircase and an extension of the kitchen-breakfast room that included the washer and dryer in a laundry alcove. Whereas the original old house was open all around, the newer addition in the rear formed an L-shaped extension that was bricked all the way to the ground and was dark as night. Obviously, the cat fled to the deepest inner sanctum of the darkest part of her hiding cave … back among the pipes to the laundry room appliances. I couldn't see the pipes but knew they were there. Thank goodness I had thought to bring along a flashlight for the early morning orange-suited crawl. I had even changed shoes so as not to ruin my military shine.

Ignoring the irritation emanating from the taxi and my own considerable angst I hurriedly crawled into the deepest recesses and turned on the flashlight. There in the very back corner among the pipes in the pitch-black darkness shown the most beautiful pair of cat eyes I have ever seen. They were panicked and paranoid eyes watching every move but they were beautiful to me. My verbal reassurances to the cat were likely melded with more direct comments suitable to my mood and situation. The cat wasn't buying any of it and seemed to inch ever farther back against the wall …. crouched to spring away if opportunity presented. I was crawling on elbows and knees, coat hanger in one hand and flashlight in the other…. trying to inch closer while simultaneously trying to present a barrier to a sudden feline bolting escape. All the while those suspicious cat eyes stared intently at my every move. I would have never caught the cat without the coat hanger and would have paid in cat scratches for the effort. As it was the coat hanger worked perfectly. You have never heard or seen more screaming and hissing, clawing and backpedaling than Gigi did in that dark corner as I pulled her out. I knew I had to keep tension of the wire just like catching fish but there was another set of worries as to what might happen when I got my hands on the cat and she in turn got her claws and teeth in range of me. I decided to just pull her on the coat hanger leash all the way out from under the house and inside the house with the door closed before trying to unhook her and again try to stuff her into the kennel.

This worked and with the kennel door finally locked on angry Miss Gigi, out to the taxi she went. I dashed back inside, shucked the orange flight suit, sweating bullets from the exertion in the June humidity. With a quick hands and face wash, shoe change and coat grab I locked the door and lunged into the taxi with the steaming menagerie. We made the plane. Today I remember those magnificent, beautiful cat eyes.

However, I am positive that at the time I did not appreciate the beauty of those cat eyes nor the humor inherent in the episode. Looking back, it would have been hilarious to a casual observer ... such as the taxi driver who probably had a great deal of difficulty controlling his expression lest he compromise his tip. Certainly, at the time I didn't realize that events such as this with family or friends are the essence of life at its richest and fullest. Adversity overcome, no matter how small and insignificant in the big picture provides the real joy of life.

NATIONAL NAVAL AVIATION MUSEUM

THE HISTORY OF NAVAL AVIATION IN ONE PLACE IN PENSACOLA

IF YOU HAVE even a small interest in Naval Aviation, this museum is a "must do." I used the word "do" rather than "see" because it is a participatory event when you visit the museum. On display are virtually all the aircraft used in the Navy since the earliest days. They are the real life, full size actual aircraft. Some are ground level; some are hanging from the overhead beams. Some are set up so you can climb in and sit as if you are flying. There are some mock cockpits arranged and powered so you can maneuver the controls and simulate flight.

The museum is located within NAS Pensacola. You must go through the checkpoint gate entrance to get on the station. On the way to the museum buildings you will pass, but not see, the hangars and headquarters of the Navy's Blue Angels flight demonstration team. When you arrive at the museum itself the collection of huge and high buildings is impressive. There are 350,00 square feet of interior space on the 37-acre grounds. Right out in front of the main entrance is a jet fighter plane mounted up in the air on a steel pedestal. The tail markings are those of the Black Aces of VF-41, one of my squadrons in CVW-7 and on the Indy.

There is a large parking lot. Inside the entrance are volunteers to greet you with information, directions and whatever assistance you may need. Admission, parking, tours and a collection of movies are all free, but donations are welcomed.

The museum is spotless with shiny floors (decks) … some are steel, some composite plastic flooring, some wood, some carpeted…. many simulate carrier decks. Displays are everywhere … all artfully arranged to draw your interest and explain their history and the many fascinating aspects of each. Visitors may wander around as they choose, follow a pattern or just go where their eyes and/or inclination takes them. The original main building is amazingly large and high inside. The expansion building behind is equally large and high with its own myriad collection of aircraft and memorabilia. There is more to see than you can easily absorb in a single visit. Plaques, photos, explanations and descriptions are everywhere to make a self-guided tour whatever you choose to make it. Formal guided tours are available if you prefer. The movie schedule is posted so you can plan around any you want to watch…. and they are excellent.

Museum Store … There is an extensive museum store with a myriad of Naval Aviation merchandise on display…. items for children, for adults with no navy experience and for former aviation personnel as well. Browsing the museum store is almost as much fun as touring the museum. Likely you won't leave without some souvenirs.

Cubi Bar Café … There is a special restaurant within the museum. When the Naval Air Station at Cubi Point in the Philippines was closed in 1992, the famous bar in the Officers Club was dismantled and shipped to Pensacola. Thousands of squadron plaques that adorned the walls were packed and sent to recreate the atmosphere in Pensacola. The décor is an amazing multitude of squadron plaques that are mounted all over the walls…. everywhere. The "feel" of the Cubi Bar Café atmosphere is that of the original Philippines site of so much R & R by naval flight officers. The food is excellent with a wide selection of appetizers, snacks, sandwiches of every kind and a selection of hot dishes prepared daily. A full bar will refresh whatever your thirst.

At certain times of the year the Blue Angels practice their Air Show behind the museum buildings and there are bleachers for observers. Try to schedule your visit to see a Blue Angels demonstration performance.

In addition to the aircraft all over the inside of the buildings there is a huge additional outdoor "air park" with dozens and dozens of different aircraft parked in rows. A rubber-tired mock trolley provides an easy way to see them. The driver/narrator on the tour explains everything.

I have been to the museum twice, not nearly enough. Once was in 1984 on the way back past Pensacola and once was in October 2019 with Gene Berry when we made it a destination trip to relive our days as Navy Flight Surgeons. An interesting thing was discovered on the first visit. The museum had and still has an F-4 Phantom on display with the wings removed and a wooden platform installed so you can climb up and sit in the cockpit. Naturally, I did that to experience that old "THERE I WUZ" feeling again. Did you know? Would you believe? When you cut the wings off an F-4, the cockpit shrinks.

NOTE: The museum closed in 2020 for the COVID-19 pandemic but has reopened with various health precautions and limited access restrictions as of this writing in December 2020. Please check on the internet for regulations and hours of access.

DENOUEMENT

AIRCRAFT CARRIERS CAN deliver military force practically anywhere in the world. That's it. There is no need to be dependent on the good will of another nation for airfields or supplies. This book has been an attempt to tell how a carrier operates, how its people live and work, some of the rewards, some of the stresses and some of the tragedies.

Naval Aviators are a special kind of people. If a physician makes a mistake, he sends his patient to the grave. If an attorney makes a mistake, he sends his client to jail. If a minister, priest or rabbi makes a mistake, he sends a person to hell. In all three cases it is someone else who pays the price of the mistake. If a Naval Aviator makes a mistake .... he is himself dead. Insurance companies have special premium supplements for military flight crew. After reading this book it should be obvious why.

Our nation is fortunate indeed to have young men and women who are willing to challenge themselves and take the risks of Naval Aviation.... and it IS a young person's game. This book is a small expression of appreciation for their collective and individual courage, talent, skills and sacrifices for their nation and its people. Go Navy.

This book is also a remembrance of half a century ago in the life of the author. Call it a memoir if you like. It is a personal recall of how it was when THERE I WUZ. (You saw that one coming.)

Concluding Thought …Perhaps a song from the operetta "The Student Prince" says it best. The music was by Sigmund Romberg with lyrics by Dorothy Donnelly. The operetta was first performed at the Jolson Theater in New York City on December 2, 1924. You may know the melody and it's okay to sing along with ….

Golden Days

Golden days, in the sunshine of a happy youth
Golden days, full of gaiety and full of truth
In our hearts we remember them all else above
Golden days, days of youth and love.

How we laughed with the joy that only love can bring
Looking back through memory's eyes
We will know life has nothing sweeter than its springtime
Golden days, when we're young …. Golden Days.

XIV

APPENDIX

NAVY ABBREVIATIONS AND SHORTHAND TERMINOLOGY

1MC	Number one Master Communications System
5MC	Carrier Flight Deck Address System
AA	Airman Apprentice
AB	Aviation Boatswain's Mate
ABE	Boatswain's Mate for Equipment
ABF	Boatswain's Mate for Fuels
ABH	Boatswain's Mate for Aircraft Handling
AC	Air Traffic Controlman
ALNAV	All Navy
ALPO	Assistant Lead Petty Officer
AN	Airman
API	Aviation Preflight Indoctrination
ASW	Anti-Submarine Warfare
AVGAS	Aviation Gasoline
B/N	Bombardier/Navigator
BAM	Bad Ass Marine
BCD	Bad Conduct Discharge (a.k.a. "Big Chicken Dinner")
BCM	Beyond Capable Maintenance (must be sent out or disposed.)
BEQ	Bachelor Enlisted Quarters
BM	Boatswain's Mate (a.k.a. Bosun)
BOQ	Bachelor Officers Quarters

BUMED	Bureau of Medicine and Surgery
BUSANDA	Bureau of Supplies and Accounts
BUWEPS	Bureau of Naval Weapons
BZ	Bravo Zulu …. meaning "well done."
CAG	Commander Air Group (Air Wing)
CAPT	Captain
CDO	Command Duty Officer
CDR	Commander
CENTCOM	U.S. Central Command
CF	Charlie Foxtrot (a.k.a. Cluster F---)
CIC	Combat Information Center
CINCLANT	Commander-in-Chief, Atlantic (also COMLANTFLT = Commander Atlantic Fleet)
CNATRA	Chief of Naval Air Training (His first name is not Frank.)
CNAVRES	Chief of Navy Reserve
CNO	Chief of Naval Operations
CO	Commanding Officer
COD	Carrier Onboard Delivery
CPO	Chief Petty Officer
CPOM	Chief Petty Officers' Mess
CS	Culinary Specialist
CSADD	Coalition of Sailors Against Destructive Decisions
CV	Aircraft Carrier (CVA = Attack … CVN = Nuclear)
CVW	Carrier Air Wing
CWO	Chief Warrant Officer
DC	Dental Corps
DD	Destroyer
DE	Destroyer Escort
DESRON	Destroyer Squadron
DILLIGAF	Does it Look Like I Give A F---?
DOD	Department of Defense
DON	Department of the Navy
DRB	Discipline Review Board

EAOS	End of Active Obligated Service (also see FUBIT)
ENS	Ensign
FAC	Forward Air Controller
FCPOM	First Class Petty Officers' Mess
FIGMO	F--- It, Got My Orders
FMF	Fleet Marine Force
FOD	Foreign Object Damage (Debris or Detection)
FTN	Forget the Navy (also ... Full-time Navy)
FUBIT	F--- U Buddy, I'm Through
GQ	General Quarters
Head	The toilet, showers, lavatories and spaces where located.
HELO	Helicopter
HM	Hospital Corpsman
HMFIC	Head Mother F---er In Charge (may refer to SOPA)
IAW	In Accordance With
ICO	In Case Of
IP	Irish Pennant (a loose thread of uniform)
JAG	Judge Advocate General
JBD	Jet Blast Deflector
JP-5	Jet Propellant No.5 (Jet fuel)
JTF	Joint Task Force
KISS	Keep It Simple Stupid
LCDR	Lieutenant Commander
LPOD	Last Plane on Deck
LSO	Landing Signal Officer
LT	Lieutenant
LTJG	Lieutenant Junior Grade (often just called a "JG.")
MAA	Master-at-Arms
MCPO	Master Chief Petty Officer
MIDN	Midshipman
MIDRATS	Midnight Rations
NAMI	Naval Aerospace Medical Institute
NAS	Naval Air Station

NATOPS	Naval Air Training and Operational Procedure Standardization
NAVAIR	Naval Air Systems Command
NAVSTA	Naval Station
NEX	Navy Exchange
NFO	Naval Flight Officer
NROTC	Navy Reserve Officer Training Corps
NS	Naval Station
NWTD	Non-Watertight Door
NWU	Navy Working Uniform
OBA	Oxygen Breathing Apparatus
OCS	Officer Candidate School (located at Naval Station Newport)
OFS	Out-F---ing-Standing.
OIC	Officer in Charge
OMPF	Official Military Personnel File
OOC	Out of Calibrations or Out of Compliance
OOD	Officer of the Deck
OPCON	Operational Control
OPNAV	Office of the CNO
OPS-O	Operations Officer (usually just called "OPS")
PACOM	Pacific Command
PAPERCLIP	People Against People Ever Reenlisting, Civilian Life is Preferred
PAX	Passengers
PCS	Permanent Change of Station
PLD	Permanent Limited Duty
PO	(3/2/1) Petty Officer (Third/Second/First Class)
POD	Plan of the Day
POM	Plan of the Month
POTUS	President of the United States
POW	Plan of the Week
POW	Prisoner of War
PRIFLY	Primary Flight Control (carriers)
PT	Physical Training

QM	Quartermaster
RADM	Rear Admiral (upper half)
RDML	Rear Admiral (lower half)
RIO	Radar Intercept Officer
RTD	Return to Duty
SAM	Surface-to-Air Missile
SAR	Search and Rescue
SCPO	Senior Chief Petty Officer
SECDEF	Secretary of Defense
SECNAV	Secretary of the Navy
SITREP	Situation Report
SN	Seaman
SNA	Student Naval Aviator
SONAR	Sound Navigation and Ranging
SOP	Standard Operating Procedure
SOP(A)	Senior Officer Present Ashore
SOPA	Senior Officer Present Afloat
SOQ	Sailor of the Quarter
SOY	Sailor of the Year
SR	Seaman Recruit
SRB	Selective Reenlistment Bonus
STREAM	Standard Tension Replenishment Alongside Method
TA	Tight Ass
TAD	Temporary Additional Duty
TLD	Temporary Limited Duty
TOPGUN	U.S. Navy Fighter Weapons School
UA	Unauthorized Absence (formerly AWOL – away without leave)
UCMJ	Uniform Code of Military Justice
UNSAT	Unsatisfactory
UOD	Uniform of the Day
USCG	United States Coast Guard
USMC	United States Marine Corps
USN	United States Navy

USNA	United States Naval Academy
USNR	United States Naval Reserve
USS	United States Ship
VAW	Fixed Wing Airborne Early Warning Squadron
VERTREP	Vertical Replenishment
VF	Fixed Wing Fighter Squadron
VFA	Fixed Wing Strike Fighter Squadron
VLS	Vertical Launching System
WO	Warrant Officer
WTC	Watertight Compartment
WTD	Watertight Door
WTF	Whiskey Tango Foxtrot (What The F---? ... also, declarative)
WTH	Watertight Hatch
YN	Yeoman

THERE ARE LOTS MORE .... SOME TECHNICAL ... WAY TOO MANY FOR THIS LIST

Also see SLANG ACRONYMS

US AIRCRAFT CARRIER FLIGHT DECK CREW JACKET COLORS

The jobs and Responsibilities of Those Wearing the Jackets.

In movies of carrier flight deck operations most have noted all the colorful jackets each crewman wears. Each person on the flight deck has specific responsibilities for which they have been trained and which duties must be carried out efficiently and correctly for safety as well as successful operations. It is exceedingly complex and all functions must be done well and coordinated. With the loud ambient noise levels communication must be visual.

Here is a list of the jacket/shirt colors and what each means. This is a broad simplification because within each group of shirt/jacket color some of the crewmen wear different colored helmets* which separate that broad group into further specialization of tasks. Everyone working on the flight deck must know what the colors (shirts AND helmets) mean and all the hand signals.

YELLOW ...   Aircraft Handling Officer
              Catapult and Arresting Gear Officer
              Plane Director ... responsible for all movement
              of all aircraft on both decks.

GREEN ...   Catapult and Arresting Gear Crew
Visual Landing Aid Technician
Air Wing Maintenance Personnel
Air Wing Quality Control Personnel
Cargo-Handling Personnel
Ground Support Equipment (GSE) Troubleshooter
Hook Runner
Photographer's Mate
Helicopter Landing Signal Enlisted Personnel (LSE)

RED ...   Ordnance Handler
Crash and Salvage Crew
Explosive Ordnance Disposal (EOD)
Firefighter and Damage Control Party

PURPLE ...   Aviation Fuel Handler

BLUE ...   Trainee Plane Handler
Chocks and Chains (entry level workers
under yellow shirts' supervision)
Aircraft Elevator Operator
Tractor Driver
Messengers and Phone Talkers

BROWN ...   Air Wing Plane Captain ... squadron personnel
who prepare aircraft for flight.
Air Wing Line Leading Petty Officer

WHITE ...   Quality Assurance
Squadron Plane Inspector
Landing Signal Officer (LSO)
Air Transfer Officer (ATO)
Liquid Oxygen (LOX) Crew

Safety Observer

Medical Personnel (white with red cross emblem)

*If you care about the helmet colors and further specialization, all the information is online.

NAVAL AVIATOR HUMOR, QUIPS, TALES AND JOKES

Some are a little "salty" and might offend a landlubbers' sensitivities.

Little boy …. "Mommy, I want to grow up and be a pilot."
Mommy's Response … "Honey, you can't do both."

Takeoffs are optional, landings are mandatory.

Heaven is crowded with civilian pilots who did not get their Instrument Rating.

Any landing you can walk away from is a good landing.

Any landing you survive for more than 24 hours is a good landing. A great landing allows one to reuse the airplane.

You can't fly unless you can land, but you can't land unless you can fly. So, which is it?

You can only tie the record for flying low.

Pilots …. looking down on people since 1903.

When you see a tree in the clouds, it's not good news.

Never fly the "A" model of anything.

God does not subtract from man's allotted time the hours spent while flying, but He exacts harsh penalties for those who do not learn to land properly.

When a pilot "buys the farm," it means his widow can pay off the mortgage with insurance money.

There are three simple rules for making a smooth landing. Unfortunately, no pilot knows exactly what they are.

Pilot dictum: Remember, in the end, gravity always wins.

Death is God's way of telling pilots to watch their airspeed on final.

The average fighter pilot despite a swaggering personality and confident exterior is capable of feelings such as love, affection, humility, caring and intimacy. They just don't involve others.

Beer was invented to make pilot stories more interesting.

It may be …. but THERE I WUZ ……. (tale follows)

Newton's Law: What goes up must come down.

Squadron Commander's Law: What comes down better be able to go up again!

FAA motto for pilots: "We're not happy unless you're not happy."

Aviation's greatest invention was the relief tube.

I'm at the age when I realize that the best thing about flying fighters was free oxygen.

A Naval Aviator walks into a bar and takes a seat next to an incredibly attractive woman. He gives her a quick glance then casually looks at his new Apple watch for a moment. The woman notices this and asks, "Is your date running late?" "No," he replies, "Just got this state-of-the-art watch, and I was just testing it."

The intrigued woman says, "A state-of-the-art watch? What's so special about it?" The aviator says, "It uses alpha waves to talk to me telepathically." Lady says, "What's it telling you now?"

Aviator: "Well, it says you're not wearing any panties."

Woman giggles: "Well it must be broken because I <u>am</u> wearing panties."

Naval Aviator: stares at watch, smirks, taps the watch two or three times and says,

"Damned thing's an hour fast."

A Young Naval Officer was in a terrible car accident and lost an ear but was otherwise okay. His career continued successfully and he was eventually promoted to Admiral. One day he was interviewing two Navy Master Chiefs and a Marine Gunnery Sergeant for his personal staff.

The first chief had a great interview, then the admiral asked, "Do you notice anything different about me?" The chief said, "Why, yes sir, I couldn't help but notice you are missing your starboard ear, but I don't know if that affects your hearing on that side." The admiral became angry at this lack of tact and threw the chief out of the office.

Next was an Aviation Master Chief who answered the same question, "Well, yes sir, you seem to be short one ear." The admiral threw him out also.

Finally, the Marine Gunnery Sergeant was articulate, extremely sharp and polite. The admiral again asked, "Do you notice anything different about me?" To his surprise the sergeant said, "Yes, sir. You wear contact lenses." The admiral was impressed and thought to himself, what an incredibly tactful Marine. "And how do you know that?" the admiral asked. The Marine replies, "Well sir, it's pretty hard to wear glasses with only one f---ing ear."

An Admiral visited one of the ships under his command and was eating breakfast with the crew. He was impressed to see that the Navy insignia was stamped on every biscuit. He went to the chief chef to ask how this feat was done so it could be used on the other ships in his command. The chief replied, "I'd be glad to share that with you Admiral. After each biscuit is cut, I just slap it here against my belt buckle which bears the Navy insignia."

Horrified, the Admiral exclaims, "That's very unhygienic!" The chief shrugs and replies, "Well, sir, if that's the way you feel about it, I suggest you avoid the doughnuts."

Do you know the difference between God and a Navy Fighter Pilot?
God doesn't think he is a fighter pilot.

How does a woman know when her date with a Navy fighter pilot is half over?
When he says, "That's enough about me. Want to hear about my airplane?"

What is the difference between an Air Force fighter pilot and his jet fighter plane?
The jet plane stops whining when you turn off the engine.

Just because there are no complaints doesn't mean that all parachutes are perfect.

How do you know service in a submarine is safer than Naval Aviation?
Because there are more airplanes in the ocean than there are submarines in the sky.

What is long, hard and full of seamen? A submarine.

A navy ship is sinking and the Captain gathers the crew on deck, asking, "Does anyone know how to pray?" One sailor steps forward and replies, "Aye, sir, I can pray." The Captain says, "Okay you pray while we put on the life jackets. We are one short."

A Navy Dentist was seen driving his car with a license plate that said, "TOP GUM."

How does the Marine Corps separate the men from the boys? With a crowbar.

In the Air Force it's 8:00 AM, in the Army it's 0800, in the Navy, it's 8 bells, in the Coast Guard, the little hand is on the eight and the big hand is on the twelve.

A Ranger, a Green Beret and a SEAL are at survival school swapping macho stories, each trying to show he was the toughest. The Ranger says, "I'm so tough that one time I had to attack an enemy headquarters alone with eighteen enemy soldiers shooting at me .... toss a hand grenade then shoot the rest of them and carry out fifty pounds of intel papers across a rocky, muddy field." The Green Beret says, "That's nothing. Two of us had to parachute into a firebase, at night, quietly kill three dozen gooks with only our knives in hand-to-hand combat. My buddy was wounded so I had to swim through a swamp with a hundred pounds of classified materials, dragging my wounded buddy." The SEAL said nothing and just stood by the campfire slowly stirring the hot coals with his male member.

Naval Aviator Fighter Pilot Crash ... After a terrible crash causing multiple serious injuries, a fighter pilot regained consciousness after several days. An attractive nurse had been caring for him and wanted to assure him that he would be all right even with some significant residuals from the spinal injuries. She leaned over and kissed him gently on the cheek and said in a soft voice, "You have had some serious spinal injuries. You will be okay but won't be able to feel anything from the waist down." The aviator said, "That's okay, can I just feel your tits?"

True Story from a Navy Supply Ship Officer ... My friend was on the bridge chatting with the OOD one night as his supply ship was cruising along making an Atlantic crossing. The helmsman on duty was apparently very tired and was probably half asleep at the wheel. One of the two officers made a comment about who was the rightful owner of something. The helmsman jerked awake and said, "Aye, aye sir, Right Full Rudder" as he cranked the wheel to turn the ship hard around. Seconds later the Captain called the bridge to find out, "What the hell is going on?" Hmmm.... "rightful owner" and "right full rudder" sound alike to a sleepy sailor.

Remember that One-liner ... "The three best things in life are a good landing, a good orgasm and a good bowel movement and a night carrier landing is one of the few times when you can experience all three at the same time."

Thirty Sailors and One Woman .... stranded on a desert island. Sorry, can't tell this one.

There are hundreds, if not thousands of jokes, sea stories, true tales, navy lore et al that would take volumes to record after lots of research. These four pages will have to suffice.

SLANG ACRONYMS

BOHICA ... Bend Over, Here It Comes Again.

Cluster F--- ... Everything just totally messed up and completely wrong.

FUBAR ... F---ed Up Beyond All Recognition. (or Recovery/Repair/Reason.)

FUBIT ... F--- U Buddy, I'm Through.

FUBU ... F---ed Up Beyond Understanding

SNAFU ... Situation Normal, All F---ed Up (from World War Two)

Imperial or Royal F--- Up .... self-explanatory.

SUSFU ... Situation Unchanged, Still F---ed Up.

TARFU ... Totally and Royally F---ed Up.

YGBSM ... You Gotta Be Shitting Me.

Sailors obviously use the F-word a lot.

OTHER SUGGESTED BOOKS

1. **Top Gun**
   An American Story
   by Dan Pedersen (Founder of the Topgun Program) 2019
   Hatchette Books, New York ISBN #9780316416269

2. **Gold Wings, Blue Sea**
   A Naval Aviator's Story
   by Rosario Rausa 1980
   Naval Institute Press, Annapolis, MD ISBN #0-87021-219-2

3. **Above Average**
   Naval Aviation the Hard Way
   by D.D. Smith Date??
   Self-published? Monee, IL

4. **Tailhooker**
   Preflight to Vietnam
   by Willard G. Dellicker 2015
   Self-published, Coppell, TX ISBN #150894234X
   13: 9781508942344

5. **United States Naval Aviation 1911-2014**

Images of War – Rare Photographs from Wartime Archives
by Michael Green 2015

Pen & Sword Aviation, Barnsley, Yorkshire, England ISBN #978-1-47382-225-2

6. **Aircraft Carriers of the United States**
Images of War – Rare Photographs from Wartime Archives
by Michael Green 2015

Pen & Sword Maritime, Barnsley, Yorkshire, England ISBN #978-1-78337-610-0

ABOUT THE AUTHOR

James Alexander White, III, M.D. was born and raised in Alexandria, LA and has lived and worked there for eighty-one years except for the fifteen years of college, medical school, subsequent specialty training...... and the active duty in the U.S. Navy which is the subject of this book. Dr. White is a 1964 graduate of the Tulane University School of Medicine and is a board-certified Otolaryngologist (Ear, Nose, Throat & Allergy Specialist) in practice since 1972. He has two daughters, Elizabeth and Lydia, and three grandchildren, Douglas, Reade and Alexandra. This book is dedicated to them and to his quarter-century-plus significant other, Linda.

Dr. White wrote this book to provide readers with insight into the medical aspects of Naval Aviation. Health and safety are incredibly important to success. The limits of human physiology and psychology are elucidated throughout the book as Dr. White discusses the intricacies of medical issues. The reader will also see inside the attitudes, emotions, risks, fears, tedium, tragedy and the humor that accompany the glamor and excitement that get all the attention.

Included are some of the nuts and bolts of Naval Air and of course its importance to the nation.

Dr. White is a Past-President of the Louisiana State Medical Society and was elected to its Hall of Fame. His is also a Past-Governor of the Louisiana-Mississippi-West Tennessee District of Kiwanis International.

Beyond medicine Dr. White has an avid passion for wine in all its aspects. The early part of this book explains how the Navy enabled his introduction to a lifetime of wine enjoyment. Dr. White was on the wine judging panel of the Los Angeles County Fair for nearly twenty years. He was a charter member of the Society of Wine Educators and taught wine classes for years. At one time he was the owner-operator of four retail wine shops, a wine wholesale company and a wine import company. Dr. White has traveled extensively in wine country all over the world for both business and pleasure.

What is the natural companion of wine? Food. Dr. White is a gourmet chef and appreciator of excellence in food and wine wherever it is found. He has pursued its discovery for many years as this book will attest. Hopefully, the reader will enjoy some of the wine and food stories sprinkled throughout the narrative. As the sayings go .... Bon Appetit and In Vino Veritas.

Author contact:
WUZBOOKS@gmail.com
www.jameswhiteworld.com